A.D.
1000

A.D. 1000

A World on the Brink of Apocalypse

Richard Erdoes

Introduction by Karen Armstrong
author of *The History of God*

Seastone

BERKELEY, CALIFORNIA

Published by: Seastone, an imprint of Ulysses Press
                P.O. Box 3440
                Berkeley, CA 94703-3440

This book is published by arrangement with HarperSanFrancisco, a division of
HarperCollins Publishers. All rights reserved.

Library of Congress Cataloging-in-Publication Data
Erdoes, Richard.
    A.D. 1000 : a world on the brink of apocalypse / Richard Erdoes ;
    introduction by Karen Armstrong
        p. cm.
    Originally published: San Francisco : Harper & Row, c1988.
    Includes bibliographical references and index.
    ISBN 1-56975-157-9 (alk. paper)
    I. One thousand, A.D. 2. Sylvester II, Pope, ca. 945–1003. 3. Civilization,
Medieval.   I. Title.
CB354.E73 1998
909'.1--dc21   98-34818
                                                                          CIP

ISBN: 1-56975-157-9

Printed in the U.S.A. by Banta Book Group

10 9 8 7 6 5 4 3 2

Design: Sarah Levin, Leslie Henriques
Cover photograph: stock montage/SuperStock
Editorial and production staff: Tom Hinds, Steven Zah Schwartz,
    Lily Chou, Patty Wakida
Index: Sayre Van Young

Distributed in the United States by Publishers Group West, in Canada by Raincoast
Books, and in Great Britain and Europe by World Leisure Marketing.

Table of Contents

Introduction
by Karen Armstrong

IN THE YEAR A.D. 1000, nobody would have predicted that the second Christian millennium would witness the spectacular rise and triumph of the West. As these pages show so graphically, Western Europe was a barbaric backwater where superstition was rife and what little culture that remained was constantly threatened by warring Slavs, Wends or Norsemen. Richard Erdoes eloquently describes the city of Rome as reduced by the end of the first millennium from its former grandeur to a collection of ruins, with its monuments of imperial might protruding poignantly from a sea of rubble. In Britain, people regarded the old Roman ruins as the work of giants, created by a race of incomparably superior mortals with skills that had passed from the world forever. To the south and to the east the great powers of Byzantium and Islam looked down on Europe with contempt. The Greek Orthodox Christians of Byzantium considered the West a pagan wilderness and its Holy Roman Emperor a barbarian unworthy of the imperial purple. In the sophisticated Islamic empire, which extended from southern Spain to the Himalayas, Europe was of no interest whatever. Muslim travelers wrote that its climate was appalling, there was no opportunity for trade and its inhabitants were on a par with the savages of sub-Saharan Africa.

The collapse of the western Roman Empire at the hands of invading Germanic tribes had been a catastrophe that made an indelible impression on the Western spirit. After the fifth century, Christianity in the West became a much darker faith than its Greek Orthodox counterpart: God was experienced through a dark night of the soul and manifest in the torn body of a crucified Savior. In Byzantium, the emphasis was on mystical light; the favorite images of Jesus were the transfigured being on Mount Tabor or the triumphant Christ Pantocrater, emperor of all things. In the year 1000, Christianity in Europe was a fragile plant. Most of the population knew so little about the official faith that some bishops noted they were unable to distinguish it from Judaism. Europeans resented the advanced culture of the Byzantines, who made them feel inferior and humiliated. We can see this in the vituperative rage of the Western legate Liutprand, quoted at length by Erdoes, during his visit to Constantinople in 968. Nobody would have guessed the despised Christians of northern Europe were about to undergo a transformation that would ultimately change the history of the world.

The rise of the West is unprecedented in world history. Nobody has managed to account adequately for the fact that an obscure group of outsiders who belonged to none of the great world cultures managed not only to catch up but eventually to overtake the advanced civilizations that preceded them. It was an achievement that arose through monumental strain. In the year A.D. 1000, though the Apocalypse did not take place as expected, the West began to find its soul and a new era started in Europe. The career of Gerbert shows the first signs of what scholars have called the Great Western Transformation. Gerbert, who became the controversial Pope Sylvester II, spent his life acquiring information and scholarship that had been lost to most Europeans during this Dark Age. He learned his science and mathematics from the Islamic world during his years in Spain; for the next two centuries other Western scholars would follow suit. Islam, which many West-

erners today regard as the enemy of decent civilization, actually helped
Europeans build their culture.

Gerbert was also passionately attached to the bygone splendor of
Greece and Rome, as was his disciple, the Emperor Otto III. This classical culture was in fact alien to the new Christian peoples who lived
north of the Alps, who sprang from Germanic or Nordic tribes that
had no historical connection with either the Romans or the Greeks.
But these were the nations—whose ancestors had helped bring Rome
down—who could create the new Western identity. They did this by
attaching themselves to the nearby Greco-Roman culture and making
it their own. At about the same time the Turks of Central Asia were
fighting their way into the great civilization nearest to them, which
happened to be Islam. They would recreate themselves as a Muslim
people in Anatolia and Asia Minor – the modern Turkey.

We can see this northern appropriation of Rome at work in the
story Erdoes presents of Gerbert and Otto. To the young emperor,
Gerbert wrote

> Italy should not deceive itself that civilization and the wisdom of
> the ancients died in the emperor's castle, and Greece should cease to
> brag of the wisdom of her ruler. Greece is in error thinking that she
> inherited the power and greatness of Rome. Ours, ours is rich and
> fruitful Italy. We possess warlike Gaul and Germany and are served
> by stout Slavs. Above all, we have you, emperor, you of Greek blood,
> towering above the Greeks, ruling Rome by rights of inheritance,
> superior both to Rome and Greece in mind and eloquence.

Here we see a divided soul. Gerbert's letter teems with resentment
for the Byzantine Greeks even while he boasts of Otto's descent from a
princess of Byzantium. He defiantly asserts a Western identity, which at
the same time is desperate to graft itself onto ancient Greco-Roman
culture to make itself legitimate.

This is a tragic story. Rome refused to accept either Gerbert or
Otto, seeing them as barbaric outsiders for all their pretensions. Otto's

last years show the strain involved in this militant creation of the new Western soul: he sank into mental illness, unable to find healing in Christianity, which he had never properly assimilated. Gerbert's prodigious foreign learning made him a demonic figure to his contemporaries. The two men existed in a transitional twilight state, never fully at home in either Italy or the north. Later generations would be more successful, and now most Western people take it for granted that their culture has roots in classical antiquity. But the strain would continue. The century that began in A.D. 1000 with an apocalypse averted would end in the apocalypse of the First Crusade—the first collective international act of the new Europe—when the Crusaders slaughtered the Jewish and Muslim inhabitants of Jerusalem like the avenging angels of the Book of Revelation. Later Crusaders would attack the Greek Christians of Byzantium, expressing in these atrocities centuries of smoldering hatred for the great civilizations, which had for so long regarded them with disdain.

Karen Armstrong
London, England
August 1998

Author Preface

THE FATEFUL YEAR 1000 stood out sharply defined from those preceding and following it: in that year many good Christians knelt trembling in their churches, waiting for the last trumpet to sound, "shedding so many tears of repentance that the tears ran down their legs, even to their toes." The central character of this period, Gerbert de Aurillac, was one of those rare human beings who emerge only once every century, usually when momentous events are about to take place. The French historian Henri Focillon called him "The Hinge of Two Worlds." Others saw in him a flash of light illuminating a barbaric age. Gerbert, also known as Pope Sylvester II, was a monk, abbot, pontiff, scholar, inventor, mathematician and astronomer, a humanist before humanism, with ideas five hundred years ahead of his time. His contemporaries suspected him of heresy and witchcraft. Some looked to him for guidance as a saint. Others called him the Antichrist, wrongfully occupying the Chair of St. Peter.

I plunged into the task of writing this book with enthusiasm and a good deal of excitement, reliving the terrors of the year 1000 in the light of my own experiences in our modern and "sophisticated" yet equally barbaric century. As work progressed, the momentarily expected and never befalling millennium occupied less and less space in the growing manuscript, and instead I became more intrigued with the ideas and doings of Gerbert's formidable supporting cast—simple serfs and murderous princes, chaste monks illuminating their parchments in gold leaf, lecherous prelates, decadent Byzantines and ax-wielding Vikings, and, particularly, the Ottoman emperors who, as Focillon remarked, started that peculiar Germanic "obsession with the Universal Empire, a taste for boundless undertakings." I delved into the emerging new thoughts and art styles of the later tenth century, the rediscovery of classic learning and literature, the end of the Age of Lead and Iron and the beginning of the true Middle Ages—in a word, the whole of human glory and destitution. Yet in the background, openly or hidden, always lurked the terror, the dread of the end of all ends.

Of course, the terror has been there from the beginning. The primordial *Weltangst* has disturbed the sleep of cave-dwelling wisent-hunting Cro-Magnon humans as well as the dreams of modern Americans, filled with images of an imminent Armageddon. Already centuries before Gerbert, learned clerics spoke of *mundus senescit*, of a world grown old and senile, ripe for well-deserved oblivion.

Sumerian seers foretold the earth's destruction from a misshapen sheep's liver or an ominous conjunction of stars. The Hindu Veda speak of *pralaya*, the dissolution of all things at the end of the universal cycle, as the *samvartaka*, or cosmic conflagration, obliterates the whole universe. The Mahabharata and the Purana tell of seven suns burning up the earth, the flames reaching even the highest realms of Brahma.

Ancient Scandinavians trembled at the thought of Ragnarök, the Götterdämmerung, the final battle of the Gods against evil monsters such as the Fenris Wolf, heralded by the appearance of the Dark Red Bird of Niflheim, a battle that will make the oceans boil amid all-killing steam. In Zoroastrian mythology a great meteor crashes into the earth, destroying all life as punishment for humankind's iniquities. The natives of Patagonia, not unnaturally, saw the ultimate calamity in an earth-covering sheet of ice.

The ancient Mayans depicted the cataclysm as arriving at the end of a 34,000-year cycle when the Goddess of Destruction with her jaguar claws, crown of writhing snakes and garments of human bones would overturn the bowl containing all the waters of the world. Montezuma saw in the coming of the Spanish *conquistadores* the long-foretold arrival of the white gods and the return of Quetzalcoatl, the Plumed Serpent, announcing the downfall of the Aztec Empire. The Aztecs also believed in a number of worlds piled one upon the other. As one world was being destroyed because of the evildoings of its inhabitants, a newly created one was promptly superimposed upon it—a belief still held by many contemporary southwestern Indians.

According to one Cheyenne tale a great pole somewhere holds up the universe, a tree trunk not unlike Yggdrasil, the World Ash of the Norse Edda myths. The Great White Beaver of the North keeps gnawing at this tree trunk, and when he has finally gnawed through, the pole will topple and the earth will crash down into a bottomless pit. Wowoka, the Paiute medicine man who founded the Ghost Dance religion, taught that the white people's world together with all their works would roll up like a carpet to reveal once more beneath it the old Indian Grandmother Earth teeming with bison, which would be hunted by dead native people come to life again.

This has a striking resemblance to a passage in the Bible: "And the heaven departed as a scroll when it is rolled together; and every mountain and island were moved out of their places." References to the apocalypse, a final battle between the forces of good and evil, and to the coming of the Last Judgment are numerous in the Gospels, and many people in the tenth century firmly believed the fatal Day of Wrath would dawn exactly one thousand years after the Savior's birth. When such prophesies failed and the appointed hour passed without the world coming to an end, new dates and new interpretations of Scripture were immediately offered by ever new prophets.

In the eleventh century a man in Cologne was so impressed by one of these augurs that he bought a shipload of anchor stones saying,

"Sin is a heavy thing, and at the last doom when good and evil deeds are weighed, those apostles who love me will cast the stones into the scale of my good deeds and thus save me." In 1843 the American Millerites or Adventists stood in nightshirts on their rooftops to be nearer to the angels who would waft them up to heaven at the hour of the Second Coming.

Today people speak again of the Second Coming—the coming of Christ, of the anointed Messiah, of the Mahdi, of the Tenth Imam, even of Buddha. A small group of Neo-Nazis is eagerly awaiting the reappearance of the Fuhrer, who will arrive from outer space and proclaim, "I am the reincarnation of Adolf Hitler and come from the planet Zeno." Sectarians go from door to door, warning that doomsday is at hand and that the rider on the pale horse is just around the corner.

Neo-Nostradamians, Paracelsians, Cagliostroans, Saucerians, Pyramidians, followers of Edgar Cayce the Sleeping Prophet, and of other sooth- or gloomsayers predict the end of the world variously as a result of a cosmic cataclysm, the assault of extraterrestrials, a sudden shift in the earth's axis or of its spinning out of orbit. Sometimes the predicted extinction is all-encompassing, the total obliteration of the universe after a collision of entire galaxies. Sometimes it is merely the expunging of our own little solar system, or perhaps of only one of the fifty states of the Union, such as the late great state of California torn from the Sierra by mighty earthquakes and hurled into the Pacific to become a second Atlantis.

But it is no longer only the sandal-clad hermits and oddballs walking the streets with placards proclaiming "the end of world" who think this puny planet of ours might not survive the twentieth century. Perfectly sane people, among them scientists and Nobel laureates, predict humankind's demise due to overpopulation, famines, deforestation, pollution, depletion of the earth's ozone layer, errors in human engineering, or simply the collapse of civilization due to the exhaustion of essential nonrenewable raw materials. The end of Christianity's second millennium is near, and A.D. 2000 is just a couple of years away. Today, as a thousand years ago, fears of the future are submerged, pushed into the background by the mundane fears of daily life—which, as Mark Twain pointed out, "is one damn thing after another."

So, of course, is capricious history. It flows unevenly by fits and starts. It might appear as a sea of still waters that, in the twinkling of an eye, are whipped into foaming, raging waves by mighty hurricanes. History is a puzzle, a kaleidoscope, a world of buried shards and broken artifacts patiently dug up or lost forever. It is seldom entirely truthful. To be objective is never easy. Two historians describing the same event from opposing points of view often seem to be talking about entirely different occurrences. The perception of history depends on such factors as the writer's age, sex, nationality, religion, political opinions, and digestion. I have tried to stick to the facts, though at times I offer my own private opinion or interpretation. I take my cue from St. Augustine: "As for all that my body's senses reach, whether earth, sky, or anything else, I know nothing at all how long they will last; but 7 + 3 make ten, now and forever. They never have made, and never will make, anything else but ten."

Luckily, I managed to unearth a mass of contemporary material. Gerbert himself was a rarity of his time—a compulsive letter writer. Much of his correspondence has been preserved. He wrote in what has been described as "a sort of Merovingian shorthand," which proved a challenge to many scholars. Besides his letters we have the tenth- and eleventh-century chronicles of such early annalists as Widukind of Corvey and Thietmar of Merseburg dealing with Ottonian Germany, Liutprand of Cremona describing affairs in Italy and Byzantium, Raoul Glaber and Richer of Rheims, Gerbert's admiring student, telling of events in France and Lorraine. More than a dozen monks and prelates, often those involved in grave matters of state, acted as self-appointed historians, writing down what they saw and heard on thick parchment with goose-quill and inkhorn, their hands stiff in winter, their eyes watering and red from smoking chimney fires and ruined by dim and insufficient lighting. One would wish to be able to conjure up their spirits and thank them for the good work done. Fortunately, most of these manuscripts have by now been transcribed into legible print and translated into at least one of several modern languages.

A year is a flyspeck in time, the atom of a flyspeck even, but it can seem like an eternity. The year 1910 bore little resemblance to 1914. The year 1945 was altogether different from 1946. The days of a year in history have to be assembled into a mosaic in which gray and color-less tesserae surround single gleaming golden titles. Each year is con-nected by its own umbilical cord to the one that gave it birth, at the same time already casting its shadow upon the year as yet unborn. The year 1000 was special, ushering in a new chapter in the human story, its mosaic aglow with many golden tesserae. It was a year preg-nant with great hopes and fears.

Tenth-century history was made by men and women as well as by economics, the improvement of trade, and new methods of agricul-ture, by old traditions and new experiments, by the primordial forest encroached upon by human works, by Christianity, Islam, and pagan-ism. The age of Gerbert proves that no century, be it the tenth or the twentieth, is ever safe; all have their violent ups and downs inflicted upon them by a cruelly indifferent past. Medieval rulers committed the same stupid mistakes as their so-called sophisticated counterparts of our times: the more things change, the more they stay the same. As in our days, the inhabitants of Europe a thousand years ago were threatened by war in all directions. They were victims of terrorism; they pined away as hostages; and they suffered from pollution caused by the soot and smoke of innumerable fires, by offal piled up in their streets, and by the lack of sanitation. They were swept away in geno-cides as men armed with lance, sword, bow, and the terrifying chemi-cal weapon called the Greek Fire killed as many people as a modern Blitzkrieg. Already they were afraid of humanity's self-destruction, and their fear proves that history always repeats itself, though never exactly in the same way.

History is essentially tragic. So is human life. The wise and the good come to the same sad end as the stupid and the bad. Gerbert, the most formidable mind of the tenth century, saw his plans come to naught by the untimely death, at age twenty-two, of his friend and pupil, Emperor Otto III. "Alas," as the chronicler lamented, "a pope too wise, an emperor too young!"

Finally, comparing the year one thousand to our nuclear age, one comes away with a sense that, above all, people, not economy or technology, make history, that the individual counts for something, be it good or bad, that even in the worst and darkest days some rare spirits are preparing the birth of a new renaissance, unswayed by the misery and destruction that surround them. Like a flower pushing its way through a crack in the pavement, life has always overpowered death and will, we hope, continue doing so in times to come—at least for another thousand years.

***

I express my special thanks to Silvio Baden, Keeper of Rare Books at the Smithsonian Institution, who kindly sent me material that would otherwise have been hard to come by.

Richard Erdoes

POPES OF ROME

John IX: 898-900
Benedict IV: 900-903
Leo V: 903
Christopher: 903-4
Sergius III: 904-11
Anastasius III: 911-13
Lando: 913-14
John X: 914-28
Leo VI: 928-29
Stephen VII: 929-31
John XI: 931-36
Leo VII: 936-39
Stephen VIII: 939-42
Marinus II: 942-46
Agapetus II: 946-55
John XII: 955-64
Leo VIII: 963-65
Benedict V: 964
John XIII: 965-72
Benedict VI: 972-74
Boniface VII: 974
Benedict VII: 974-83
John XIV: 983-84
Boniface VII: 984-85
John XV: 985-96
Gregory V: 996-99
John XVI, Antipope: 997-98
Sylvester II: 999-1003

EMPERORS OF THE WEST

Charles III, the Fat: 881-87
Guy of Spoleto: 891-94
Lambert of Spoleto: 892-96
Arnulf of Germany: 896
Lambert of Spoleto: 897-98
Lois the Blind,
    king of Provence: 901-2
Berengar of Friuli: 915-24
Otto I: 962-73
Otto II: 967-83
Otto III: 996-1002

EMPERORS OF THE EAST

Leo VI: 886-912
Constantine VII,
    Porphyrogenitus: 913-59
Romanus II: 959-63
Nicephorus II: 963-69
John I, Tzimesces: 969-76
Basil II: 976-1025

KINGS OF GERMANY

Charles III, the Fat: 882-87
Arnulf of Carinthia: 887-99
Louis the Child: 900-11
Conrad of Franconia: 911-18
Henry I, the Fowler: 919-36
Otto I, the Great: 936-73
Otto II: 961-83
Otto III: 983-1002

KINGS OF FRANCE

Carloman: 879-84
Charles III, the Fat: 885-87
Odo of Neustria: 888-98
Charles the Simple: (893)
898-922
(923)
Robert I: 922-23
Raoul of Burgundy: 923-36
Louis IV, D'Outremer: 936-54
Lothair: 954-86
Louis V: (979)
986-87
Hugh Capet: 987-96
Robert II, the Pious: (987)
996-1031

KINGS OF ITALY

Charles III, the Fat: 879-87
Berengar of Friuli: 888-89
Guy of Spoleto: 889-94
Lambert of Spoleto: 892-96
Arnulf of Germany: 894
(rival king): 896
Lambert of Spoleto: 897-98
Berengar of Friuli: 898-900
Louis of Provence: 900-902
Berengar of Friuli: 902-22
Rudolph of Burgundy: 922-26
Hugh of Arles: 926-47
Lothar,
son of Hugh of Arles: 931-50
Berengar of Ivrea: 950-61
Otto I: 961-73
Otto II: 973-83
Otto III: 983-1002

THE OTTONIAN HOUSE

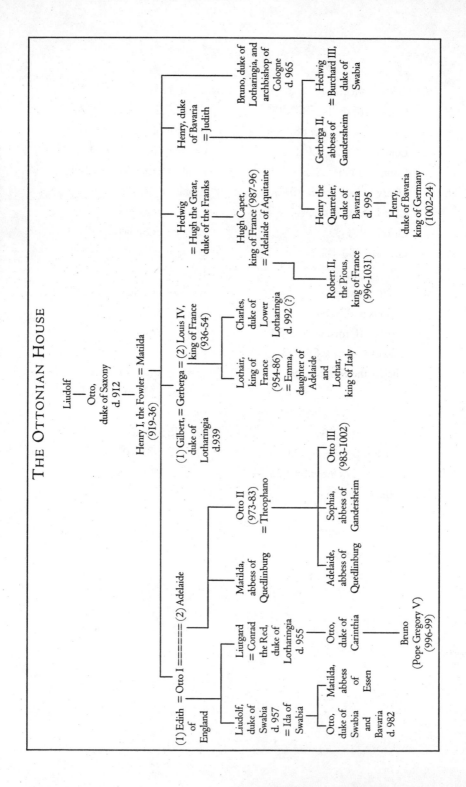

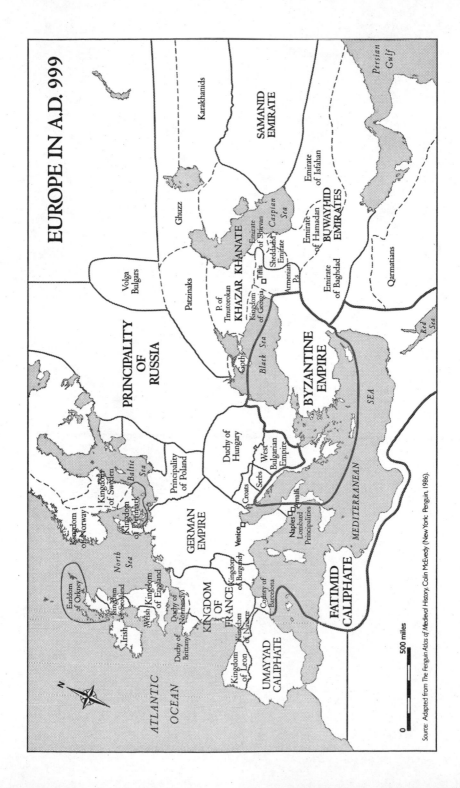

EUROPE IN A.D. 999

ATLANTIC OCEAN

Earldom of Orkney

Kingdom of Scotland

Irish

Welsh Kingdom of England

Duchy of Brittany

Duchy of Normandy

KINGDOM OF FRANCE

Kingdom of Burgundy

Kingdom of Navarre

Kingdom of Leon

UMAYYAD CALIPHATE

County of Barcelona

GERMAN EMPIRE

Venice

Naples Amalfi

Lombard Principalities

FATIMID CALIPHATE

MEDITERRANEAN SEA

North Sea

Kingdom of Norway

Kingdom of Sweden

Kingdom of Denmark

Baltic Sea

Principality of Poland

Duchy of Hungary

Croats

Serbs

West Bulgarian Empire

BYZANTINE EMPIRE

PRINCIPALITY OF RUSSIA

Patzinaks

Volga Bulgars

Goths

P. of Tmutorokan

Black Sea

KHAZAR KHANATE

Kingdom of Georgia

Tiflis

Armenian Ps

Emirate of Shirvan

Sheddadid Emirate

Caspian Sea

Ghuzz

Karakhanids

SAMANID EMIRATE

Emirate of Isfahan

Emirate of Hamadan

BUWAYHID EMIRATES

Emirate of Baghdad

Qarmatians

Red Sea

Persian Gulf

0   500 miles

Source: Adapted from *The Penguin Atlas of Medieval History*, Colin McEvedy (New York: Penguin, 1986).

CHAPTER ONE

Fear and Trembling
at the Stroke of Midnight

ON THE LAST DAY OF THE YEAR 999, according to an ancient chronicle, the old basilica of St. Peter's at Rome was thronged with a mass of weeping and trembling worshipers awaiting the end of the world. This was the dreaded eve of the millennium, the Day of Wrath when the earth would dissolve into ashes. Many of those present had given away all their possessions to the poor—lands, homes, and household goods—in order to assure for themselves forgiveness for their trespasses at the Last Judgment and a good place in heaven near the footstool of the Almighty. Many poor sinners—and who among them was without sin?—had entered the church in sackcloth and ashes, having already spent weeks and months doing penance and mortifying the flesh.

At the altar the Holy Father, Pope Sylvester II, in full papal regalia, was celebrating the midnight mass, elevating the host for all to see. Many did not dare to look, lying face down upon the multicolored marble floor, their arms spread out in the shape of a cross. A few were seized by holy ecstasy, waiting to be united with Christ. As the minutes passed and the fateful hour was about to strike, a deathly silence filled the venerable basilica. Only the voice of the pope was heard intoning the hallowed phrases, and, at the words *ite missa est*, the great bell began to ring.

The crowd remained rooted, motionless, transfixed, barely daring to breathe, "not a few dying from fright, giving up their ghosts then and there." This description was written from hearsay, and things might not have happened just that way, but it gives a good idea of the all-pervading dread of the apocalypse that held humankind in its grip. Legends set the period against an apocalyptic background and associate the end of the first millennium with some vague terror of judgment day. The historical truth is that not only the year 999, but the whole century that preceded it was a period of obscurity during which people, "blinded with blood, groped their way fearfully through a quagmire of filth."

This is not to say that everybody believed in the impending doom. Many did not. Prelates and abbots inveighed against the belief that the earth was about to burn up. But the common people, the lower nobles, village priests, and peasants, took it as an absolute truth that the "nightfall of the universe was at hand."

Some were certain that the Second Coming of Christ would fall on the last day of the year 999, at the very stroke of midnight. Others were equally convinced that Armageddon would happen a little earlier, on the eve of the nativity when "the Children of Light would join in battle with Gog's army of hellish fiends." Some fixed the date on the day of the summer or winter solstice in the thousandth year after our Lord's passion.

In France and Lorraine wise men scoffed at the idea. They had it on good authority that the end would come when the Feast of the Annunciation fell on a Good Friday "when darkness will cover the earth and the stars fall upon it." Though people quarreled about the exact day and hour, they all agreed, in the words of Raoul Glaber, that "Satan will soon be unleashed because the thousand years have been completed."

This Raoul, author of *Tales* and known by the nickname of Bald-pate or Glaber, was very much of his time. He was a restless, insufferable monk whom no abbot could keep within the rule and who all his life jumped from one monastery to another. A semivisionary, ever haunted by superstitious fears, he "saw the Devil at every turn of the road."

Many expected the Last Judgment to be held at Jerusalem, and, throughout the year 999, the number of pilgrims converging upon the Holy City were compared to an immense, desolating army. Often these pious wayfarers had also sold their worldly possessions to finance their pilgrimage.

As Glaber described it: "On the threshold of the aforesaid thousandth year, so innumerable a multitude began to flock from all parts of the world to the Sepulchre of our Saviour at Jerusalem, as no man could before have expected; for the lower orders of men led the way, and after them came those of middle rank, and then all the greatest kings, counts and bishops; and lastly many noble ladies and poor women. For many purposed and wished to die in the Holy City. . . . Many who had studied the matter, being asked about the significance of this great wandering to Jerusalem, answered with some caution that it portended the advent of Antichrist, whose appearance at the end of this world is prophesied in Holy Scripture."

And so the pilgrims thronged the miserable roads. On foot, in carts, riding horseback, and singing psalms, they fearfully scanned the sky, which they full expected to be rent asunder at any moment.

"Every phenomenon of nature filled them with alarm. A thunderstorm sent them all upon their knees in mid-march. It was the opinion that thunder was the voice of God announcing the Day of Judgment."

Signs and prodigies prompted faith in the apocalypse. If one is to believe contemporary chronicles, many such signs appeared. One early scribe told of the sky splitting open, letting fall down to earth a gigantic torch, which left behind it a long trail of light like a lightning bolt. Its thunderclap frightened not only people surprised in the open fields but also those who at the moment were safely indoors. The gap in the sky closed again, but then the shape of dragon with blue feet appeared, its head continuing to grow until it filled the horizon from end to end.

In England a meteor caused much fear and trembling. A fiery lumen appeared in the month of September. It shone so brightly that it turned night into day. It vanished at cock's crow, but whether this light came from God or from the devil the people did not know. French nuns saw "fiery armies fighting in the sky." They started a procession and said many prayers to ward off the dreaded ultimate ruin.

In Aquitaine, the sky rained blood, spattering people's clothing with crimson spots that could not be expunged. This caused apprehension that great wars and bloodshed were about to occur—a surefire prophesy in an age of uninterrupted violence and warfare. Not only the victims of soldierly brutality but also the soldiers themselves took fright in the face of such omens. In 968, the men of emperor Otto I, marching against the Saracens of Calabria, panicked when an eclipse darkened the sky. They dove head first into empty wine barrels and supply chests or crawled underneath their carts. "Fanatic preachers kept up the flame of terror. Every shooting star furnished occasion for a sermon, in which the sublimity of the approaching Judgment was the principal topic."

Many signs and omens were seen in Italy, not surprisingly, as many people believed that the dissolution of the world would begin at Rome and spread out from there until all of the earth should be consumed. Raoul Glaber took note of this: "For in the seventh year before that date A.D. 1000, Mount Vesuvius, which is also called Vulcan's cauldron, gaped far more often than its wont and vomited forth numberless vast stones mingled with sulphurous flames which fell to a distance of three miles around; and thus by the stench of its breath, like the stench of hell, made all the surrounding province uninhabitable. . . .

"It befell at the same time that most of the cities of Italy and Gaul were ravaged by flames of fire, and that even the greatest part of Rome itself was devoured by a conflagration. The flames caught the beams of St. Peter's church and began to creep up to the bronze tiles and lick the carpenters' work. When this became known to the watching multitude, being quite helpless to avert the disaster, they turned with one accord, and crying with a terrible voice, hastened to crowd before the image of the Chief of the Apostles, crying upon him with curses that, if he watched not over his own, nor defended his own church, many throughout the world would abandon the faith and fall back into paganism. Whereupon the devouring flames at once left the wooden roofbeams and died away."

Among lesser signs mentioned was an image of Christ that wept crimson tears and a wolf who crept into the church to adore it. The pious beast seized the bellrope between its teeth and rang the church bell, which caused great unease among all who heard it. Also, in the castle of Joigny, belonging to a certain Sir Arlebaud, it rained stones of different sizes for three long years. Eleven sons and grandsons of Arlebaud died during that dismal time, which surprised nobody; had it not rained stones?

Near Chalons, a man called Leutard dreamed that a swarm of bees had entered his body and emerged through his mouth. Leutard claimed that the dream was real, and he showed many bee stings to prove it. The bees had revealed to him that he was to do things that were impossible for ordinary men. He went to the nearest church and trampled underfoot a cross and an image of Christ, claiming at the same time that it was sinful and ungodly to pay tithes and taxes. He was subdued and killed, but his behavior was explained as still another sign of coming calamities.

Another madman was suddenly possessed by a fiend who made him plunge a lance between the ribs of the saintly Père Abbon of Fleury. The murderer had his hands cut off and was burned. This too was a bad omen, as the assassin had no discernable motive.

In 960, a preacher from Thuringia, named Bernhard, told an assembly of bishops and laymen at Würzburg that God had appeared to him in the flesh, revealing to him the exact day and hour in which the world and all who lived on it would be obliterated. He insisted that the hour was at hand. At first his listeners were frightened, but when the false prophet began drooling, capering, and making faces, they saw that he was just a fool, and the crowd mocked him, pelting the poor wretch with offal. Often such madmen were tortured—not to punish them, but merely to torment and drive out the indwelling demons, thereby rendering a kindness to the bedeviled victim.

The tenth century has been called the Century of Lead and Iron. The barbarian invasions were not yet finished; Europe was still besieged, with horde after horde continuing to fling themselves against its walls. Western Europe was beset on all sides by fanatic Saracens, Spanish Moors, Thor-worshiping Vikings, pagan Bulgars, and fierce Magyar horsemen—the proverbial Scourges of God. Christian barons slaughtered each other with a vengeance over pieces of land, killing their enemies' serfs—men, women, and children—to weaken them economically, burning villages and crops, and cutting down fruit trees for good measure.

In Rome, rival popes imprisoned, starved, mutilated, castrated, blinded, and assassinated each other. Sons murdered fathers, husbands killed wives, sisters fought brothers for possession of a castle or manor. As early as 909, at the Council of Trosly, Hervèe, archbishop of Rheims, lamented, "The cities lie in ruins, the monasteries are burned or destroyed, the country far and wide reduced to a lifeless desert. Like the first people of earth, men live without law and fear of punishment, abandoning themselves to their passion. Everyone does as he pleases, defying the laws divine and human, as well as the orders of their bishops. The strong oppress the weak. Everywhere there is violence against the poor who are helpless to resist—and equally helpless the churches and cloisters who cannot defend what is theirs. And we ourselves, bishops, shepherds of the people, we who should correct, protect, do not fulfill our task. We neglect to preach, see our flock abandoning God and wallow in vice without speaking to them, advising them, offering them our hands. They tell us that the burdens we lay upon them are too heavy, that we do not even offer them our little finger. And therefore the flock, our Lord's sheep, perish by our silence. In the meantime we think only of our own well-being. But the moment approaches when we must give accounts. Soon we shall see approach the day, majestic and terrible, when we, together with our flock, shall stand before the Great Shepherd of all."

Such warnings occurred again and again throughout the century. Glaber wrote, "Close to a thousand years after the Virgin gave her son to the world mankind threw itself into the most fatal errors. The people were bound for evil from childhood, like a dog returning to its own vomit, sinning again and again like a swine that was washed wallowing once more in the muck. They waxed fat and proud, and kicked against God's laws. For even princes and bishops had their hearts set on ill-gotten riches, turning to theft and greed. And the lower sort of people followed the example of the higher so that never before had there been such base crimes of incests, adulteries and fornications between close kindred, such immorality and keeping of concubines."

Elsewhere he lamented, "A mixture of frivolity and infamy corrupts our way of life; therefore our minds have lost their taste for what is serious and dwell upon what is shameful. Honor and justice cannot be had now at any price. Women walk about in shortened dresses, moving wantonly. Among men, degeneracy gives way to effeminacy. Fraud, violence and every imaginable vice vie with each other for dominance. Not even the ravages of the sword, famines and pestilences can keep men from sinning and if the goodness of the Almighty had not suspended His anger, hell had already swallowed up mankind in its bottomless pit. Such is the power of crime that the more evil one commits the less one fears repeating it and the more one doubts the Last Judgment."

Violence, however, was not the only source of fear. Recurrent famines added to the general misery. The result of the new invasions—as well as of feudal wars—was a terrible decline of agriculture from the days of Charlemagne. In the most fertile plains, forest, heath, and marsh resumed the offensive. Moreover, famine was rife on badly cultivated land, the produce of which was continually threatened. In certain years famine became general; it happened at least five or six times during the century. Starvation wandered ceaselessly from one region to another, thanks now to a bad harvest, now to an invasion, and now to war. "Men believed that the orderly laws of nature had been suspended, that the natural flow of the seasons, which until then had ruled the earth, had fallen into utter disorder foretelling the end of all mankind."

The famines brought on by droughts, floods, and wars resulted in widespread cannibalism. Parents ate their children. Robbers not only waylaid hapless travelers, but also devoured them. Glaber relates tales of hosts murdering their guests for their flesh. He mentions parts of human bodies sold on markets and buried corpses being dug up and roasted. He tells of starving people eating unclean beasts and creeping things. A man who sold human flesh on the market of Tournus was strangled and burned. Another wretch who dug up the man's corpse and cooked it was burned at the stake. A charcoal burner installed himself inside an abandoned church and murdered and ate persons who went there to pray. A husband and wife who stopped there to ask for shelter surprised the cannibal, who was surrounded by forty-eight human heads while gnawing on the forty-ninth. The pair managed to escape and report their grisly discovery. The culprit was caught, smeared with pitch, and set aflame. People found themselves reduced to eating earth.

Wars and famines were followed by epidemics. "At this time a horrible plague raged among men, namely a hidden fire which consumed and sloughed off all the limbs of the body it attacked. A single night sufficed for this frightful evil to entirely devour its victims." This might very well have been the dreaded St. Anthony's fire which, all during the Middle Ages, killed thousands of people. It was caused by ergot, a fungus of the rye plant not easily detected by the naked eye. People eating bread made from diseased rye first experienced a tingling sensation, as if thousands of ants were crawling over their bare skin. In severe cases, affected fingers and toes gangrened, turned black, and fell off. This was sometimes accompanied by respiratory failure, hallucinations, madness, and death. For this and other diseases of the Middle Ages there were no remedies and not even a way of diagnosing the cause. Medicine was still mainly a matter of magic, and treatments were determined by grotesque superstitions. Illness was usually looked upon as divine punishment or the effect of malevolent forces.

While some saw the approaching doom in signs and portents, others were convinced by Scripture, quoting Revelation: "And when the thousand years are expired, Satan shall be loosed out of his prison, and shall go out and deceive the nations which are in the four quarters of the earth, Gog and Magog, to gather them together to battle: the number of whom is as the sands of the sea."

Many trembled at the prospect, but others rejoiced in the knowledge that the Second Coming was near. The empress Adelaide told Odilo, abbot of Cluny, "As the thousandth year of our Lord's becoming flesh approaches, I yearn to behold this day, which knows no evening, in the forecourt of our Lord. I want to be dissolved in Christ."

There was a yearning for the liberation from earthly shackles, an eagerness to see the face of God, a universal cry of "Veni, Domine Jesu!" (Come, my Lord Jesus!) The hope of a better world to come filled many with a euphoric feeling of jubilation. People were wont to quote the prophet Joel: "It shall come to pass in that day that the mountains shall drop down new wine and the hills shall flow with milk." Such hopes were echoed in the *Baruch Apocalypse*, which held that "the day is coming when every vine shall bear a thousand shoots, every shoot a thousand clusters, every cluster a thousand grapes, and every grape shall yield a ton of wine."

Pessimists pointed out that before the advent of the hoped-for millennium, Antichrist would, at least for a while, rule the world with a rod of iron. From the earliest days of the church the appearance of the Man of Sin had been awaited with trepidation. Passages in the Bible and the writings of the church fathers had been studied word by word to find a clue as to when Antichrist would appear, so that humankind should not be caught unawares.

In Brittany, people convinced themselves that they had already seen Antichrist in the shape of a black, dwarfish homunculus lurking among prehistoric cairns and megaliths of ancient heathen. Many believed that the proverbial ship of faith and true belief would be swallowed up by a boiling sea. The sun would blacken, the moon cease to shine, and the stars fall from heaven. But after a time of tears and terror Christ, so they hoped, would descend to avenge the blood of the saints by destroying Antichrist, and a new and better world would be born.

The Evil One was supposed to arise out of the Tribe of Dan, because of the Biblical passage: "Dan shall be a serpent by the way, an adder in the path," and also because none of the Danites had acquired the seal of adoption that the servants of God had received on their foreheads. Some believed Antichrist to be a phantom demon, others that he would appear as a fiend—a true man and true devil—"not as Christ assumed humanity, so the devil will become human, but the MAN will receive all the inspiration of Satan, and will suffer the devil to take up his abode within him." People of the tenth century who believed this saw no dearth of men around who fit that description.

Satan was supposed to take possession of Antichrist from infancy and train him for his office, instilling in him cunning, guile, cruelty, and the pride of Lucifer. "He will make a show of godliness whilst denying the power thereof. He will sow doubts about God and Christ in men's souls. Antichrist will exalt himself to sit like God in the Temple of God, the ultimate abomination standing in a holy place. He will find a pope who will ally himself to Antichrist and be his servant. Such a pope himself will become the Man of Sin, the beast and the harlot."

The Holy Father in 999, Pope Sylvester II, intoning the midnight mass, fulfilled the dark prophecy for many of the prostrate believers. There were some who believed him to be Antichrist appearing in the shape of a pontiff. Did he not voice disbelief in the imminent end of the world? Had he not introduced evil wisdom gotten from Jews and Moors? Did he not practice black arts such as astronomy? It was rumored that, in Spain, Sylvester had taken a Mahometan witch for his mistress who had taught him to fly through the air and foresee the future. He was said to have made an artificial man who could speak and answer questions put to him with a yes or a no. He was making spheres depicting the world as an orb. Surely this was blasphemy. It was thought that he had sold his soul to the devil in order to obtain knowledge and honor. And so the worshipers trembled in fear.

But when the fatal hour passed and the earth did not open to swallow up church and worshipers, and when no fire fell from heaven burning everything alive to ashes, all stirred as if awakening from a bad dream.

Then everybody breathed a great sigh of relief amid much weeping and laughing. Husband and wife, servant and master embraced and even unreconciled, enemies hailed each other as friends and exchanged the kiss of peace. Then all the bells of St. Peter's, of the Lateran, of the Aventine, of every church upon the Seven Hills of Rome, began to ring, praising the Lord as with one single voice. The bitter cup had passed, the world was like reborn and all humankind rejoiced, as related by many ancient chroniclers.

Before he was raised to the papal throne, Pope Sylvester II was known throughout Christendom as Gerbert of Aurillac, a learned monk, full of wisdom.

CHAPTER TWO

Of Poor and
Humble Parents Born

THE CHILDHOOD AND ORIGIN OF GERBERT, the "most accomplished man of the Middle Ages," is hidden in a mist of obscurity. We do not know the year in which he was born, the place of his birth, or the name of his parents. He himself said only that he was the son of poor and humble folk. His pupil Richer wrote that Gerbert "was from Aquitaine." And that is all. One gets a first faint glimpse of him as an oblate, a child reared in a monastery to become a monk, in the abbey of St. Gèraud, at Aurillac, a town in the Auvergne.

Gerbert of Aurillac, as he became known later, has been called "a child of the rich soil of the Midi—that joyful landscape not made for ascetics or downcast spirits," a hill country of wine and ripening grain fertilized by Greek, Roman, and Arab culture. It was a land jealous of its individuality, proud of never having been altogether assimilated into the French mainstream. The high-hearted and hardworking inhabitants had never been easily intimidated and always quickly recovered from the ravages of ferocious Arab, Norman, and Hungarian raiders. Their churches and monasteries were promptly rebuilt after being torched by pagan tribes.

At the time Gerbert entered the Abbey of St. Gèraud, it was a "little kingdom of peace, a seat of learning, untroubled by war." Its monks working in the scriptorium were famous for their calligraphy; its sole resident scholar, Raymond, was respected for his knowledge of grammar as well as for his elegant Latin, which Gerbert acquired from him. Today nothing is left of the monastery burned by Huguenots in 1569, and a half-ruined castle is one of the few relics surviving from Gerbert's time. There is, however, his bronze statue, erected in 1851, to remind us of Aurillac's most illustrious son.

The Benedictine cloister of Aurillac was founded by Count Gèraud who "died in the odor of sanctity" and was later duly canonized. Gèraud acted in obedience to a vow when he bestowed his "fair domain of Aurillac with all that will be needful to support an abbot, thirty-nine monks, and such other persons, cleric or laic, employed in the service of this house."

By this magnificent gift the count thought to ensure for himself the favor of heaven, particularly of his patron saint who, he fervently hoped, would intercede for him on the day of the Last Judgment. He also founded the abbey to have monks praying for him and his soul in perpetuity. He probably also intended his abbey to be a good spot in which to place as abbots the younger sons of his descendants. As a good Avernian it is likely the count had not only the salvation of his own soul in mind, but also the well-being of his family and heirs. Yet Gèraud likewise intended to find a center, not only for piety, but also for learning, and he spared nothing to make his monastery splendid.

Soon after 910 the monastery accepted the Cluniac reforms and rules. The famous House of Cluny, which gave birth to the great monastic reforms of the tenth century, was founded seventeen years after the Abbey of St. Gèraud by William the Pious, count of Auvergne and duke of Aquitaine. It is interesting to learn in somewhat more detail the wording and the thoughts behind William's donation.

"It is manifest to all who ponder seriously, that they can earn everlasting rewards by a good use of the things which are their transitory possessions. This is shown convincingly by God's word: 'The ransom of a man's life are his riches.' Therefore I, William by God's grace, count and duke, intent to provide for my own salvation while there is yet time, have thought fit to spend for the benefit of my soul a small part of the wealth which has been granted me in this world. Be it known therefore that I grant of my own free will, to the holy Apostles Peter and Paul, some of my rightful possessions; namely Cluny with all that belongs to said village: manors, chapels, serfs male and female, vineyards, meadows, woods and waters, corn mills and fields tilled and fallow.

"All this do I, William, and my wife Ingelberga, first for the love of God, and also for the health of our bodies and souls, on this condition, that a monastery shall be built at Cluny wherein monks shall live according to the role of St. Benedict, which monks shall have and hold these possessions for all time; provided also that busy petitions and supplications be addressed to the Lord, both for myself and all others mentioned herein. If perchance, which God forbid, any man of what condition soever, attempt to encroach this testament, let him incur the wrath of God Almighty, and may the Lord expunge him from the land of the living and erase his name from the book of life, and let him suffer everlasting damnation. Let the earth swallow him up so that he may be sent down alive into the yawning maws of hell and thrust into bonds of eternal torment."

Nor did pious William forget earthly punishments, adding as an afterthought, "Moreover, by the laws of the world, let the judges make him pay a hundred pounds of gold to the monks against whom he has trespassed." Evidently the early founders were not men to leave anything to chance.

As a result of such bequests, monasteries, like feudal lords, owned lands, estates, forests, cattle, and serfs and, in some cases, had vassals who did them homage.

Not all founders were known for their kindness. Fulk of Anjou, plunderer, murderer, robber, and swearer of false oaths, a truly terrifying character of fiendish cruelty, founded not one but two large abbeys. This Fulk was filled with unbridled passion, a temper directed to extremes. Whenever he had the slightest difference with a neighbor he rushed upon his lands, ravaging, pillaging, raping, and killing; nothing could stop him, least of all the commandments of God. This appalling man had countless crimes upon his conscience, but when seized with a fit of remorse he abandoned himself to incredible penances. Thus the very tomb of St. Martin, whose monks he had ill-treated, saw him prostrate, with bare feet and in penitent's dress; and four times during his life he went to Jerusalem as a devout pilgrim, treading half-naked the sorrowful road of the passion while two of his servants flogged him until the blood flowed, crying, "Lord, receive thy perjured Fulk!" When contemplating the torments of hell, vividly depicted in paintings, sculpture, and illuminated manuscripts, even the greatest sinners sometimes became meek as lambs doing good works, particularly when they were getting old and sick. Cruelty and piety went hand in hand, sometimes even overlapped.

Together with land, a wealthy donor sometimes also bestowed precious wonder-working relics upon a favorite monastery, and their display immediately attracted crowds of pilgrims, which were a welcome source of added income.

Men became monks for many reasons, but at the core was a belief that life on earth—this vale of tears and corruption—was merely a severe preparation for eternal life in heaven. After all, true human happiness was rare during the Century of Lead and Iron. Life on earth was important only as a foundation for afterlife in which a poor soul might be rewarded, if very lucky, for starvation and oppression suffered on earth.

Rewards in heaven were best gathered by withdrawal from the world which alone ensured serenity and peace of mind. Asceticism, the conquest of the flesh by renunciation of otherwise lawful pleasures enabled the soul to focus on God and salvation. A hairshirt swarming with vermin, or a knotted girdle of thorns worn underneath one's robe helped the pious to concentrate on matters divine.

There were, of course, other reasons. The church or monastery offered the only chance to the poor and lowly to gain some learning, a meal and a roof over one's head, sometimes even to live well and make a name for oneself. To many the cloister opened a wider vista than the village or the small nascent city. Inside its walls one was considerably safer than inside a peasant's hovel, though only comparatively. The many abandoned ruins of ransacked cloisters testified to this.

Originally, the forerunners of medieval monks and nuns had been solitary anchorites and hermits living in caves. Later, the rule most widely accepted by those fleeing the things of the world was that of St. Benedict, the Father of Monasticism. Shunning Rome because of its wickedness, Benedict made his abode inside a grotto in the hills outside the city. After years of solitude he was joined by three others wanting to share his life of abnegation and devotion. Thus a small community of believers came into being. It grew until caves became too small to contain it, and in 529 Benedict built his monastery on Monte Cassino, south of Rome.

The rules St. Benedict established at Monte Cassino were adopted by most European monasteries. They were severe, and nothing was further from the founder's mind than attracting men to submit themselves to the discipline he had laid down. Becoming a Benedictine monk was to be made as difficult as possible, to ensure that only the most dedicated should enter the brotherhood.

First it should be ascertained that the spirit that moved an applicant came truly from God: "Let him persist in knocking at the gate from four to five days and patiently bear all the injuries inflicted upon him, and if he still persists, let him be in the guest's house for a few days . . . Let there be put before him all the hard, rough things through which lie in the path to God. And let the rules be read to him after two months, and if he stands firm, let him be conducted to a novice's cell and have his patience and humility tried for another four months."

After months of hardship, scrutiny, and observation, the candidate was finally received into the community "knowing himself now established by the law of the Rule so that it is not lawful for him from this day forward to leave the monastery, nor to free his neck from the yoke of the Rule which it was permitted him after such prolonged deliberation to refuse or accept."

Gerbert did not have to knock for four or five days for admittance. He entered St. Gèraud as an oblate, that is, a young boy destined to become a monk. Parents gave their children to an abbey to acquire merit in heaven or simply to know them safe and cared for. Sometimes an abbey received a younger son barred from inheritance, for whom there was no place else. Some married priests, or those who had illegitimate offspring from concubines, gave their children to be monks in expiation of their own sins. It was the custom to give a donation together with the child, usually a deed of land.

We do not know at what age Gerbert became an oblate. Raoul Glaber, the monk-chronicler, was twelve years old when he was given to his monastery. Perhaps Gerbert was of similar age. On admission the oblate underwent a solemn ceremony designed "to cut him off henceforward irrevocably from the world."

After Gerbert became a famous teacher, abbot, bishop, and pope, many historians engaged in speculation about the date and place of his birth and parentage. Some said that he was born in 938, others in 945, 950, or somewhere in between those dates. One chronicler said that he was born in the village of Becciac, another maintained that he entered the world at Quercy, because of a nearby forest called Bois de Gerbert and an old manor named Maison du Pope. Early writers invented distinguished ancestries for their hero, saying that he was descended from the famous Romans Cicero and Caesius or even from Hercules. That he had been born noble was inferred from a letter in which the emperor Otto III wrote to him: "We are of the same blood." It was even surmised that Gerbert was the emperor's father, but Otto had meant only that they were related through their love of science and philosophy.

Such wild guesses bring to mind a pious bishop of the period who manufactured out of whole cloth the biographies of saintly men of whom not much more was known than their names because he thought it was fitting that something should be related of their lives.

He said that he wrote only after much time spent in prayer and meditation, putting down only what was inspired by God.

More plausibly, it was affirmed that his father was a certain Agilbertus or Ughelli, "a poor serf employed by the monks of St. Gèraud," a shepherd "grave and meditative amid his simple tasks." A few writers theorized that he had to be a bastard "because otherwise he would surely have related something about his parents," but this is mere speculation. All that is certain is what he himself wrote: that he came from poor and humble parents.

Gerbert's life as an oblate, or child monk, must have followed the customary pattern. Usually, when a boy was offered for holy orders, his parents brought him to the altar after mass had been said and had him make an offering. They then gave him into the hands of the officiating priest, who made the sign of the cross over him. If they desired him to become a monk on the same day, they let the abbot bless him and pour holy water over his head, after which his hair was cropped with shears amid the singing of psalms. The oblate was then stripped and clothed anew with the cowl, his monk's habit, while a prayer was said over him. When the boy reached the age of reason he had to make his profession like any adult, except for the benediction of the cowl, which he had already received as an oblate.

The life of a young would-be monk was austere, nor was he spared the proverbial rod. "If the boys commit any fault in their psalmody or other singing, either by sleeping or such like transgression, let there be no delay, but let them be stripped instantly of frock and cowl, and beaten in their shirt only with supple and smooth osier rods provided for this purpose . . . If any happen to linger after rest, let them be smartly whipped; for children need custody with discipline and discipline with custody. Let their chastisement be either to be beaten with rods or to have their hair pulled strongly; but never are they to be disciplined with kicks or fists." On the other hand, a weak or sickly boy might, now and then, be "heartened" with a loving cup of hot spiced wine.

The day-to-day life of an oblate was never easy. They had to be up at dawn, wash and dress quickly, work and study hard, and never speak to each other without leave. At meals they had to sit "each on his own tree trunk without ever touching each other." They ate and slept little. They were never without supervision and always spied upon. The ever-threatening pliant, supple osier enforced strict obedience.

The rules governing the upbringing of oblates seem to have been designed to prevent the evils of masturbation and sexual experimentation, though that is never openly said. At night, one or more masters was supposed to stand between the beds with a rod in one hand and a lighted candle in the other, watching like hawks over every sound and movement. When drying their hands "let the oblates wipe their hands as far as possible one from the other at opposite ends of the towel. When sitting down, let not even the skirts of their robes touch."

Naturally, discipline varied from cloister to cloister. At St. Gèraud it seems to have been relatively mild because, in later years, Gerbert always remembered Aurillac with nostalgia and gratitude. Some of the monks he had known there remained his lifelong friends. Gerbert was also lucky because St. Gèraud had accepted the Cluniac reforms, its monks were hardworking, frugal, and very pious, contrasting in this respect from other monastics elsewhere who led vicious lives.

Benedictines were required to work, some in fields, some in workshops, and some, most important from Gerbert's point of view, in the scriptorium, copying books and manuscripts. A Benedictine cloister was self-supporting. The rule regulated in minute detail the monks' daily work and prayers. Every hour, one could almost say every minute, of the brothers' life was strictly prescribed.

Upon entering a monastery, the novice took the threefold vow of obedience, poverty, and chastity. In the case of an adult he was obliged to distribute all his worldly goods to the poor, or more often to surrender them by way of a solemn grant to the monastery, before he was admitted to holy orders. The rule did not permit a monk to own anything: "Let not any one presume to give or accept anything without the abbot's orders, nor to have anything of his own, neither book, nor writing-tablet, nor pen; no, nothing at all, since indeed it is not allowed for them to keep either body or will in their own power, but to look to receive everything necessary from their monastic father; and let not any one be allowed to have what the abbot has not either given or permitted. And let all things be common to all, as it is written: 'Neither did any one of them say or presume that anything was his own.'"

Architecture also followed a rigid pattern. South of the church was the cloister—four long, sheltered arcades forming a square, in some cases surrounding a fish pond. Grouped around the cloister were the main buildings: the refectory in which the brothers took their meals, the chapter house in which the abbey's business was conducted and the dormitory in which they slept. There was a kitchen, a bakery, and, not seldom, also a brewery. Beer was brewed commercially by monks as early as A.D. 800. Each house produced its own distinctive brew. Most offered two types—great beer, strong and full-bodied, reserved for the good brothers and their favored guests at one gallon per day apiece, and small beer, for common pilgrims and such. The brewers even had their own, somewhat questionable, patron-saint: St. Gambrinus. During the late Middle Ages the figure of the red-nosed jolly monk became a stereotype. An old proverb said,

> To drink like a Capuchin is to drink poorly.
> To drink like a Benedictine is to drink deeply.
> To drink like a Dominican is pot after pot.
> To drink like a Franciscan is to drink the cellar dry.

At the head of the monastery stood the abbot, whose sway was absolute. If an abbot died the monks elected a new one from among themselves—if the rule was adhered to. In some parts of Europe a suspiciously large number of abbots and abbesses were the sons and daughters or other close relatives of kings, dukes, and counts. Though ruling with unquestioned patriarchal authority, the abbot was supposed to make no important decision without consulting his monks, even the youngest brother. He was answerable to God for the souls of all his monks and was not to "overdrive" them or give them cause for "just murmurings." He was to be chosen for his "worthy manner of life and wisdom," even if last in the abbey's order of seniority. He was to be well versed in divine laws, chaste and sober minded—not "full of commotion, nor anxious, jealous, or overly suspicious, because such a one is never at rest." Above all, he was to "exalt mercy above judgment, that he himself may attain it." However, to the modern mind, punishments meted out by a "merciful" abbot for minor infractions seem very severe.

To help him, the abbot had a precentor who supervised the services and music; a sacrist who looked after the church and its treasures and saw to the ringing of the bells; a cellarer who watched over the food and drink supply; a chamberlain who was in charge of all clothing, including its washing and repair; an infirmarer who cared for the sick; an almoner who distributed gifts to the poor, mostly in the form of food; and a hospiter who saw to the needs of the ever-present guests.

A large amount of time—some four or five hours on weekdays, as much as eight hours on Sundays—was devoted to religious services, such as the recitation of the hours at which psalms were said, hymns sung, and prayers offered. Shortly before midnight the bell rang, and the monks rose, dressed, and went silently to the church for matins, the first office of the day. After a short interlude lauds were said, after which the monks returned to bed. At six in the morning they rose again for prime, followed by early mass, a frugal breakfast, and meeting in the chapter house to discuss the business of the day. At nine o'clock Tierce was said, followed by high mass. From then on until about five in the afternoon the monks pursued their daily tasks in fields, workshops, or scriptorium. It must be said that the lowliest work was left to serfs and lay brothers. At five, the monks assembled in the refectory for the single real meal. The fare was plain, coarse, dark bread, the staff of life. Red meat was forbidden.

During the meal one of the monks read aloud a chapter of the Bible, or from the works of one of the church fathers. At table silence was enforced, and unnecessary talk was discouraged at all times. A system of signs evolved as a substitute for speech. For instance:

"For the sign 'fish' imitate with your hand the motion of a fish's tail in water. For pike make the sign for 'fish' and then put your outstretched fingers before your mouth to indicate a pike's protruding teeth.

"For 'milk' grasp the little finger of your left hand with all the fingers of the right, and pull as one who draws milk from a cow.

"For 'book' move your hands as if turning pages.

"For 'bed' make the sign for house, put your right hand under your cheek and close your eyes.

"For 'cold' make a show of trembling and blow on your hands.

"For 'hot' wave your right forefinger about as if burned and then put it in your mouth."

And so on. Some monasteries had signs for hundreds of words.

Meals were followed by a short period during which the monks could talk or play games if they wished. Then came the last office of the day, compline, and by nightfall the monks were all in bed observing the "time of the great silence" until the bell rang for matins.

Alms giving was a sacred duty—"Alms in kind every day, alms three times a week, alms to all passersby, general alms on Sunday, alms to all who shall ask."

At the Cluny Hospitium, the *granaturius* gave one pound of bread to all comers on the first day of the week, a half-pound thereafter, also fish, vegetables, meat, wine, and, when available, a penny.

As to the monks' cleanliness, and medieval cleanliness in general, there is a great deal of contradiction. It is said that in Gerbert's days people washed and bathed more often than commonly thought. The Rule of St. Benedict provided that monks should wash the feet of guests promptly on arrival, but this might have been done more in imitation of Christ's washing the feet of his disciples than for reasons of cleanliness. In England, some of the old Roman baths were still in use, and elsewhere pious donors left money for maintaining public baths "so that also the poor may clean themselves." In Benedictine houses the masters saw to it that the oblates washed themselves upon rising, and streams were diverted into water ducts to flush out the drains and latrines, the so-called necessaria, to carry off the wastes and "leave everywhere neat and spotless."

In contrast, there are many indications that too much cleanliness was held in low regard, if not considered outright sinful. The faithful were warned that hell contained a bath of fire, hotter than molten ore, and wider and deeper than the ocean. It was reserved for those who bathed too often out of vanity and carnal delight, people who slept on soft featherbeds, dreaming unchaste dreams.

Odo of Cluny quoted St. Jerome's praise of Hilarion the Anchorite: "He cut his hair once a year, on Easter day . . . When once he had clad himself in sackcloth, he never washed it . . . lest so great a desire for cleanliness infect your soul with uncleanliness."

Of Adelbert of Bremen and Bruno of Cologne it is said with special praise that they were very saintly men because they eschewed the pleasures of the bath. The church looked with disfavor on bath houses on account of their supposed immorality. Public baths, in which men and women bathed naked, were already—quite unsuccessfully—forbidden in 745 by St. Boniface. A proverb said that the public bath "was a great place for a woman to get with child." The medieval words for bath—*bagnio* and *bordello*—eventually came to mean houses of prostitution.

Volumes could be written about the church's, and particularly the monks', attitude toward women and sex. Woman—the diabolic female principle—was considered the deadliest of all obstacles to the soul in search of salvation, womanly beauty a satanic distraction, a woman's charm the devil's snare to lure men into sin. It was seriously debated by learned scholars whether women had souls. It was, after all, "a single woman, Eve, through whom Adam was banished from Paradise, by which she brought about original sin and condemned Christ to suffer on the cross." Women were the accursed "daughters of Eve who, in league with the Serpent, tempted man to eat the forbidden fruit."

Some historians ascribed the idea of woman as the great temptress, manipulated by Satan to ensnare poor, sinful man, to Jewish biblical writings, a general male fear of woman, and the guilt feelings of early ascetics and pious hermits.

In the words of William E. H. Lecky: "Woman was represented as the door of hell, as the mother of all human ills. She should be ashamed at the very thought that she is a woman. She should live in continual penance on account of the curses she has brought upon the world. She should be ashamed of her dress, for it is the memorial of her fall. She should be especially ashamed of her beauty, for it is the most potent instrument of the daemon."

Women were the "inferior sex," and "great was the peril and temptation they caused to men"—the "superior sex." It was said that "the badness of men was yet better than the goodness of women." Judicially, women had few rights. In certain places a seven-year-old son was given guardianship over his widowed mother. In most parts of Germany, a husband had the right to sell his wife. Men were exhorted to physically punish their wives, short of breaking bones and knocking out teeth, for nagging, talking back, or being disobedient. In the Nibelungen Saga, the hero, Siegfried, belabors his beloved Kriemhilde, daughter and sister of kings, with a stout club for annoying him with her chatter. The confessor of St. Elizabeth, not only a queen but eventually a saint, frequently chastised her by slapping her face.

To the Christian teachers, every sexual act was inherently dangerous and sinful, because "the devil dwells below the girdle." The woman's sexual organs were called the "gate of hell." Her very glances could kill. Proverbs of the time maintained that it was "better to go mad than give free rein to desire" and that "if a woman is chaste, it is only for lack of opportunity."

Odo of Cluny often enumerated to his monks the wiles of the daughters of Eve: "Their shiny shoes, by their very creaking, excite wanton eyes to feverish desire. Their hair falls down for a little, and is gathered up again. Neck and throat are casually bared by letting fall away their cloak, and are hastily covered again as though they had not meant them to be seen."

To resist the allure of sex was regarded as heroic virtue, and heroic were the means to avert it by fasting, bathing in icy streams, scourging oneself until the blood flowed, and other mortifications of the flesh. One dying ascetic, having separated from his wife forty years before, when she came to visit him, cried out, "Take the straw away, woman, begone! Take the straw away, there is fire yet!"

Of St. Hugh of Grenoble, "a man of wondrous modesty and chastity," it was said that in all his life he knew only one woman by sight. Some prided themselves in their power to withstand carnal temptation. Ancelin, bishop of Beccy, boasted, "I for my part can look indifferently upon any woman whatsoever; because I instantly flay them all," by which he meant that in his imagination he stripped off their skin, contemplating with pious satisfaction "the foul corruption beneath it."

There are, however, contradictions in attitudes, typical of the tenth century. One commentator considered woman "superior to man because Adam was made of mere clay, but Eve from man's side; superior in place, because Adam was fashioned outside Eden, and Eve within; superior in conception, because the Virgin conceived Christ which no man could do; superior in apparition, because the Savior appeared to Mary Magdalen before HE appeared to HIS disciples; superior in heaven, because the Mother of Christ was exalted above the choirs of angels."

Not all priests and monks shared in the detestation and avoidance of the "vessel of corruption called woman," and not all monasteries were as devout as St. Gèraud. Universal terror and a fear of the apocalypse pervaded the tenth century, and many monks lived as if they expected no tomorrow. Comparatively few among them were endowed with heroic virtue. Their licentiousness was proverbial. Many had wives or kept concubines. As a matter of fact, the well-regulated Benedictine abbey with its hardworking, devout, and chaste monks was the exception rather than the rule. It was principally because so many tenth-century monasteries had become "cesspools of vice" that Cluniac reforms had been instituted.

Gerbert's pupil Richer mentioned in his chronicles monks who squandered their cloisters' revenues, forgetting all discipline, preferring the tournament to the church, ending up as robbers and thieves in monks' habits. He described communal life abandoned, days and nights filled with drinking bouts, revels, and debauches.

"At St. Ghislain the clergy lived in the cloister together with their wives and children; the sacred relics were only there to entice from common folk gifts which were spent on carousals. At Lobbes the worst scenes were enacted. When he tried to recall the monks to the observation of their Rule they ill-treated their abbot Erluin. He tried to banish those who would not reform; whereupon three of these outcasts fell upon him, cut out his tongue and blinded him."

Farfa was one of the richest Italian cloisters. Situated in the Sabine hills, it was destroyed by Arabs in 925. After it had been rebuilt the monks began to "live riotous and depraved lives." They murdered one of their abbots because he tried to force them to conform to the rule. The monks then made themselves masters of the abbey. They called themselves abbots, divided the monastery treasure, and acquired wives and mistresses. One monk named Campo fathered three sons and seven daughters, setting them up with money from the treasury. Another monk had so many illegitimate children that "there was not enough money left to enrich them all." The monks took up their abodes in villas around Farfa. They destroyed their cloister cells "so that nobody should be able to force them to live in them again." They melted down holy vessels and utensils to make jewels for their wives and concubines. Rome sent pious monks to reform Farfa. They were manhandled and fled in terror. The pope installed a new abbot by force or arms, but he was promptly poisoned. Another abbot appointed by the pope thought it prudent to make common cause with the monks, joining them in their debaucheries "in order to survive," as he informed his superiors in Rome. He did it with such gusto that he was taken in flagrante delicto committing adultery. Rome let him off with a hefty monetary fine, which says much about the morals of the capital.

In 972, Adalbero of Rheims, who was to become one of Gerbert's closest friends and allies, struggled vainly against his monks' obsession with fine clothes: "They wear little mirrors on top of their shoes so that with each step they have an opportunity of admiring themselves . . . Their habits are as tight as those of women, so that they exhibit the shape of their arse. They walk about in costly stuffs and furs, all colored like peacocks." Adalbero also thundered against "shoes with ears" and breeches or tunics of "luxurious linen, so fine it scarcely hides the shameful parts."

Fortunately, such things did not happen at St. Gèraud, "the abode of piety and learning," when Gerbert lived there. Young Gerbert was launched upon his illustrious career when, one day, he chanced upon his abbot, Gerauld de Saint-Cléré (or Céré), who was taking a walk in the cloister garden. Noticing the boy's precocious intelligence and eagerness to learn, the abbot decided to entrust him to the monastery's scholar, Brother Raymond de Lavaur, who taught him the trivium—grammar, rhetoric, and dialectic. Raymond must have been no mean scholar. He instructed Gerbert so well in these subjects that he never had to study them again with other masters.

It was said of the seven liberal arts making up the sum total of tenth-century higher learning that "grammar speaks; dialectics teach truth; rhetoric colors words; arithmetic deals with numbers; geometry measures; music sings; and astronomy looks to the stars." The first three subjects were the basics, the so-called trivium. The other four constituted the quadrivium and were not taught at Aurillac.

A pupil was first of all instructed in grammar, which, in the words of a ninth-century scholar, Rabanus Maurus of Fulda, "Is a science which teaches us to know the poets and historians, and instructs us in the art of speaking and writing correctly." Grammar was taught in Latin, the universal language of the church. The student had to learn poems, psalms, passages from the Bible, and writings of the church fathers by heart. He might get a generous dose of Boethius and Erigena without being exposed to such pagan writers as Cicero, Livy, or Ovid, acquaintance with whom, it was thought at the time, would endanger his immortal soul.

Rhetoric was an adjunct to grammar. It not only stressed oratory, a highly respected art when speech was almost the only form of communication, but also the *ars dictandi*, that is, the art of writing a good letter. Dialectic was akin to logic, the art of clear and concise thinking, taught mainly by studying Boethius's commentaries on Aristotle's logical treatises or his *Consolation of Philosophy*.

Raymond taught a "particularly elegant Latin" for which Gerbert later became renowned among learned people. He also mastered the art of oratory "necessary for those who may be called to preach," and in later life he astonished his listeners with "the distinction and elocution with which he was wont to explain to his students the authors of antiquity."

"It is Raymond," Gerbert used to say with some exaggeration, "to whom I owe all that I know."

It was said that young pupils in monasteries learned not through their brains but through their buttocks, "that part to which the rod of wholesome discipline was most liberally applied." At St. Gall, the supple osier was so vigorously wielded that it left the pupils bleeding profusely and so angry that they set fire to the cloister. We can imagine Raymond as having been lenient in the use of the whip, because Gerbert always mentioned him with great affection. When Gerbert himself had become a famous teacher he wrote to his old master, "The love I bear you is known to all, Latins as well as Barbarians, who share in the fruits of my labor." When the abbot Gerauld de Saint-Céré died in 986 and Raymond was elected to succeed him, Gerbert, ever the diplomat, managed to express at the same time his grief for the first and his joy for the second event: "When death robbed me of my most illustrious father Gerauld, it felt as if I had lost a part of myself. But when, in conformity to my wishes, you, my most beloved, were chosen to succeed him, I was again wholly reborn as your son."

Thus Gerbert entered his real callings, the worlds of learning and, later, diplomacy. He must have made the scriptorium with its precious library his domain. Books were very valuable because at every stage they had to be made laboriously by hand. They were produced almost exclusively by monks. Every larger monastery had its scriptorium in which the brothers carefully, word by word, copied texts put before them—a psalter, the life of the saints, or even a scientific treatise, though worldly science, in the time of Gerbert, was looked upon with great suspicion.

Some monks carefully prepared the parchment and cut it to size. Others scraped unwanted texts from the precious vellum so that it could be used again. Certain monks did only the lettering. The script at that period was still the uncial derived from and closely resembling the old Roman letters. Specialists did the embellishing and illuminating, still others the stitching and binding. A very few made costly covers of wood, leather, and metal, encrusted with gold and precious stones, though probably not at St. Gèraud.

It was because making a book took so much time, patience, and effort that books were treasured. For fear of fire no lit candles or fireplaces were allowed in the scriptorium, and many were the complaints of monks whose fingers were frostbitten. At the cloister of Emmerau one monk went blind after copying missals for lack of candles.

So highly regarded was the transcribing room and the work done in it, that at its consecration an abbot uttered a special prayer: "Deign, oh Lord, to bless the scriptorium of thy servants, that all which they write there may be comprehended by their minds and realized in their works." Another prayer, expressing the thought that learning always came second after piety, was "Oh, Lord, give me both knowledge and goodness, but if I am not worthy to possess both, give me goodness so that I may possess eternal life."

A monk-scribe was highly respected, his work sacred. As one of them wrote, "We use our fingers gloriously in place of our tongues to combat, with pen and ink, the ravings of the devil." Or, "As I dip my pen into my goat's horn filled with ink, for every word of holy scripture I write, a wound is given to the devil." Some thought that for every line written, a sin was forgiven them. One proverb maintained, "He who does not turn up the earth with a plough ought to paint the parchment with his pen."

Inside the scriptorium absolute silence was the rule, as nothing was permitted to distract the monks from their work. A brother, when asking for a book, made the sign of extending his hand, making motions as if turning the pages, but in order to indicate a pagan work, he was also told to "scratch his ear as a dog does—because, says the regulation, unbelievers may well be compared to a dog." Convents also had their scriptoria where learned nuns were at work, such as the famous poetess Hroswitha, who lived in the days of Gerbert.

Books were so expensive that some monasteries put them under anathema, that is, forbade their being lent or borrowed on pain of excommunication. In other cloisters certain books were reserved only for the use of the brothers while the less valuable could be lent to the studious poor, "seeing that such a loan is one of the chief works of mercy and a deed of great merit before God."

The scribes firmly believed that devils, devilkins, imps, and hobgoblins were forever trying to hinder them in their holy work. One monk was convinced that the many fleas whose bites diverted him from copying, induced him to make many mistakes, and, by his scratching, caused him to spill ink over his manuscript, were in reality little devils masquerading as fleas. Another studious brother was sure that his falling asleep over his writing was the work of playful, mischievous imps that kept pulling down his eyelids. One monk who was plagued by a sparrow that forever pecked at him and his pen recognized in the bird the devil in clever disguise and plucked it alive saying, "There, small fiend, creep away naked and begone!" Still another scribe was visited by a devilkin that took up its abode inside the poor man's belly making "rumbling noises like a toad which, for hours, distracted all who were working in the scriptorium."

Such evil spirits were admonished and exorcised with appropriate curses: "Away, you lean sow, you devil's arse, you fiends' excrement, ordure, obstinate accursed fly . . . out, out, out! Don't kick against the prick! Away, loathsome cobbler, stinking he-goat, sooty spirit from tartarus, away! Back into thine infernal kitchen, you bestial vomit!" But usually the fleas continued to bite and the belly to rumble.

If hobgoblins ever prevented Gerbert from studying, he never mentioned it, nor is it likely that he took fleas for devils. His was a cool, critical mind, atypical of that unhappy time. He had apparently gone as far as he could in his studies with the limited resources of Aurillac. Though it is said that the cloister school of St. Gèraud had many excellent copies of the classics, they were still too few for the young future bibliomaniac who "lusted after books as a lecher after voluptuous women."

Of the seven liberal arts only three—the trivium—were taught by Raymond. The quadrivium—arithmetic, geometry, astronomy, and music—was not taught at all at St. Gèraud for the simple reason that in the whole of France and Lorraine there were then only four masters capable of teaching it, all of them far away from Aurillac. Gerbert was at a dead end. Of mathematics and astronomy, two sciences to which he felt irresistibly drawn, he knew next to nothing. Of music he knew only psalms and plain chants that the monks used in their liturgy.

If fate had not intervened, Gerbert probably would have spent his whole life at Aurillac, eventually replacing Raymond in teaching the trivium to young oblates, lording over the scriptorium, enriching the library, possibly even becoming abbot, but still "a universal mind imprisoned in a too small space." But good fortune arrived in the shape of Borrel, count of Barcelona, duke of Hither-Spain and lord of Catalonia. Together with a large entourage this mighty personage appeared at St. Gèraud in the course of a pilgrimage. We may surmise that the abbey possessed wonder-working relics that could attract such a great baron, though it is not known what they might have been. Borrel was received with due honors, making himself comfortable in the hospitarium, probably sampling the cellarer's excellent wine.

The abbot Gerauld and Brother Raymond had been for some time concerned about Gerbert's further development, having "imparted to him all the spiritual food and sweet skills in their power to bestow." Gerauld asked the count whether he had in his country learned men capable of teaching the quadrivium, particularly arithmetic and astronomy. Borrel replied that, indeed, there were such men in Catalonia. Gerauld said that he had in his care a young monk, still a mere youth, but exceptionally gifted and intent to study the subjects mentioned. Would Borrel consider taking the young brother along and finding a teacher for him? The count said he would, and thus the matter was settled.

In all this a contemporary chronicler saw "the finger of God, the hand of providence and a true miracle." And so Gerbert, in 967, flew the nest. Always he remembered "that most holy company that had nourished him and brought him up." Forty-six still existing letters addressed to Gerauld are proof of his lifelong affection for his old abbot. In one of them he wrote, "No better gift has God given to man than that of friends . . . Happy was the day, happy the hour in which I had the good fortune to meet with a man whose name is enough to drive all care from me . . . Ever firmly fixed in my breast is the face of my friend, of Gerauld, at once my master and my father."

Many years later, as bishop and finally as pope, Gerbert still remembered the monastery of St. Gèraud, furthered its cause, and sent gifts to the friends of his youth. He left, as the old saying goes, "with one moist and one dry eye," a little reluctant, perhaps, but also eager to leave Aurillac's confining walls behind and embrace a new world.

CHAPTER THREE

Like a Falcon Unleashed

"LIKE A FALCON, UNLEASHED AND UNHOODED, flown from his master's fist, gamboling in the air, diving and tumbling, feasting his eyes on woods, meadows, and all of God's world. . . ." So Gerbert set out to try his wings. He left behind him the narrow but comforting world of Aurillac, the only one he had known—the monastery, the hamlet, and the surrounding fields. Naturally curious and blessed with a keen, inquisitive mind, he must have been filled with awe as he set out on his journey into the unknown.

Traveling in the tenth century was perilous. Those who could avoid it did. Roads, where they existed, were atrocious, and there were no inns. The greater part of Europe was still covered with wild, un-drained bogs and primeval forests in which the wanderer encountered packs of roaming, ravenous wolves and ferocious grunting boars able to disembowel a victim with one swipe of their curving tusks. Travelers might even come face to face with an aurochs—a wild species of oxen resembling the buffalo—which, in those days, still foraged the countryside and survived in Poland until the fifteenth century.

One French traveler was set upon by a monstrous wolf which, he guessed, "took me for a ram." Luckily, the man was a stout fellow, well armed and protected, and he owed his life to his fine coat of mail covering not only his body but also his throat. With dagger, sword, and ax the man finally got the better of the beast. When the wolf was skinned and his belly opened "there were found in its stomach parts of human limbs."

More dangerous than wild beasts were wild humans who waylaid, robbed, or killed unwary wanderers and, in times of famine, even made meals of them.

Experienced wayfarers gave the rude castles a wide berth and hid themselves at the approach of riders, because strangers were fair game for anyone stronger who might take a liking to their wallets, clothes, or shoes, leaving them naked in the road. People set out on a journey well armed with shield and spear. According to the rule of the road, travelers walked or rode on the left to have their right hands free to wield lance or battle-ax against possible assailants.

The king or local duke had little power beyond his own ancestral domain. A strong central government did not exist. Some so-called highroads were so narrow that two horses were scarcely able to pass each other. The only halfway passable roads were the old Roman ones and those near monasteries, because keeping them in good shape was a pious deed and pleasing to God. An old chronicle tells what happened to a peasant lad working for an abbey: "A boy from another monastery was sent by the prior to bring green hay from the meadow. The servants loaded this upon an ass which, on the way homeward, passed through a certain sunken way, where the load was caught between the banks on either side and the ass, slipping away, came home without the boy's knowledge. He stood by the hay, smiting it oftentimes and threatening the ass (which he did not know had got away) as best he could. Nor did he stir from the spot until the brethren came out to find him, who could scarce persuade him that the ass was clean gone and that the hay could not walk without a beast of burden."

The king and the great nobles were forever feuding among themselves and had no armed men to spare to police the roads. Fords were usually unbridged, while ferrymen were notorious for holding up passengers in midstream for extra payment or simply robbing them while holding a knife to their throats. Feudal lords fleeced all persons passing through their domains. A tax called *pontage* was leveled for allowing travelers to use the local bridge. Cheaper was *rivage* or *travers*—a toll for simply wading across. A local magnate might even force travelers to cross by bridge rather than wading, or use a toll road instead of just making their way through the forest in order to make them pay up. Lowly peasants or peddlers, carrying their bundles to market, still had to pay the *péage*, as a sort of foot tax for walking on the owner's land. Such payments were usually lumped together under the name of *maltotes* or "bad tolls" on account of their unpopularity.

Travelers usually went on foot or horseback because most roads could not be negotiated by carts. They went from monastery to monastery because a cloister was the only place where wanderers could feel safe, get a meal and a cheering cup of hot mulled wine to restore them from the rigorous journey, and, finally, a sack of straw to sleep on.

Richer, Gerbert's student, gives us a glimpse of what a short, unusually peaceable and uneventful journey was like. Richer tells of traveling from Rheims to Chartres to attend lectures on medicine and philosophy by the saintly and learned cleric Heribrand. He had to cover some 120 miles of flat country in what was then the best developed and settled region of western Europe. Yet Richer speaks of "this far and difficult voyage." He complains that his abbot had let him have only one packhorse, no money at all, and, worse, not even a change of clothes. Richer was accompanied by a serf to help him, and for greater security, he teamed up with a horseman also bound for Chartres.

On the first day they got as far as Orbais, where the abbot received them hospitably. The next day, on the way to Meaux, they got lost in a thick forest and wasted six miles and much time groping blindly in the wilderness. Near Chateau-Tierry they were surprised by a storm with rain coming down in torrents. The overworked packhorse collapsed "as if hit by lightning" and gave up the ghost. The servant "was discouraged," and Richer left him with the baggage after telling him that no matter how tired he might be, he must on no account fall asleep, but stay awake and watch the baggage. Soaked to the skin, Richer then doubled up behind his mounted companion.

When they got to Meaux not a single light was showing. It was so dark that they could not see the bridge, which was in any case so full of holes that even in daylight the locals, who knew it well, did not dare to cross. The two wanderers looked for a boat but could not find one. They decided to try the bridge after all and discovered it at last after much searching and groping. Feeling his way across, Richer's resourceful companion covered hole after hole with his huge shield, guiding the hooves of his horse. "With the help of heaven, now bent over, now upright, at times going forward, and at others backwards, he finally, wondrously got me and his mount across." Totally exhausted they reached the church of St. Faro, where the monks refreshed them with "the cup of friendship."

Outside the darkness was "absolute and abhorrent," but Richer's companion volunteered to go back and fetch the serf with the baggage, whom he found after much searching and "hallooing back and forth." The rider did not dare to face the dangers of the bridge a second time. He and the serf found a peasant's hut to shelter from the rain, though the owner, "having no food to spare did not invite them to dine." Both men, together with the horse and baggage, arrived at St. Faro in the morning, bedraggled and ravenously hungry. The kind abbot fed them and even the horse was given oats and straw. Richer had not slept a wink, worrying how it would all turn out.

Richer left the useless servant at Meaux and finally arrived safely at Chartres. It had taken him a whole week to reach his goal. What had frightened him the most, Richer admitted, was being caught in the open after nightfall "when it is pitch dark and one cannot see the hand before one's eyes." Richer could count himself lucky. He had encountered only the usual trials and tribulations of medieval travel, had not met up with robbers or wild animals, and had been only moderately inconvenienced.

The great mass of people did not dare to travel at all. Their village was the only world they knew. And yet a few traveled far and wide—clerics, pilgrims, and traders. Two hundred years before Gerbert, Charlemagne and the caliph Harun-al-Rashid exchanged embassies and gifts. German kings sent ambassadors to the emirs of Cordova or to the rulers of Byzantium. Being ambassadors, however, did not always protect men from being abused, plundered, or imprisoned. Some German rulers married Anglo-Saxon or Byzantine princesses. Vikings sailed down the rivers of Russia to the Black Sea to fight in the pay of Byzantine emperors against Saracens in Asia Minor. Arab traders and voyagers commented favorably upon the Russian steambaths which "in a country of icy wastes warmed up the despairing wanderer's frozen bones and stiffened limbs." Muslim merchants reached the shores of the Baltic Sea and ventured into the arctic regions of Scandinavia, trading for furs and amber, bringing back tales of northern lands "where the sun shines only one hour in a day and where, in winter, shaggy, blond-haired unbelievers cower in near endless darkness as then the sun does not rise at all."

Few maps existed, and those that did were hard to read. One showed the earth as a flat disk surrounded by limitless waters, held up by the Savior and by saints taking turns so that the world should not fall into the bottomless nothing. Tales of headless people in Africa or people in India with only one eye in their foreheads were readily believed, as were stories of giant ants mining for gold and diamonds, which they had to guard against fire and poison-breathing basilisks.

Gerbert's first great adventure was considerably longer than Richer's journey. From Aurillac to Barcelona was about 140 miles as the crow flies, but, unlike crows, Gerbert and his companions could not fly over the Pyrenees.

This rugged range was only sixty miles wide, but its mountain passes were so steep that even goats and mules experienced difficulties getting through them. Although Gerbert left no record of the crossing, perhaps the company chose to take the one fairly easy pass in the west, the famous gap of Roncesvalles where Roland, Charlemagne's famous paladin, died loyally fighting Saracens.

Gerbert's crossing was undoubtedly helped by traveling in the train of a great lord, protected by Count Borrel's well-armed retainers. Most likely his patron also provided him with a mount, even if only a mule or donkey. Thus, after what must have been a hazardous crossing, the whole cavalcade descended into the Catalan plains, the "land of castles." Catalonia was then considered to be a frontier district of France, the Spanish March of Hither-Spain, established by Charlemagne as a bastion against Moorish incursions. Its mountains, during times of war, were a haven for Christian refugees.

Here people spoke Catalan—"Cato's Latin"—a patois introduced by Roman legionnaires, mostly barbarian mercenaries. The nobles spoke the now extinct *langue d'oc*—the "language of yes"—the speech of southern France where "yes" was pronounced "oc," in contrast to the northern *langue d'oil*, where it was pronounced "oil," which in time became the modern oui.

The country had seen many conquerors come and go, from prehistoric bison hunters to Celt-Iberians, Basques, Carthagenians, Romans, Jews, Visigoths, Arab Muslims and Franks. The inhabitants were described as a people of mixed ancestry, hardheaded, sharp-witted, stubborn, proud, and rebellious. Others thought of Catalonia as a "country partially aboriginal, partially romanized, with a germanic veneer."

The roots of Christianity were as yet feeble. Hidden mountain valleys served as shelter for all sorts of folk not wanted elsewhere, some of these given to the worship of female demons. As late as A.D. 900 Bishop Nantigis of Urgel went up into the high country "to consecrate heathen temples where idols were worshipped"—a strange ritual for a Christian bishop to perform. Indeed, all through the tenth century faithful monks talked about heathen living in dark and hidden places adoring the images of goddesses with pendulous breasts and gravid bellies, practicing fire rituals, unchristian burial ceremonies, and other abominations. This was still a wild border country forever under the threat of Moorish invasions.

The mountains were full of game at the time of Gerbert's arrival, and people hunted and trapped their food. Local lords reserved for themselves "one haunch and all four feet of any bear" killed within their domains, "and one quarter of any other wild beast." In many places sword and knife were still the law. During incessant seigneurial wars nobles battled over a piece of pasturage "which wouldn't have fed a sick goat." The strong robbed and despoiled the weak, Christians and Muslims conducted raids into each others' territories, towns were conquered and reconquered, houses and farms burned, the peasants raped and slain. Men were murdered, mutilated, castrated, or had their hands hacked off. Women were not only raped but sometimes had their breasts cut off. Behind such atrocities was the understanding that peasants and serfs were equivalent to livestock and by killing or mutilating them a petty lord harmed his enemy—another petty lord—economically.

One gets an idea of the suffering this perpetual state of guerrilla warfare inflicted on rich and poor, townsfolk and serfs alike by looking at a Catalonian decree intended to bring about the Truce of God. Among deeds abhorrent and unlawful were listed: fighting on the sabbath and holy days, killing or maiming people who had sought sanctuary inside churches, violating nuns and wounding unarmed clerics, burning cloisters, destroying crops, and cutting down olive trees. The decree also stipulated that one should at least leave a poor peasant one horse for plowing and not mutilate him severely for "trifling reasons," nor take all of his and his wife's clothes and all the wax and honey from their beehives. Also, one should leave good Christians in peace from sundown to sunup so that they could sleep without fear during the hours of darkness, and, if it was necessary to plunder and harass them, to do so only in daylight. Thus it was considered acceptable to burn and ravage on weekdays, steal a man's livestock so long as one left him a single nag for plowing, rape women if they were not nuns, take a man's last shirt but leave him his loincloth, and mutilate a man lightly, perhaps by putting out only one of his eyes instead of two.

Decrees like this Truce of God were promulgated again and again throughout the tenth century without making the slightest impact.

"The man on horseback, protected by helmet and chain mail, armed with lance and sword, could defend himself, but against him there was no defense. He took what he liked. Taking was his only work, the one he did not despise." In later years Gerbert was to lament, "We live in a world of recklessness. Divine and human laws are violated due to the greed of wicked men and only what passion and force extorts is deemed right, after the manner of wild beasts."

Borrel, count of Hither-Spain, duke of the Spanish March—La Marca Hispanica—lord over the counties of Barcelona, Gerona, Ausona, and Urgel, was, for his time, a good and enlightened ruler, *un chef unique*, as one French historian described him. He tried to keep the peace in his domains, and he was pious and much given to pilgrimages, though usually he combined them with practical business and politics. He was the type of ruler expected to personally lead his men into battle, wielding sword and battle-ax. Owing only nominal allegiance to the French king, he was the fount of all justice and head of the Catalonian church insofar as he named his own bishops and abbots, often relatives, loyal and sure.

Such prelates were often men of the sword rather than men of the cloth, delighting in the hunt and in war, besieging and defending towns. On one such occasion, the archbishops of Barcelona, Gerona, and Vich died in battle against the Arabs of Cordova, "laying about him manfully, slaying pagans by the score, dying gloriously."

Borrel also installed one of his own sisters as abbess at St. Jean. In this he did better than one of his ancestors who gave the same job to one of his mistresses "so that both could enjoy the income from that nunnery." Monks and priests knew very well to whom they had to look for rewards and punishment, and they flattered Borrel and, later, his son and successor shamelessly, calling them "light of the land, glory of the world, prince illustrious throughout the universe." Thus the good Count Borrel, son of Sunifred or Suner, ruled happily on the whole, from 948 to 992, the third of a dynasty that had been founded by his grandfather Guifred the Hairy, of whom little is known except that he was "exceedingly unkempt and shaggy."

Borrel was married to a woman named Lutgarde, of whom we know only her name. Presumably, she was pleasing to her lord, and their marriage was one of the reasons for her husband's pilgrimage to St. Gèraud—a sort of honeymoon, perhaps, which providentially resulted in Gerbert's coming to Catalonia.

Below the count, considering themselves his equals in lineage, manliness, and pride, came his self-willed, scheming nobles. Their motto was "My horse, my son, my wife"—in that order. The horse, a man's most prized possession, came first. The son of his loins, whose task was to perpetuate the bloodline, came next. The wife ran a poor third. One hapless woman was captured and held for ransom by the Saracens. Her husband, a proud lord, considered the price far too high. He proclaimed that he carried the instrument to sire more sons between his legs and that he had no need of that particular wife. Any wife would do, and getting a new one would be no problem. Perhaps the ransom price was reduced.

The nobles lived in small, rude castles built on the most inaccessible rocks available. Rooms were tiny, bare, and uncomfortable. In cold weather they were full of smoke "with everybody's eyes red, dripping, and smarting." The words *noble, lord,* and *chatelain* evoke visions of splendor, perhaps images from the golden age of chivalry. In reality, the Catalan lords of the tenth century were a poor lot. To be a lord, it was said, one needed only one halfway presentable steed, a lance, a sword, a helmet, a shield, and a tent while on campaign. The worldly possessions of Guitard, lord of Barbera, consisted of one pair of shoes, one shirt, and a single pair of pants. Feeling his end near, Guitard had to sell his helmet and lance to insure for himself a decent funeral.

The baron Adalbert, a viscount's son, left to his heirs "all his furniture, to wit: one featherbed, three coverlets, two rugs—one of felt and one not of felt. Likewise all his money, namely forty silver pennies." Adelbert would have been considered wealthy because he possessed some coined money. Most of his contemporaries counted their wealth in heads of horses and cattle, in pigs and goats—"money that could walk on four legs."

The nobles' main amusements, in order of importance, were fighting and raiding, taking peasant wenches to bed, hunting and falconry, gaming, drinking bouts, and watching jugglers. Exploited and harassed by the nobles, the Catalan peasants were famous for their tenacity in struggling with unyielding soil and for, as a proverb had it, "making bread out of stones." They were called *villanos*, *pecheros*, or *pageses de remense*—peasants bound to the soil—and their lords had the right "to treat them well or ill according to their will." These peasants, or serfs, grew wheat, oats, and rye. A gruel made of cereals was their usual daily meal. Olive trees were still something of a rarity. A single, well-bearing tree made its owner a desirable son-in-law. Peppers (*pimientos*) and salt were the only spices. Mutton fat was used as grease, medicinal balm, and cooking medium. Wild chestnuts were a welcome addition to a meager diet. Pork was the preferred meat of free people.

Bad harvests were frequent, famines endemic. On holidays counts, bishops, and abbots distributed *pain et vin*, the proverbial bread and wine, to the poor, since wine was considered indispensable to a meal even for recipients of charity. The poor and starving were without numbers. In times of dire need many Catalans exposed their newborn children—"so many hungry mouths which could not be fed"—to die in some wild, out-of-the-way place, an evil custom also practiced in other parts of Europe, though the church frowned on it.

Lower still than the peasant was the slave "left over from a ruder age." Slaves were often valued less than mules or fat pigs. For the most part they were descendants of Roman and Visigoth slaves, prisoners of war, or wrongdoers condemned to servitude for the crimes of homicide and adultery. In Gerbert's time, their numbers had greatly diminished, and they could buy their liberty or become free simply by helping fight the Arab infidels. Throughout Europe outright slavery in the traditional classic sense decreased while, with feudalism establishing itself, more and more free peasants were made into serfs. The slave was no longer needed. Serfs were legally not slaves, but many a poor villain, bound to the land and at his lord's mercy, would not have seen much difference.

In 967, Borrel's capital of Barcelona was a city encompassing a mere twenty-five acres, on which huddled slightly under one thousand inhabitants. To young Gerbert, after little Aurillac, it must have appeared as a large, exciting metropolis, with its cathedral, abbey, and nearby port, its Roman-built aqueduct, and its stout Roman walls interspersed with more recently erected Frankish towers.

It was an ancient city, founded, it is said, by Hamilcar Barcas, Hannibal's father, who gave it his family's name, Barca, which in time became Barcino and, finally, Barcelona. The site on which it stood, watered by the Llobregat and Besos rivers, had already attracted Neolithic shore dwellers. The Carthaginian Barca was held in awe by the primitive native tribes surrounding it, the abode of a race of magicians and superhumans. The townspeople contributed their quota of stone slingers to Hannibal's army marching on Italy.

After Rome had conquered Carthage, Barca became a colony of Roman war veterans, who renamed it Barcino. They laid out a Roman-style city, complete with gridiron streets, temples, a forum, and a circus in which gladiators dutifully fought wild beasts and killed each other. The colonists enjoyed a number of basic amenities, such as public hot and cold baths and many comfort stations, as well as oil-burning street lamps—luxuries long forgotten in the days of Gerbert.

A Roman woman touring the outlands once complained that nothing ever happened in Barcino, a very boring city. For centuries of Roman occupation the city had no walls, precisely because nothing ever happened, and the city consequently did not need them. The Roman woman would have had no reason to complain of ennui once the time of the Great Migrations saw Germanic barbarians burning and sacking the defenseless town. The citizens belatedly encircled what was left of Barcino with massive walls of imposing height and thickness. In A.D. 415 the Visigoth king Ataulf, a semibarbarian married to the Roman princess Galla Placida, the great Theodosius's daughter, took Barcelona, probably by guile and diplomacy rather than by storm. He did not enjoy his city for long, as he was assassinated by rival chieftains. In 713, Barcelona was stormed by Arab Muslims who renamed it Bardjaluna, and in 801 it was occupied by the Franks and became the chief town of the Marca Hispanica. From 850 to 852 it was once more in the hands of the Moors.

Gerbert's sojourn in Spain coincided with the beginning of the so-called *Reconquista*, the reconquest of the Iberian peninsula by the Christians, who had once been driven by the Arabs into a small northwestern corner of Spain, the rugged mountainous region called Asturias. As the Islamic tide ebbed, the Christian expanded, though most of Spain was then still in Muslim hands.

Gerbert found the city at peace. Relations with the caliphate of Cordova were cordial, trade with Muslim Spain flourished. The Moorish danger seemed a thing of the past, and, behind their thick walls, the people of Barcelona felt smugly safe. Under Borrel's rule, the city was cosmopolitan. Good Christians dwelled in houses around the cathedral and near churches. Among them were Catalans and Franks from the Auvergne and Provence, many speaking the "language of yes," as well as a few visitors from Poitou and Burgundy. Walking in the streets one met Greek, Byzantine, Syrian, and Venetian sailors, even an occasional Viking or two, who were regarded with a good deal of suspicion. Always one encountered Moorish traders with silken stuffs, brocades, damascened swords, and thin-walled, iridescent glassware. Jews had their own quarters, protected and even welcomed during the reign of the tolerant Borrel. Among these Christians, Moors, and Jews many trembled at the thought of the approaching apocalypse because they had seen in the sky or in their dreams infernal beasts and demons heralding the day of doom. Some drew what they had seen on walls or sheets of parchment.

Most important, from Gerbert's point of view, were the many learned men one could find in Barcelona and elsewhere in Catalonia, men who had something to teach him. In the scholarship of its clerics, influenced by the wisdom and science of the Arabs, Catalonia was far advanced compared to the rest of Europe. In the words of the French historian Henri Focillon, Catalonia was "the region whose vitality in the tenth century is extraordinary. The monks who built the first vaulted churches of the West—St. Cecilia of Montserrat, St. Mary of Amer, St. Stephen of Baryoles, St. Martin of Canigou—were also men made for authority and for the high adventure of the mind."

CHAPTER FOUR

A Passion for Learning

IF A PASSION FOR LEARNING BOILED within Gerbert's heart, as his student Richer tells us, or as others wrote, "that he thirsted for knowledge as a wanderer in the desert for water," then Catalonia was the ideal place for him to quench his thirst. It was said that the Spanish March formed a bridge for Muslim science to cross to the West and that the Catalan earth was fertilized by both, the East and the West, and watered by the wisdom of three continents. Others called Hither-Spain "a door open to the glorious past—to the works of Greek and Latin philosophers and poets of antiquity."

The famous Catalonian libraries in the abbeys of Vich, Ripoll, Montserrat, and Cuxa, both in the numbers of books as well as in their variety, by far surpassed those of France and Germany. Nicolau d'Olwer, an expert in the matter, describes "the Vergilian glossaries and the commentators on Vergil in the library of Ripoll," works not available in the Cluniac abbeys of France. At Vich and Ripoll, in contrast to the monasteries east of the Pyrenees, the quadrivium as well as the trivium, the entire cycle of the seven liberal arts, was taught and taught well.

What distinguished the intellectual life in Catalonia from that of the rest of Europe was its tolerance and unorthodoxy.

The orthodox world, in Gerbert's age, was, on the whole, hostile to science. A papal chancellor condemned the sciences as "tricks and foolishness." It was preached that the yearning for knowledge was a sin if pursued "for any other purpose than to know God." Studies were considered of value if undertaken for the sake "not for this, but for that other, heavenly world." Reason was to be subjugated to faith, dialectic used as a game to "prove revelation out of reason."

Throughout the tenth century Christian thought in the West was dominated by the Cluniacs, who were armed with papal privileges and approval and who propagated their own ideas with tremendous force. It was said that the greatness of Cluny was really the greatness of its early abbots, four of whom—Odo, Majolus, Odilo, and Hugh— became venerated saints. "They were men of noble birth and unyielding character, born to command, educated to the highest level of the culture of those times; taking part in all the great movements of ecclesiastical and temporal politics."

While they had cleansed and revitalized a monasticism that had grown degenerate and corrupt, and therefore deserved the praise heaped upon them, these abbot-saints, "men of iron anti-humanism," had no use for classic learning or pagan authors. St. Odo held up the example of a dream he had experienced, a terrifying vision after reading one of Vergil's poems. Half awake and half asleep he beheld a wonderfully precious vase from which crawled loathsome, poisonous serpents, winding themselves around him and strangling his limbs. Fully awakened from this nightmare he perceived that the magnificent vase represented the work of enchanting seducers—the pagan authors— and that the snakes crawling from it were the pernicious heathen doctrines contained in their writings.

Odo at once renounced these profane masters, vowing to devote himself henceforth exclusively to the study of the Bible and sacred texts. His successor, abbot Aymar, also agonized over having "perused the lies of Vergil" and strictly forbade his monks to taste such forbidden fruits. St. Odilo likewise forbade the study of profane works. St. Gervin, abbot of the famous monastery of St. Riquier, "the ornament of Christendom," also confessed to having "lost himself in the study of profane authors" but then abjured all their books as coming from the devil and endangering his immortal soul.

Luckily for the development of Western thought, Gerbert did not share such fears but, swimming lustily against the mighty stream of orthodoxy, determined to study the ancients "with holy fervor," intent to "hone his mind as a knife is sharpened on a whetstone." Count Borrel again helped, acting as the instrument of providence, recommending the young monk to the scholarly Hatto, bishop of Vich, later known as the "teacher of the pope."

Under Hatto, Gerbert studied the quadrivium, delved into Boethius, Cassiodorus, and Isodore of Seville, contemplated the works of Vergil and Horace, and plunged into his favorite subject—mathematics. At Vich, he probably first became acquainted with the *gobar* or *gebar*, the system of arabic numerals that he later introduced into western Europe. *Gobar* derives from *grobar*—dust—because early Islamic mathematicians used to trace their signs on tablets covered with dust or fine sand. To Arab science, also, Europe owes the introduction of the decimal system. Many words connected with mathematics, such as *zero*, *cipher*, *algebra*, *almanac*, *alembic*, and *zenith*, are Arabic. At the time, arithmetic was still frequently referred to as "algorish," after the famous Islamic mathematician Al Khowarizmi. Gerbert played a major part in bringing Moorish science to France and from there to Germany and Italy at great risk to his reputation and danger to his life.

The young monk also studied astronomy, which had stirred his imagination since early youth, even though astronomy in his time had a bad reputation. It was often confused with the pseudoscience of astrology, anathemized by the church as a forbidden, accursed, and occult art. Gerbert rather agreed with those teachers who held "that God himself had set His seal of approval upon astronomy when He made use of the stars in the heavens to mark the birth of His Son."

Gerbert saw the world not as a flat disk surrounded by endless waters, which was then the prevailing view, but as an orb, and he con-

structed a sphere to support his view. In later life he constructed a sophisticated sundial, complete with written comments and much admired for generations. He was also famous for having, with his own
hands, made an astrolabe and written a long treatise on its use. The astrolabe, before him unknown in the West, has been called "the pocket
watch and slide rule of the medieval world." Invented in Greece—its
invention has been credited, falsely perhaps, to Ptolemy of Alexandria—
it was greatly improved upon by Islamic scholars. With it one could
measure the elevation of sun and stars, compute latitudes, and determine the moments of sunrise and sunset. The Muslims used the astrolabe mainly for fixing the time for prayers, for the beginning of
Ramadan, and for finding the direction of Mecca, which they faced
when praying to Allah. Here, too, Gerbert was an innovator, as he used
the astrolabe for strictly scientific purposes.

In the opinion of William of Malmesbury, an English historian
who had not much good to say about him, Gerbert "surpassed Ptolemy
with the astrolabe, and Alcandreus in astronomy, and Julius Firmicus
in astrology." The first two appraisals were compliments, the last was
not.

Gerbert also brought back with him from Spain the abacus, and,
unlike other scholars who only theorized, "with hammer, tongs, and
file he created at his own workbench many of these marvels."

Besides Bishop Hatto, Gerbert met with many learned men. Among
them was a certain Lupito, or Llobel, archdeacon of Barcelona, from
whom he begged "by reason of your nobility and affability" a treatise
on astronomy and astrology translated from the Arabic (*Liber translatus
do Astrologia*), which he used in writing his own dissertation on related
subjects. Gerbert seems to have made to Lupito, in return, a gift of
one of his own books. This Lupito was probably the translator of the
treatise, and quite possibly he was the son of a certain Abdallah Mo-
hammed ibn Lupi, one of several Moorish scholars at the court of
Alonzo of Asturias to whom this king confided the education of his
son Ordono.

From Joseph the Spaniard, also known as Joseph Sapiens or His-panus, a converted Mozarab Jew, who translated Islamic books into Latin, Gerbert likewise received a book on mathematics and geometry.

A sure friend was Guarino, abbot of the Mozarabic monastery of San Miguel de Cuxa, who at a much later time suggested to Gerbert that he come stay with him, since the one-time monk from Aurillac had become famous but also disgusted with life in France and Italy. Gerbert was interested and frequently thought of ending his days in Hither-Spain, but, of course, fate arranged things differently. At any rate, Gerbert always remembered his days in Catalonia and kept in touch with his friends by corresponding with them to the end of his life. As Gerbert's scientific work was so heavily influenced by Moorish works, there has always been speculation that he had at some time traveled to the court of the caliph at Cordova and there "imbibed the wisdom of the infidels at the source." Adhemar de Chabannes asserted that Gerbert had gone there "for the love of science." William of Malmesbury was positive that Gerbert went to Cordova "to study the accursed black arts." La Salle de Rochemore theorized that Gerbert had kept his visit to the Moorish capital secret in order not to run afoul of the church, which might have looked with disfavor on such a journey.

Gerbert himself wrote nothing about his years in Spain. His pupil Richer mentions only that he had gone to Catalonia with Count Borrel, studied under Bishop Hatto at Vich, and then had accompa-nied both men of their journey to Rome. Much that one would like to know remains hidden. It is possible that he went to Cordova, but not likely. For a Christian, particularly a monk, it would have been a dangerous undertaking. Those who did go to Cordova never knew whether they would be permitted to leave, or indeed if they would still have a head on their shoulders at the end of their journey.

However, Gerbert did not have to enter Moorish Spain to acquire Islamic learning. There were plenty of Moorish prisoners in Cata-lonia as well as ransomed or escaped Christians who had spent years in Arab captivity. The libraries contained scholarly Islamic works both in the original text and in translation. After all, Barcelona, Gerona, and other Catalan cities had been conquered and occupied for long periods of time by the Saracens. Finally, men like Gerbert's friend Lupito-Llobel were themselves of Moorish, or partially Moorish, origin and fluent in both Arabic and Latin.

Gerbert stayed in Catalonia from 967 to 970. The knowledge he gained and the inventions he conceived in three years were remarkable and largely due to the magnificent culture of Islam—itself so anachronistic in the general decadence of the tenth century—that surrounded him and fascinated him. He then traveled to Rome, where fate launched him upon a wondrous career.

The Lure of Cordova

IN VIEW OF THE INFLUENCE Arabic scholarship and science had upon Gerbert, it is tempting to speculate how much more he might have learned had he been able to live and study freely in the world of Islam.

The tenth century has been called barren, a wasteland of the human mind, when all the teachings of the ancients had been forgotten and "there was scarcely a man of worth to be found in all of Europe"—Christian Europe, that is. In Islamic Spain, Al Andalus to the Moors, philosophy, literature, poetry, and the arts flourished. Its splendid civilization rested upon the country's wealth which came from agriculture, manufacture, and trade.

The Moors of Spain were, above all, tillers of the soil. In a country partially arid, watering the fields was of the utmost importance, and the Arabs excelled at it. Abd-Er-Rahman III introduced a hydraulic irrigation system. One underground aqueduct at Maravilla was one mile long and thirty feet wide. The Moors constructed dams more than 800 feet long and reservoirs with a circumference of more than three miles. Abd-Er-Rahman also "ordered the making of vast troughs of stone for the use of cattle, and watering places for horses also." Under such care, fields yielded three crops every year, and "the soil fed thirty million people which, after conquest by the Spaniards hardly furnished food for six million beggared folk."

Moorish agriculturists were far more accomplished than their Western counterparts. They rotated crops, terraced hills, and were experts at grafting and pruning. They introduced into Spain—and consequently Europe—such plants as cotton, flax, hemp, sugar cane, olives, buckwheat, asparagus, pomegranates, artichokes, melons, oranges, apricots, plums, and coffee.

The Arabs were also exceptional stock raisers, horse breeders, and sheep herders. Hundreds of villages devoted themselves to sericulture, while Màlaga and Xerez provided dry and sweet wines, though the Qur'an forbade their use to the faithful. In reality the joys of wine-bibbing became a favorite subject of Islamic poems.

Moorish economy was far advanced. At a time when minted coins were extremely rare in the West and most people spent their lives without ever having experienced the sensation of rubbing one between thumb and forefinger, money circulated freely throughout Moorish Spain. Products manufactured and exported to Europe, Africa, and the Middle East included embossed Cordovan and Moroccan leather from "the best tanneries in the world"; damascened sword blades from Toledo, famed for their beauty and temper; carpets from Teulala; dyed woolens from Baza; fine glassware from Almeria; paper, as substitute for parchment, from Jativa; silk, often transparent, from Granada; arms and armor from Seville.

The Moors also traded with minerals gained through active mining operations, including gold, silver, lead, copper, iron, and mercury. All these products from Al-Andalus were shipped from the country's chief ports of Seville, Almeria, and Malaga. Unlike the feudal world of the West, Islam honored traders, as the prophet Muhammad himself had been a merchant for the greater part of his life.

The wealth derived from land, enterprise, and ingenuity supported learning and the arts. It is true, however, that these learned Moors exhibited a good deal of snobbishness toward those who worked with their hands rather than their heads—soldiers, artisans, and peasants alike. As one of the savants, Sayid Ibn Ahmed of Toledo, put it: "Even the most accomplished builder must look with envy upon the hexagons constructed by bees in their hives. The greatest hero, once bereft of his armor and weapons, trembles before the lion, and in their amorous vigor men are much inferior to the average billy goat, while teachers, philosophers and poets are the true lights of the world which, without them, would sink into the swamp of ignorance."

Scorned also was the would-be scholar, the idiot-savant, who was said to be like an ass loaded with books. Islamic scholars were proud and had good reasons to be. They were not afraid to make jokes at the expense of their rulers who had the power to have their heads cut off, nor to teach them lessons in humility. One famous, traditional story tells how the great caliph Harun-Al-Rashid exclaimed, during an excursion into the countryside, that he would give an empire for a cool glass of water. "And what would you give, Oh Caliph," the learned Ibn-Al-Samak asked, "should you not be able to pass from your body this water after you have drunk it? What would you give to end such baneful suffering?" "The whole of my kingdom," was the answer. "And are you then so overly proud being the ruler of a realm that is worth less than a sip of water and a piss?" An excessively forward remark—but the scholar not only avoided retribution, but was often quoted by the caliph.

One Islamic sage of the tenth century was Razi or Rhazes, called the experienced and the New Hippocrates. His greatest work, *The Secret Of Secrets*, was a truly overwhelming encyclopedia of all that was known of healing among Greeks, Arabs, Indians, Syrians, Africans, and Persians, a book that contained "all the world's wisdom."

Equally famous was Al-Farabi. Continuously traveling from place to place, interviewing scholars and philosophers upon every conceivable subject, he was known as the Arab Aristotle. No hardship or danger could keep him from the pursuit of learning. He wrote a lengthy treatise on the agreement of the philosophy of Plato and Aristotle, and he translated the works of the classic Greek philosophers, scientists, physicians, and poets, thereby introducing them to western Europe where the knowledge of Greek had become almost extinct.

Strongly influenced by Al-Farabi was Ibn Sina, better known as Avicenna, "the Galen of the Mahometans" and Prince Among Philosophers. By the age of twenty in 999, he was already famous. A child prodigy, he knew the entire Qur'an by heart at the age of ten. While still a mere boy he cured the ailments of the sultan of Bokhara who, in return, gave him access to his library. Ibn Sina completed the most famous of his works, the *Canon of Medicine*, while, under Islamic law, he was still a minor. He is said to have espoused pantheism, a belief that identifies God with the universe and the universe with God.

Mafati-Al-'Ulum was a renowned tenth-century mathematician, the author of a work called *The Keys of Science*. He has been credited with the invention of the *sifr*—the little circle representing the power of ten.

Al-Hallaj, more of a mystic than a scientist, taught that Allah continuously and endlessly creates and recreates atoms, arranging them according to his pleasure to form transient bodies of fleeting existence. Only the atom exists, was, and always will be. The universe, a human being, a crystal are nothing but atoms assembled and disassembled as God wills.

Geography was a favorite subject of the Arabs. Islamic scholars of the ninth and tenth centuries compiled guides for travelers that described foreign lands, peoples, and customs. They informed travelers of the waterless deserts, frozen mountain ranges, and other dangers they were likely to encounter when taking the Great Silk Road to China. They acquainted merchants with the strange habits and even stranger foods they were apt to find among a shaggy, lumbering people called Rus, and they warned of the bone-chilling cold and eternal night to be endured among the Norse, whose ax-wielding men sacrificed people and horses to their fierce gods but were willing to give much precious amber in exchange for a silken scarf or curiously wrought glass, and whose white-skinned, blue-eyed women gave their bodies freely for a trifle—though one should keep an eye on the husband with his wicked ax.

Muslim astronomers constructed spheres and used pocket-sized astrolabes to determine latitudes and tell the time. They are even said to have invented the seafarer's compass.

Tenth-century Islamic physicians were far ahead of their Christian contemporaries. Western healers, hampered by theological scruples and largely influenced by superstition, put their faith in medicaments such as "powdered unicorn's horn" and "basilisk teeth," or compounds of newts' eyes and pigeon dung. Muslim doctors relied upon common sense and experience. They practiced in the belief that a reasonable diet, exercise, and fresh air were the best medicine. One of their proverbs was "Eating sparingly, walking often and briskly, putting your cares away when going to sleep, will make us doctors poor and idle."

They knew that in order to cure the body one also had to heal the mind. In Spain, doctors had to be licensed and to undergo an examination in anatomy, herbalogy, and chemistry. Since, like Christian physicians, dissection of the human body was forbidden to them by their faith, they learned their anatomy by dissecting apes and certain kinds of four-footed animals.

Much of their work was based on clinical observation. *El Hawi*, Razi's vast medical encyclopedia, dealt with case histories. He wrote a profound dissertation on smallpox. In order to find the healthiest spot for his hospital in Baghdad, he kept dangling pieces of meat in various parts of the city and started building at the spot where the meat rotted most slowly.

Surgery was practiced with success. Muslim physicians trepanned, excised tumors, and used anesthetics, mostly opiates, to deaden their patients' pain. Specialists in eye disease performed cataract operations. Interestingly, Gerbert was fascinated by the subject and owned a book on ophthalmology. Such was the fame of the Muslim doctors of Cordova that Christian Spanish rulers journeyed to the Moorish capital to be treated by pagan practitioners rather than by their own doctors at home. They once concluded a truce in the midst of war and gave away castles and even a city in exchange for being healed. In 956, King Sancho the Fat of Navarre, who was so obese that he could not walk without being supported, was made well by Hasdai of Cordova, a Muslim-trained Jewish physician, by means of a sensible diet, drinking mineral waters, relieving himself regularly, and being instructed by Hasdai in a new attitude toward life.

The practice of Moorish physicians strikes us as curiously modern. Bedside manners were stressed: "Console your patient with a promise of healing, even in cases where you are in doubt, for in this way you may strengthen his will to get well." Social conscience was promoted: "Neglect not to visit and treat the poor, because nothing pleases Allah more than this." Advice on receiving prompt payment for services rendered was not neglected: "Ask for your reward while your patient is still suffering. Once cured, he will soon forget what you did for him."

Among the arts, music and poetry went hand in hand and were highly esteemed. At a time when poetry, except the religious sort, hardly existed in western Europe, Moorish poetry and love songs appealed to the heart and to the senses. Spanish Moors loved music also, and musicians performed their art with the help of a great variety of wind, stringed, and percussion instruments. Gerbert, who brought with him from Spain new theories of music, might have been acquainted with the works of such Muslim musicologists as Ibn Firnas and Maslama Al-Majriti. Arabic virtuosos were lavishly rewarded, and some grew rich by performing before emirs and caliphs.

Hispano-Arabic learning was so all-pervading and overpowering that Christian Spaniards complained that the most talented among them knew only Muslim authors, studied only Islamic science, and knew how to express themselves elegantly only in Arabic. Muslim learning penetrated into southern France. Some historians maintain that the town of Montpellier and its great learning center, the most famous of the early Middle Ages, was founded by Saracen refugees after their own city of Maguelone had been destroyed. Muslim science also influenced one of Gerbert's contemporaries in Catalonia,

Rabbi Menachem Ben Saruk, who lectured on Islamic culture in his synagogue at Tortosa—a good example of the amalgam of Christian, Jewish, and Arabic learning in Catalonia.

Cordova, the Moors' capital, was the most populous and cultured city in Spain. Its inhabitants boasted that "Cordova is the Bride of Andalusia. To her belong all the beauties which delight the eye. Her necklace is strung with the pearls her poets gathered from the ocean of language. Her garment is made from the banners of learning, embroidered by the masters of every art known to mankind." The Moorish author Al-Makkari quoted a visitor who, in Gerbert's days, had counted the houses in Cordova, all 260,377 of them. If there were really that many, even including the poorest, smallest huts, then the generally accepted number of 500,000 inhabitants might be too low. At the same period no single city in all of western Europe could boast a population exceeding 30,000. Cordova's dwellings and gardens stretched for some twenty-seven miles in all directions, and its walls were pierced by seven huge gates. In A.D. 999 the town had 80,455 shops and 4,300 markets, large and small. Its army of artisans included gold- and silversmiths, workers in copper and brass, glass-blowers, tanners, ivory carvers, and not fewer than 13,000 weavers. It took 5,000 mills to grind the grain for all the people. Cordovans were famous for their courteous and refined manners, their learning, their exquisite taste, the beauty of their women, the spirit of their horses, the sumptuousness of their meals, their rich dress, and the sweetness of their music.

Streets were paved, lit with oil-burning lamps, and regularly flushed and swept. Sidewalks were raised so that, unlike in French, German, or English cities, pedestrians need not soil their feet in mud or offal. Pure water was brought to the city in lead pipes. Waste was removed through large underground sewers "so wide that a cart and bullock could move in them." Western Europe did not know such amenities for centuries to come.

In innumerable gardens, palms, cedars, decorative shrubs, roses, and other flowers sweetened the air with their fragrance. To Muslims, more than to any other people, cleanliness was next to godliness. Their faith imposed upon them ritual ablutions through which they purified themselves before prayer, washing arms, hands, feet, face, and hair to be pure in mind and clean in body before God. Women had to take a ritual bath after menstruation. Cordovans had no fewer than 300 *hammans*, or public baths, in which to immerse themselves. A Moorish proverb had it that "a hungry beggar would rather spend his last *dirhem* on a cake of soap than on a meal."

Muslim attitudes toward cleanliness and sanitation contrasted starkly with those of their feudal non-Muslim neighbors. Of Spanish Christians, Stanley Lane-Poole wrote that "their fanaticism and cruelty were what might be expected from such uncouth barbarians, and where the habits of the people were as foul as the garbage-sodden mud that lay in their streets." One Christian woman of the tenth century boasted that in all her life she had never washed any part of her body except the tips of her fingers before going to mass and taking the host. Whether she died in the "odor of sanctity" is not known. Spanish knights were wont to say that "bathing weakens the flesh and spirit of men for war," and after the conquest of Granada all public and private baths in the city were destroyed. Gerbert's fastidiousness and fondness for washing led to rumors that he had fallen under the spell of unbelievers to the peril of his soul.

Cordova's architectural wonders included the great mosque to which the caliph retired on Fridays, the Muslim sabbath, on pavements covered with rich carpets. The roof of the mosque was supported by 1,293 columns carved and inlaid with gold and lapis lazuli. The walls were of marble and adorned with rich mosaics of gold and glass tiles, while the pulpit (*mihrab*) was made of ebony and ivory, encrusted with semiprecious stones. The interior was lit by hundreds of brass lanterns made from Christian church bells, while the huge candelabra suspended from the ceiling's center contained no fewer than 1,454 separate cups filled with lamp oil. One traveler described the mosque's interior as a "dark colored, golden-glinting brocade in stone." The work involved in building this marvel can be inferred from the fact that it took two hundred workers and a team of seventy bullocks a full twelve days to transport a single block of marble from a distant quarry.

Famous for their beauty were the three abodes of the caliphs, the Palace of Flowers, the Palace of Contentment, and the Palace of Love. The most admired edifice was the immense Palace of Ez Zahra—"The Fairest"—built three miles outside of the city by Abd-Er-Rahman III in honor of his favorite sultana.

Begun in 936, it took 25,000 workers twenty-five years to finish. It was built on three terraces. The lowest was covered with gardens, the middle contained the apartments of the courtiers, while the highest was reserved for the caliph's private palace proper. Its roof and main ceilings were supported by 4,300 columns of Spanish, African, Italian, and Greek marble. The main hall was decorated by an army of imported craftsmen, including a number of specialists from Constantinople lent to the caliph by the Byzantine emperor. These craftsmen constructed walls of multicolored marble inlaid with gold arabesques. The woodwork was of ebony with inlaid ornaments of ivory, turquoise, onyx, and lapis lazuli. Prominently displayed in the hall's center was "a monstrously large pearl, lit up by a hundred lamps."

The walls of Abd-er-Rahman's bed chamber in which, one supposes, he dallied with his "Fairest," were made of onyx, with columns of alabaster and rock crystal. In the middle of the room was a fountain of mercury and a basin of green malachite and red gold supported by the images of twelve animals, possibly representing the signs of the zodiac. Besides the caliph's favorite wife, the palace housed 6,314 women of various kinds comprising Abd-er-Rahman's harem, attended by 3,350 pages and eunuchs.

Andalus was, above all, famous as a land of scholars, libraries, book lovers, and book collectors. One book collector refused an invitation to become the vizier to an eastern sultan because transporting his library, from which he would on no account be separated, would have required a caravan of four hundred camels. When Gerbert was studying at Vich, the libraries of Moorish Spain contained close to a million manuscripts.

In countless reading rooms scholars could lose themselves in the Greek and Roman classics, all translated into elegant Arabic. If they happened to be linguists they could read them in the original. At book auctions collectors outbid each other. One scholar complained that a rich merchant bought a rare book he himself could not afford "merely to fill a space on his wall." It was said that in Cordova books were more eagerly sought than beautiful concubines or jewels.

The city's glory was the great library established by the Caliph Al Hakam II, Abd-Er-Rahman's son and successor who ruled from 961 to 976. Founding it "Al Hakam made Cordova shine like a light-house upon the darkness of Europe." The royal bibliophile devoted his life to building up the greatest library the world had ever seen. Ultimately it contained 400,000 volumes at a time when the greatest libraries in France and Italy thought themselves rich if they had four or five thousand books on their shelves. On the opening page of each book was written the name, date, and place of birth as well as the ancestry of the author, together with the titles of his or her other works. Forty-four weighty catalogues, incessantly amended, listed and described all titles and also contained instructions on where, among this mass of manuscripts, a particular work could be found.

Unlike manuscripts in western Europe, which were written on parchment, Arabic books were made of high-quality paper with exquisitely tooled bindings. In one single year no fewer than 70,000 copies of manuscripts were made at Cordova. Attached to the library was a large staff of copyists, illuminators, bookbinders, and translators. The head librarian was Talid, a eunuch as well as bibliophile. His deputy was a scholarly woman named Labna, while a certain Fatima, herself a well-known author and book collector, acted as the caliph's agent, scouring Cairo, Damascus, and Baghdad for rare books, which she bought with seemingly inexhaustible funds to send to Cordova. It is reported that Al Hakam's city boasted of a number of literary-minded women who preferred a writing career to marriage.

During its golden age, Cordovan society was relaxed and tolerant. It consisted of Arabs and Berbers proper, Christians converted to

Islam, unconverted Christians, and Jews. Those belonging to the last two groups could aspire to the highest offices, even becoming viziers or army commanders. Religious taboos were not always taken seriously. "The cultured Ommayads of the time paid scant attention to the prohibition, either to depict humans and other living creatures, or to drink wine." Two red porphyry columns in the great mosque were decorated with the story of the seven sleeping Ephesians and Noah's dove and raven.

Although winebibbing was strictly forbidden to the faithful, fine wines were one of the country's chief exports, and the cheering cup of sweet tawny or bright ruby was enjoyed by all but the most orthodox. When, in a moment of piety, Al Hakam was about to forbid wine drinking, his treasurer pointed out to him that this would result in a disastrous shortfall of taxes that might prohibit the large extension of the library. The caliph quickly gave up the idea. Some zealous imams criticized Al Hakam for having in his library many erotic books, some of them "explicitly" illustrated, besides works of Christian and Jewish authors whose writings were at variance with the teachings of the Qur'an. The caliph merely shrugged his shoulders. In indulgent Cordova, women went about unveiled, their eyes outlined with kohl.

The skeptical Moors did not share the belief of most Christians that the end of the world would come with the dawn of the year A.D. 1000. To them it was merely the year 388 after the Hegira— Muhammad's flight from Mecca to Medina. Though a Last Judgment was also one of Islam's articles of faith, Moors were comforted in the thought that only Allah knew the appointed day and hour.

The three caliphs who dominated Spain during the tenth century were Abd-Er-Rahman III, 912-961; Al Hakam II, 961-976; and Al Mansur, who died one year before Gerbert. Abd-Er-Rahman III succeeded to the throne when only twenty-one years old and died at the age of seventy. He was an army commander par excellence, but he has also been eulogized as the mildest, most enlightened caliph that ever ruled a country. It should be said that he was also a crafty politician who knew how to get rid of dangerous opponents.

In 953, the Saxon emperor Otto the Great sent an embassy to this caliph led by Johannes of Gorze, a fanatic monk. He brought with him a letter from Otto to be personally delivered into the hands of Abd-Er-Rahman. It contained an offensive diatribe against Islam and praise for Christianity as the only true religion. A certain Spanish priest found out about the insulting passage before it was delivered and notified the caliph in order to incur his favor. Abd-Er-Rahman thereupon refused to receive the letter, and the monk of Gorze had to camp for three long years outside Cordova, neither allowed to see the caliph nor to go home.

Abd-Er-Rahman sent the Jewish rabbi Ibn Chasdai to reason with Johannes, begging him to resolve the conflict by delivering the letter without the offending passage. The stubborn monk indignantly refused. The caliph threatened to kill all Christians in Andallus unless Johannes relented. The caliph represented to Johannes, via Ibn Chasdai, the great guilt the monk would have to bear if he caused such horrendous bloodshed. The monk replied that it was better for hecatombs of innocents to perish than for Abd-Er-Rahman to continue in the falsehood of his beliefs. It took three years of messages going to and fro between the Cordovan and Saxon courts before an order from Otto finally arrived ordering Johannes to deliver the emperor's letter without its exhortation. Then the German embassy was, at last, received with great pomp and left laden with gifts.

Al Hakam II, the caliph who reigned during Gerbert's stay in Spain and who built the great library, was forty-eight years old when he succeeded his father. He managed to combine piety with tolerance. Buried in his books, he left business to his vizier, though, when needed, he made vigorous war upon Castile, Leon, and Navarre, whose rulers he forced to sue for peace.

Ibn Abi Amir, better known as Al-Mansur Billah, the "Victorious by the Grace of Allah," was, strictly speaking, not a caliph. Son of a lawyer of good but not influential family, knowledgeable and crafty, he managed to win the favor of the court, particularly that of the women of the royal harem. At the age of thirty-one he had already held the position of chief judge and commander of the bodyguards. As finance minister he gained the confidence of the boy caliph Hashim's mother, a Basque woman named Aurora-Ssobsh, who became his mistress. Al-Mansur soon made himself de factor ruler and commander in chief of the army. He then became the most brilliant commander in the history of the Spanish Moors. He stormed and sacked Barcelona some thirty years after Gerbert had left it and also took Santiago de Compostela, which sent shock waves through all Christendom.

Nothing lasts forever. Eventually the Almohads, fanatic Berbers led by fundamentalist prophets, plundered Abd-Er-Rahman's wondrous palace, leaving it in blackened ruins, while most of the books of Al Hakam's famous library were burned as superfluous if they contained what was in the Qur'an and harmful if they did not.

Meanwhile, in 970, Count Borrel of Barcelona set out for Rome to obtain the pope's consent to make Vich an archbishopric and his Catalonian church independent from the prelates of France. The count took Bishop Hatto with him, who, in turn took Gerbert. Though he must have come to love Catalonia, the gifted young man surely welcomed the opportunity to travel to the capital of Christendom and the throne of St. Peter. In the annalist Richer's opinion it was God himself who had brought the monk from Aurillac to Vich and was now bringing him to Rome and who was, with infinite divine mercy, brightening his journey for the glory of science and the enlightenment of all Gaul. Gerbert was taking with him out of Spain the little spark which would light up the mighty flame of learning in the schools of Christendom.

CHAPTER SIX

An Empress Among Cities

"AND SO THE NOBLE COUNT, the bishop, and the monk, young in years but old in wisdom, journeyed to Rome, following in the footsteps of Hannibal, but without elephants." Actually, nobody knows by what route Borrel, Hatto, and Gerbert traveled to Rome, but the route most often taken was the one trodden by the great Carthagenian and his pachiderms in 213 B.C.—over the Alps and into the valley of the Pa. Richer said nothing of the dangers of the trip, but only remarked, "Because HE wanted that Gaul, still covered with darkness, should be lit up by a great light, all-knowing GOD put it into the count's and bishop's mind to take with them to the eternal city the young man whom it had pleased HIM to give into their care."

Gerbert must have been overwhelmed at his first sight of the city spread over its seven pine-studded hills. Rome was the see of God's Vicar on Earth; it was known as Caput Mundi (the Head of the World), Domina et Princeps Urbium (Mistress and Prince Among Cities), and Caput Orbis Terrarum (Ruler Over All the Earth). It stood proud in the safety of its 381 massive towers and 46 strong castles. But even at first glance, Gerbert must have noticed that the mistress of the world wore soiled and ragged garments. The urbs had fallen on bad days. As Charles the Bald had written, "In ruin lies the mistress of nations, the queen of cities, the mother of churches."

Like owls and ravens nesting in nooks and crannies, patricians and prelates had built their rude palaces into the noble structures of the fallen empire, such as the theater of Marcellus or the thermae of Constantine. The vaults and portals of decaying temples stared like empty eye sockets and were inhabited by bats. The ground was strewn with fragments of smashed statues of the gods. To the lime kilns and sewers had been consigned the works of ancient sculptors. From the Colosseum and the Baths of Caracalla papal workers pried the marble blocks to build churches. No longer able to properly dress stones, the Romans of the tenth century dismantled and plundered the relics of a splendid past, using slabs of the finest marble to construct crude dwellings, though most of the city's houses were then built of wood.

And yet "neither the vandal hand of zealous Christianity nor centuries of ignorance could blot out the memory of greatness. Titus was forgotten but the "Arch of the Seven Candlesticks' still looked down upon the city." The Forum of Augustus was choked with weeds, the Forum of Trajan covered with debris. Ancient thoughts, ancient names were rapidly submerged, but like moss there clung to the city memories of Rome's past." While on the one hand images of the old deities were hacked to pieces, on the other hand a temple of Janus still stood at the foot of the Ianiculus, where people continued to pray to the doublefaced god, one of the oldest in Latium. Likewise in the very shadow of the Lateran, near the Tiber River, was a grotto sacred to Priapus, whose statue, with oversized, strutting membrum virilis, stood in the cave's darkest, farthest recess. The statue's erect symbol of masculinity, travelers reported, was always garlanded with fresh flowers, wound around it by Christian matrons wishing to conceive.

Some of the feasts and pageants in which even popes participated were entirely pagan, going back to the dawn of history. Gerbert must have witnessed, and later as pope must have taken part in, the Festival of Fools and Asses, called Coromannia. During this rite of spring, the archdeacons of Rome's eighteen parishes rang the church bells and summoned the people. Garlanded with flowers, his head adorned with a ram's horns like Silenus of old, a sacristan headed the parade. Bearing a staff covered with small bells, followed by priests in full ornate, he led the people to the Lateran. There the crowd clamored with much noise and shouting for the pope to come out of his palace. As soon as the Vicar of Christ made his appearance, the celebrants danced around him in a circle, intoning the laudes "to honor him to whom have been given the keys to rule over all things." Gamboling and shaking his bells "in a very earthy way" the sacristan performed a solo dance with movements very much like "a rutting billygoat." Then the archpriest, amid much laughter and guffawing, mounted an ass with his face toward the tail, bending backward to fill his hands with coins held aloft in a silver bowl by the pope's mayor domo, who walked backward in front of the ass. The coins would be flung to poor folk and beggars. The pope then received the gift of a dove and a cock, after which he gave the crowd his blessing—all very reminiscent of ancient Rome's Lupercalia and Saturnalia with their erotic caperings.

Romans might well amuse themselves while they could. They had little enough to laugh about in the tenth century—Rome's and Europe's darkest age. The strong oppressed the weak, made war upon each other, hovered above the city in houses made into fortresses, and ambushed their rivals in narrow, winding alleys that now covered the Roman squares and gardens of former times.

The church itself gave the worst example. Rather, Bishop of Verona, described the life led by prelates and high churchmen: "They walk in cloth of gold brought from Constantinople and Baghdad, dine richly while lying upon upholstered benches like the heathen Romans of old, while listening to obscene songs and watching lascivious dances. They delight in the hunt, riding with falcons on their gloved hands and travel around in gilded carriages, looking down upon common folk. At nightfall they gorge themselves once more with dainty dishes and stagger drunkenly to their beds to awake with curses and blasphemies on their lips." Some of Gerbert's contemporaries stated bluntly that Rome had become a cloaca, the papacy a cesspool, that some cloisters had become brothels, their abbots whoremongers.

According to tenth-century sources, many priests were obsessed with sex. In its early days the church had preached that life existed not to be enjoyed, but for daily mortification. Sex, even inside marriage, had been deemed "intemperance," a form of pollution that was unfortunately hard to avoid. A second marriage after the death of a spouse had been condemned as "decent adultery" or outright fornication. Sex, it was taught, was a consequence of Adam's fall, marriage an inferior state, and "to cut down with the axe of virginity the wood of marriage" a desirable goal.

In tenth-century Rome such ideas were laughed at. One Italian bishop complained, "If I were to enforce the canons against unchaste men administering ecclesiastic rites, none would be left but young boys; and if I would enforce the laws against bastards, then I would have hardly any priests left in my diocese."

Countless clerics were married or lived in open concubinage. An archdeacon at Ravenna publicly flaunted his wife and many children. One abbot had seventeen children in one village alone and was highly praised for supporting them. Not for nothing were clerics jokingly called "the true fathers of the country." It was worse that married priests, prelates, and bishops sometimes tried to make their offices hereditary, provided for their children out of church funds, and became involved in bloody fights, started by their sons, over church property.

During one synod, held in France, one bishop spoke of the throne of Peter as "glistening with the gold of pride and the silver of avarice, without love and puffed up with vain knowledge." He warned that if things went on as they did, the pope would be turned into Antichrist, and he lamented that asking advice from such a one was like petitioning dead, cold marble. "Where to turn?" he exclaimed loudly, "where to get help? Not from Rome which is for sale!"

Tenth-century Rome, the historian E. B. Osborn said, was "a derelict city, a Vesuvius of furious feuds constantly in eruption, set in a desolate, disease-ridden countryside. . . . It scoffed at the sacred things which were its livelihood, and fleeced the pilgrims which were its paymasters. Huge square brick keeps, family fortresses, were the only architectural achievements of medieval Rome. It was, in fact, a decapitated head."

The history of the papacy in the Century of Lead and Iron, or rather the "Pornocracy," as some called it, makes sorry reading. One particularly disgusting example of its degeneracy came when the corpse of Pope Formosus, who occupied the Chair of St. Peter from 891 to 896, was exhumed by his political enemy and successor, Pope Stephen V, who dressed the corpse in pontifical robes, placed it upon the papal throne, and solemnly put his dead predecessor on trial for having allowed himself to be made pope against canon law. To give the affair a semblance of legality, a deacon was appointed to plead the corpse's case, which he did with much trembling and stammering and to no avail. The dead Formosus, who could plead his own case but poorly, was pronounced guilty by Stephen, while the assembled crowd of church dignitaries cried aloud, "So be it!" Forthwith, his papal robes were torn away, and three fingers of his right hand, which the deceased had used to bless the Romans, were hacked off. The decomposing remains were wrapped in sackcloth and thrown into the Tiber. Not long after, as the political climate changed, Stephen himself was thrown into prison by a Roman mob and there was strangled by unknown assassins.

In quick succession followed a number of pontiffs: Boniface VI, who enjoyed his elevation for a mere three weeks; Romanus, who occupied the chair for less than four months, and Theodore II, pontificating for exactly twenty days. Some of these, it was said, might have died natural deaths, but then again, they might not have. Their successor, Leo V, was jailed by an antipope named Christophorus, who, in turn, was deposed by Sergius III, who had been made pope by Theophilact, financial manager of the curia and, more important, commander of the Roman militia. Sergius had both Leo V and Christophorus thrown into a subterranean dungeon and there murdered.

With Theophilact began the rule of "fearful, man-mad women." Theophilact made his wife, Theodora, a senator and himself consul, dux, and senator.

From Theodora, in the space of a hundred years, descended five popes and a number of sovereign counts. She was an ancestor of the powerful Crescentii and Colonna families who "considered Rome a toy to be played with." The couple had two daughters—Theodora and Marozia—nymphomaniacs who dabbled in politics and poison. The blunt, down-to-earth Bishop Liutprand simply called them whores.

At this time popes were not necessarily elected by a collegium of cardinals but installed by powerful nobles who seated and unseated them at their whim. For thirty years after Theophilact's death, his wife Theodora and her daughters, the younger Theodora and Marozia, disposed of the Holy See and filled it with their paramours, children, and grandchildren. The whole clan installed itself in the Castle of St. Angelo, originally the mausoleum of the emperor Hadrian, a "frowning, storied fortress" whose thick walls hid a multitude of crimes and orgies.

The mother Theodora first promoted one of her lovers to the papal throne under the name of John X. He was a warlike pope who took the field against the Saracens of Sicily and southern Italy and defeated them in a great battle near the Garigliano River, laying about him lustily with "a great, sharp sword." His mighty weapon was, however, of no use against the intrigues of the younger Theodora, who had him either smothered with pillows or killed by starvation, to put in his place Leo VI, whose reign lasted less than six months. He was quickly followed by another nullity, Stephen VII, a protégé of Marozia, who quickly established herself as the most formidable woman of the clan. Marozia, "whose sensuality put Aphrodite to shame," put her own bastard son, fathered by Sergius, upon the see of St. Peter at the age of twenty-one, but the young man was more interested in fornication and horses than prayers.

Besides her innumerable lovers, Marozia also had three legitimate husbands. The first was Alberic, count of Spoleto, a ferocious Lombard. Among several children of this union was a certain Alberic II, nicknamed the Serpent Child. After her first husband's death, Marozia married a Count Guido of Tusculum, who perished during a street battle. Finally Marozia married Hugh, self-styled king of Burgundy. Her bastard son, Pope John XI, presided over the nuptials. This Hugh, himself a man of amorous appetites, maintained three mistresses simultaneously, whom the Romans referred to as Venus, Juno, and Semele. He followed Marozia's practice by making his numerous offspring patricians, senators, and bishops. Marozia's own son, Alberic II, the Serpent Child, did not get along well with his latest stepfather. Annoyed by Alberic's arrogance during a festive dinner, Hugh smashed his fist into Alberic's face, who "took it very ill." The resentful son raised the Roman mob against his mother and stepfather. "What," he harangued the crowd, "for the lust of an ancient hag, you suffer the rule of this stranger, one of those Burgundians who once were your slaves?"

Alberic II personally led the rabble against the Castle of St. Angelo. Hugh did not await the outcome but fled, letting himself down by a rope from the castle's walls and leaving his wife, his mistresses, and the hapless John XI to the tender mercies of Alberic, who had made himself master of the city. John XI was allowed to linger on as a deposed pope and prisoner and was probably murdered in the end. Marozia disappeared forever into one of Hadrian's tomb's innumerable dungeons, and nothing further was heard of her.

After making a few nonentities pope, Alberic II died naming as his successor his son Octavian, who, in 955, at the age of sixteen, became Pope John XII. This was the worst of all the pontiffs descended from Theophilact and Theodora.

"His palace was the scene of scandalous licence, while his public acts were those of a tyrant. He desired to be both pope and prince, but utterly failed to be either." John XII converted the Lateran into a bawdy house, committed adultery on countless occasions, consorted with prostitutes, and was "a danger to every virgin and virtuous matron." It was said that respectable women of foreign nations "were afraid to go to Rome on a pilgrimage on account of the lascivious advances of this depraved pope." He made his dead father's mistress his own, raped nuns, and was accused of incestuous relationships. He was "more addicted to horse-breeding and hunting with hound and falcon than to spiritual matters." He blessed and installed deacons in a horse stable. He sold the great offices of the church to the highest bidders, consecrating a ten-year-old boy bishop of Todi. He walked about like a common soldier in armor, sword in hand. He drank wine in honor of the devil, toasting the Prince of Darkness with raised cup, and he invoked Jupiter, Venus, and Mars while playing at dice. He failed to celebrate matins and the canonical hours and was never seen to bless himself with the cross. He was guilty of arson and ordered the eyes of his godfather to be put out, causing the poor man's death. He had a Roman priest who dared to criticize him castrated, and he put a great number of opponents to death.

Events finally took the course that changed Gerbert's life. Despised by all, threatened by revolt inside the city and by powerful nobles outside its walls, John XII urgently appealed to the Saxon king Otto I for help. The pope hoped to acquire a powerful protector in the person of the mightiest ruler in Europe, and Otto I, who coveted the crown of empire, heeded his call.

In 962 Otto crossed the Alps and marched on Rome, and on February 2 he and his wife Adelaide were crowned emperor and empress of the Roman Empire with a solemnity not unworthy of Charlemagne. Thus was founded what would soon come to be known as the Holy Roman Empire of the German Nation.

Otto had sworn: "To thee, John, Lord and Pope, I, King Otto, do promise and swear in the name of the Father, the Son, and the Holy Spirit, and on the relics of the Saints, that I will glorify God's Holy Church and thee, its ruler, to the utmost of my power." Privately he whispered to his sword bearer to have his weapon ready, as he did not trust the Romans.

The pope and the people on their part swore fidelity to the emperor, and within a few days a formal alliance was concluded. It was to be of short duration, since each man wanted to use the other for his own purposes, and both were strong-willed men. Seeing Otto settling down as de facto ruler of Rome and Italy, the angry pontiff waited only for Otto to absent himself from the city to instigate a revolt against him. Pope John XII even begged his erstwhile enemies—the Byzantine Greeks and barbarian Magyars—to help him defend Rome, but eighteen months after his coronation Otto recaptured the city, and John fled with his papal treasures.

Otto promptly had John put on trial as a "monster, deaf to virtue and given to commit the most heinous crimes—a criminal who is no stranger to any known vice." After John had been duly deposed, the emperor put a pope of his own choice, Leo VIII, on the throne, compelling the Romans to swear never again to elect a pontiff without his consent.

In the meantime John was biding his time "lurking like a wild beast in the wilderness," somewhere in Campania. With the help of a certain Pietro, nicknamed Imperiola, who made himself city prefect, John stirred up a new revolt. The Roman mob rang church bells and blew trumpets to summon support in attacking the Vatican, occupied by Otto and his retainer. The German knights beat off their assailants with great slaughter, leaving the area around the Vatican littered with corpses. As soon as Otto left again on campaign, John returned once more with an army of adherents. Leo VIII, whose backside, it was said, had hardly begun to warm the Chair of St. Peter, was himself deposed and forced to flee while John was reinstalled with great pomp. He immediately took vengeance upon his enemies. One cardinal, who had testified against him, had his offending tongue and nose cut off. One bishop lost his right hand, while a German prelate was scourged with leaded whips. Many of John's opponents were killed outright, but John himself did not enjoy his reinstatement for long. "On a beautiful night, in the month of May, Pope John, going to visit one of his mistresses, a married woman, found in her bed chamber, instead of his beloved, her husband, who gave him such a terrific clout on the head that he died within a few days of his injury." Exit John XII, who had loved neither wisely nor well and had come to a fitting end on the fourteenth of May, 964.

In John's stead the Romans elected Benedict V, against the emperor's wishes and in spite of having pledged themselves never to do such a thing. Once more Otto was obliged to march upon the capital of Christendom. Again his enemies scattered as chaff before the wind. The hapless Benedict was publicly divested of his office, his papal insignia torn from his body. On his knees he had to beg forgiveness of the emperor, who spared his life but exiled him to faraway Hamburg, "a mean, cold and barbaric city where he died."

Leo VIII was restored to the papacy, but still the Romans resisted a pope imposed upon them by strangers. In 966, after Leo's death, Otto enthroned the bishop of Narni as Pope John XIII, and the Romans promptly rose against him, driving him from the city. For the fourth time, Otto and his army made the long march from Germany to repair the situation. Terrible was the emperor's anger. This time there was no forgiveness for those be considered traitors and oath breakers. The gallows, the sword, blinding, and the mutilating knife were their lot. The prefect Pietro was hanged by his hair from the equestrian statue of Marcus Aurelius, then placed naked on an ass, his face toward the tail. In this manner he was led through the city, an object of derision and a warning to all who harbored evil thoughts against their Saxon masters.

The quickly reinstated John XIII was a vast improvement upon most of his predecessors, and even Italian historians admit that, on the whole, Otto and his descendants put worthier men upon the papal throne than the Theophilacts, Alberics, and Morozias. The thirteenth John, though he could be vengeful on occasion, was pious and had no spectacular vices. In 967 he crowned Otto II—then twelve years old—as his father's co-emperor, Caesar and Augustus. He was still pope when Count Borrel and his party arrived in the queen of cities.

Count Borrel successfully conducted his affairs, managing to make his Catalonian church independent from the See of Narbonne. The good Bishop Hatto was elevated to the rank of archbishop but had little time to enjoy his new rank, dying soon after of an unspecified illness while still in Rome. Quite possibly Gerbert participated in the delicate negotiations between Borrel and the pope. He was at any rate introduced to the pontiff, who was much impressed by the young monk's good manners, tact, ability, and scholarship and wished to attach him to the papal court. Count Borrel demurred, but fate intervened in the person of the emperor, who was providentially in Rome at the time.

Pope John XIII diplomatically mentioned to Otto that the count had in his entourage a young man who had studied mathematics, astronomy, and music in Spain. The pope also suggested that Gerbert might make a fine teacher for Otto's son. The elder Great Otto immediately ordered the pope to prevent Gerbert from leaving Rome. John negotiated with his usual finesse, representing to the count that the emperor only wished to have Gerbert for a short time, and that the count might profit from the arrangement by ingratiating himself with Europe's most powerful monarch. John also personally guaranteed that Gerbert would be returned to Borrel presently.

Borrel could not resist. The pope had given him everything he had requested and now demanded his quid pro quo. He left Rome alone, never to see Gerbert again.

Soon after, Gerbert had a long interview with the emperor, who tested his knowledge. Gerbert explained frankly that although he knew a great deal about mathematics and astronomy, he as yet knew little of philosophy or logic. All the same, he was retained to tutor the young Otto II, "a prince singularly cultivated for his time."

The almost two years spent with the two Ottos had the most important consequences for Gerbert's career. He never forgot the kindness shown him by the emperor and attached himself irrevocably to the cause of the Saxon Ottonians. At the end of his life he took pride in the fact that amid trials, afflictions, and wars he had always been faithful to them. Still, he was determined to complete his education. In 972, an embassy of Lothaire, king of the Franks, arrived at Otto's court. Among the members of the embassy was Gerannus, archdeacon of the cathedral of Rheims, a most sacred city famous for its school in which Gerannus—"the man most skilled in logic among all scholars"— taught philosophy. Gerbert decided that he should go to Rheims with Gerannus. He must somehow persuade Otto to release him from his duties. It must have been with a great deal of trepidation that he approached the great Magnus Otto, the world shaker who had smashed the wild, leather-clad Magyars, pressed back the Slavs and Norsemen, and made his kingdom the one truly organized state of that time. Otto growled and muttered but, in the end, gave Gerbert leave to depart.

CHAPTER SEVEN

Magnus Otto, Maximus Otto

WHILE GERBERT BEGAN A LIFE of scientific inquiry, scholarly research, and philosophic debate, the Saxon emperors strengthened their rule in Germany and Italy, posing as protectors of the church and of European Christendom against the ravages of pagan Slavs, Magyars, and roving Vikings. The most powerful of these sword-wielding rulers was Otto I the Great, Magnus Otto, Maximus Otto, a sturdy, broad-shouldered fellow well able to bear the burden of his kingship. Not exactly a genius, he was, however, a crafty, far-seeing politician and a mighty man in war. The most powerful ruler in the West, he was depicted in illuminated manuscripts sitting upon his throne with the orb, symbol of world rule, in his right hand and the scepter of authority in his left, with his feet planted firmly on Terra, the inhabited Christian earth, and his kingdoms in the shape of noble women bowing down before him, while the protecting finger of God touched his forehead. He was extremely pious after his own fashion, never letting piety stand in the way of committing the sins of fornication, pride, and overindulgence in rich foods and even richer wines.

Young Otto's kingdom was still a wild country of forests, interspersed with clearings and villages, some open fields, herds of grazing sheep, half-wild swine feeding on acorns, a few towns here and there, abbeys, and solidly built minsters. One imagines him in his youth, stalking wild boar in primeval forests with his *saufeder*, or boar spear, and riding on lonely, barely discernable paths with a falcon on his wrist.

In German lands the king was still a semi-nomad, trekking with his retinue from one *pfaltz* to the next, without a definite capital, having a number of *Kaiserpfaltzen*—stark and unadorned timbered halls—to tarry in for a while during his incessant wanderings. At the beginning of the Ottonian Age, his subjects showed him little respect, thinking themselves almost as good as he and remembering the old Saxon days when their kings were elected in the open field. In those days no one was born to the crown, and only those who could hold on to what was theirs, the tallest and the brawniest, were raised upon the shield.

And so the first rulers of the tribe trekked from *pfaltz* to *pfaltz*, from one fortified monastery to the next, over moor and heath, from Lorsch to Fulda to Quedlinburg to Ingelheim to Fritzlar to Paderborn to Aachen, feasting when not hunting, hunting when not drinking, fighting when not praying, because they were both a devout and a warlike lot. The Saxon kings did their wandering in order to impress upon their subjects that they were rulers over Swabians, Thuringians, Bavarians, and Wends, as well as over their own Saxons. Wherever the king happened to be, there was the capital and seat of government. There he gave great feasts, reveled in gargantuan drinking bouts, listened to musicians and watched jugglers or contortionists, received and gave presents, but also sat in judgment, raised tribute, received ambassadors, and took counsel with the local lords, who were rude men, still "brothers to the tree, the rock, and the brook." The people complained loudly of the "presents" he extracted from them in order to maintain his court; on the other hand there was no regular system of taxation, and he protected them against the onslaughts of Hungarians, Slavs, Danes, Vikings, and horse-worshiping Wends. The Saxon rulers also needed money to battle among themselves—son against father, brother against brother, duke against duke.

They had advanced in the world since the breakup of the Carolingian Empire, rising somehow from among the battling barons contending for bits and pieces of Charlemagne's crumbling realm. It all started with a certain duke, Otto the Illustrious, who managed to hold on to what was his and to grab what was not and, on the side, to father Henry I, surnamed the Fowler. Henry was so named because his favorite sport was catching birds with a *leimrute*, a stick smeared with glue, and because, so the tale went, he happened to be snaring birds when his nobles came to inform him of his election to the throne.

Henry the Fowler had married a certain Matilda, who traced her descent to the legendary Saxon chieftain Widukind, who had defied Charlemagne and his Christianizing in battle after battle. Hanging on grimly to his old gods Wotan and Thiu, Widukind put up such a fierce resistance that Charlemagne took desperate steps. Frustrated that he could not make good Christians out of heathen Saxons, the great Charles beheaded 4,500 of them in a single day at Verden, in the neighborhood of Bremen. Disheartened by such measures, Widukind finally allowed himself to be baptized, but not before bequeathing his sturdy, stubborn genes to some of his Ottonian descendants.

Although Henry the Fowler earned his election the hard way, his son would inherit the kingship by right of birth. This was because Henry fought Franks and Gauls, Danes and Magyars, Slavs from beyond the Elbe who worshiped gods named Svantepolk and Bog, ax-wielding Danes, and rival Bavarian dukes. He was successful in his battles because he was very careful, never trying to chew what he could not swallow. He always remained duke of Saxony first and foremost, and king of Germany second. He has been credited with founding many cities where, before him, there had been none. He also organized his dukedom's armed host, making it into a formidable fighting force. He ruled in harmony and, together with his barons and prelates, secured the borders of his kingdom against foreign invaders. He bequeathed to his son, the first Otto, a reasonably well-ordered realm, which is not saying much in that darkest century of the Dark Ages.

It was Otto I who really ushered in the Ottonian Age, and his story must be told in order to understand what impact his life had on Gerbert and on the tenth century in general. His chronicler, Widukind of Corvey, has left us a vivid impression of what Otto was like. "At the very first glance Otto appears as a born ruler. Old age only lent him more majesty. His body was strong and firm but not without a certain grace. Even in his later years he remained a rugged hunter and agile horseman. From his sunburnt face shone light and lively eyes. Sparse gray hair covered his head and his beard, after the Saxon manner, flowed long and mighty over his chest which was very hairy-like a lion's mane. He wore Saxon dress and shunned foreign splendor. He only spoke his native Saxon language, but had some knowledge of Roman and Slavic speech. He divided his days between work and prayer, matters of state and the service of God. He slept sparingly, and as he used to talk in his sleep, seemed always awake. Open-handed, accessible, and friendly he attracted many hearts and yet was more feared than loved. His anger was hard to bear though for many years he had tried to curb it. The old emperor could be severe unto harshness, even the young emperor trembled at the old lion's growl.

"Otto had a will of iron, from youth to old age. He kept faith with the path he had laid out for himself to accomplish great and worthy deeds, and youthful ardor filled his veins even in his old age. And he still had all the virtues for which he had been praised when he was a youth—rock-like fidelity to his friends, magnanimity toward his humbled foes—both remained the ornament of his later days. He never remembered a wrong done to him once he had forgiven it. Of his royal and imperial dignity he was ever conscious and ascribed it to God's favor. He never placed the crown upon his head without having first fasted and prayed. In those who rose up against his majesty he saw offenders against God's law.

"His mind is worthy of admiration because after the death of his first queen, Edgitha, he learned what he had not done before, to read and write. He hunted as often as he could, loved to play chess and games of draught and sports which could be done on horseback. He loved to wander alone into the forest singing to himself all the time. Some said that his eyes had something terrifying about them." German historians describe him as a real *Waldmensch*—happy only in the woods among mighty oak trees. Though not much of a scholar himself, he took a lively interest in the arts and furthered learning in the many monasteries founded by him, which was probably the reason why he and Gerbert took so quickly to each other.

Otto's brother, Bruno, archbishop of Cologne, was a noted scholar, grammarian, and linguist who brought many learned and distinguished men to serve and aid Otto: Bishop Liutprand of Cremona, diplomat and diarist; Willigis, bishop of Mayence; and Thietmar of Merseburg. The play-writing poet and nun, Hroswitha of Gandersheim, who wrote a rhymed history of Otto in Latin, contributed her share to Saxon culture. The Ottonians did more than just hew enemies asunder or quaff mead from enormous drinking horns.

In the words of Widukind of Corvey, who was twelve years old at the time and might very well have been an open-mouthed witness, "There were assembled the dukes and powerful counts together with the leading warriors in the hall of columns right next to Charlemagne's church and there placed Otto upon a throne and put their hands in his and swore to be true to him and made him king after the ancient Saxon custom.

"Clad in gold-glittering vestments, crosier in hand and mitre on his head, the Archbishop Hildebert of Mainz presented Otto to the crowd, calling out to the people: 'Behold, I am bringing to you him whom God Himself has chosen and whom all the princes of the realm made and acknowledged their true king. Lift your right hands up to heaven as a sign that you agree with their choice.' Then all the folk assembled raised their hands high and with loud, strong shouts wished the new king good luck.

"Then the bishop took him to the altar and girded him with the sword, put on him the royal robes, bucklers, clasps, and bracelets, placed into his hands orb, staff, and sceptre. Handing him the weapon he exhorted Otto: 'Take this sword and with it drive away the enemies of Christ, barbarous heathens and bad Christians, because by God's mandate has been given thee the power to vouchsafe peace to all good people.' Then Hildebert clad him in the royal mantle, saying: 'May this noble robe, reaching to the ground, remind thee to shelter beneath it the people and the faith evermore.' Then he took up the sceptre and the staff, admonishing the king: 'With this staff may you discipline your people after the way of a good father and protect the servants of God, and stretch out a pitying hand to all widows and orphans.'

"Then the bishops anointed and crowned the king, afterwards leading him to a high place between two beautiful marble columns where he could be seen by all. The Te Deum was sung and a solemn mass held. Then followed the sumptuous feast at the *pfaltz*. A marble table was set for Otto, royally decked out, and trestle tables beside, and the new king sat himself down with his nobles and all the folk to great eating and drinking during which mighty dukes attended him as cup bearers, butlers and stewards, and when the meal was finished the king smiled."

Thus the ceremony had unfolded itself, symbolically divided into three parts like the Holy Trinity. First came the election under the open sky in the ancient Saxon manner, the sword-girt nobles choosing a king from among themselves and doing homage to him as good vassals should while the common folk raised their hands aloft in agreement. The second part translated the king's election into spiritual terms, as he was wedded to his bride *ecclesia*, the church, a union blessed by God himself. Finally, guests stuffed and quaffed as a symbol of the king's worldly role as nourisher and giver and provider, while dukes cut the king's meat and poured his wine as a sign of their voluntary submission to royal authority.

They did not submit for long. Soon the old Teutonic habit prevailed again, and the dukes began looking askance at their ruler, thinking that, after all, he was not much better than they. Many believed they had as much right to sit on the throne as this twenty-four-year-old stripling. Most probably his vassals started plotting against him before they had digested the meal. A whole series of revolts that would plague Otto for years broke out almost at once, partly because, unlike his father, he was not satisfied with being a king in name only. From the start, he asserted his authority over his unruly nobles. He punished Duke Eberhard of Franconia for infringing on his kingly prerogatives and for the same reason deprived another Eberhard, duke of Bavaria, of his fief. His elder brother, Thankmar, rejected as candidate of the throne because he was a bastard, rose against him with the help of powerful barons, taking Otto's younger brother Henry prisoner and holding him as a hostage. God-fearing and pious as Otto was, when Thankmar was defeated, Otto killed him even though Thankmar had taken refuge in sanctuary. Once freed, the ungrateful brother Henry tried to replace Otto as king, helped by that old plotter Eberhard of Franconia and Giselbert, duke of Lorraine. Otto defeated them in battle. Eberhard was slain, while Giselbert drowned crossing a stream in hasty flight. Pardoned, Henry was soon involved in a conspiracy to murder Otto. It was discovered, but Henry was once more forgiven.

In 952, Otto's own son Ludolph rose in arms against him, aided by Duke Conrad of Lorraine and Frederic of Mayence. They managed to seize the king and for a while kept him prisoner, forcing him into agreements that Otto promptly broke as soon as he was free. It was not until 955, almost twenty years after he had been crowned, and after many bloody battles, that Otto at last, once and for all, managed to stamp out the rebellions of his relatives. With good reason he lamented that his own kinsmen—children, brothers, and inlaws—were a greater trial to him than the heathen barbarians raiding across his borders. Once finally defeated, however, many of the rebels became faithful friends.

Harder to subdue than Otto's own Saxon kin were the Danish and Norwegian Vikings who still practiced human sacrifice, hanging their victims from the branches of sacred oak trees or burying them in bogs, where their bodies still are found in a remarkable state of preservation. Equally dangerous were the slavic Wends, likewise worshiping alien gods. Otto defeated them all in a long series of engagements and, in the end, managed to keep them outside his borders.

Worst of all were the Hungarians or Magyars, the "scourge and terror of all Christendom, enemies of God and humanity." Emerging from the steppes of Central Asia, they forced their way into Europe toward the end of the ninth century. Their mounted hordes appeared suddenly, as out of nowhere, burning a town here, sacking a cloister there, disappearing with their loot and prisoners as swiftly as they had come. No corner of Europe was safe from their depredations. They learned to ride before they learned to walk and "cooked" their meat by putting it under their saddles. If on a raid one of them ran out of food he opened a vein in his horse's neck and sucked out a little blood. They drank mare's milk and made a kind of cheese from it.

Calling themselves the offshoot of a Hunnic tribe, the Hungarians were divided into clans named after wild beasts and birds of prey. The men advanced into battle under their totem-standard with the image of a Turul bird, or raven, carrying a piece of meat in its beak. Their favorite weapon, which they wielded from earliest youth, was a short but powerful horn-backed bow. For this reason some chroniclers called them the Bow-bending People. Already Henry the Fowler had battled them with uneven success; and Otto himself, from the very first days of his reign, had his hands full trying to stem their never-ending onslaughts.

Liutprand called them an evil folk: "No thirsty man is so greedily yearning for a cool cup of water, as this cruel people is always yearning for a fight. Among them it is the custom of mothers to cut the faces of their newborn sons with sharp knives so that, even before their first suck of mother's milk, they learn to bear wounds. They also cut and slash themselves to show their grief at the death of a relative. Having neither god nor conscience they shed blood instead of tears."

Against such fierce foes Otto carried into battle a victory-bringing talisman—his famous Sacred Lance, the Dominica Hasta, containing one of the nails that had pierced the hands and feet of the Savior. The emperor Constantine, it was said, had carried this Holy Lance in his battle against Maxentius, which ended in the triumph of Christianity over Roman paganism. "Much gold, silver and Swabian land, even the good town of Basle," had Henry the Fowler given for it to Rudolf, king of the Burgundian. For a king wanting to reestablish Charlemagne's empire, it was a powerful thing to own this divine and mythical link to the mighty Constantine, making the Ottonians his spiritual heirs.

When the wild Magyars once again swarmed burning and plundering in terrific numbers across Bavaria, Otto vowed "that he would rather die than tolerate such evil," while the Hungarians on their part, swore "that the earth would open up and the sky fall upon them before they would yield to any man born from woman." On the tenth of August, 955, on the Lechfeld, an open plain near the town of Augsburg, Otto's army met these enemies for one last decisive battle.

Otto was facing the Hungarians with eight legions of mailed, brave, and battle-scarred men lined up along the banks of the river Lech. Three of these legions consisted of local Bavarians led by their own nobles. The fourth was made up of Franconians commanded by their duke, Conrad, Otto's son-in-law, once a rebel, now a faithful vassal. The fifth legion, the king's own, was formed of hand-picked, experienced men led by Otto in person. The sixth and seventh were brought into the field by the duke of Swabia, while the eighth was made up of Bohemian Slavs whose newly acquired Christianity was somewhat suspect, under their Duke Boleslav I, of equally suspect loyalty. On this day, however, Saxon and Slav had a common interest in stemming the Magyar tide.

The great battle took place on the feast day of St. Laurentius, called the Vanquisher of Fire, since the emperor Valerian had sentenced him to die by roasting on a gridiron, which later became his symbol. Since the Hungarians were burning every hut and castle in their path, this seemed a propitious sign. Otto took communion and vowed to found a bishopric and minster in honor of the saint if God would vouchsafe him the victory. Holding the Holy Lance aloft so that all could see it, Otto exhorted his men in a loud voice that carried to every man in the Christian host: "The accursed heathen are many, but poorly armed. We are the better men and wear better armor. Let us rather die like men than live as slaves of these barbarians!"

With the banner of St. Michael, captain of the heavenly host on the final Day of Judgment, fluttering by his side, the king then ordered his legions to advance against the foe. The Germans sang the kyrie eleison; the hundred thousand Hungarian horsemen roared their war cry: "Hooy, hooy!"

At first the battle went badly. One large wing of Magyars fell upon Otto's rear, howling like wolves and raining a shower of arrows upon the Bohemians, who broke and ran like hares, involving the Swabians in their rout. Luckily, the Hungarians stopped in their pursuit to plunder Otto's camp and baggage. The king sent Duke Conrad to restore the situation. Otto and Conrad then managed to encircle the Hungarians and, after much desperate fighting, shatter their forces and put them to flight. Then the slaughter began. Only those Magyars who got back across the river managed to escape, and that for a short while only, with Otto's men pursuing them down the Danube all the way to Regensburg.

All Magyar leaders who fell into Otto's hands were hanged in full sight of the army. Many prisoners were buried alive, and others were tortured to death to make them pay for their misdeeds. Among those executed were their commanders in chief, the *kakhan* Bulczuk and the *khan* Lehel, the latter having been captured while pinned beneath his dead horse.

About this Lehel and his ivory bugle horn grew up a legend according to which he was brought before Otto, who sentenced him to die for his depredations. Lehel protested that he deserved to be put to death, but for losing the battle. As a last favor the khan begged to be allowed to blow his famous horn one more time. Otto was enraptured by its sound, which was "like the roar of a mighty lion." Wounded Magyars heard it and died with a smile on their lips. But Lehel, seeing his special enemy, Duke Conrad, among the onlookers, suddenly used his huge and heavy horn to beat in the skull of the brave Conrad, crying aloud, "Thou shalt go before me and be my slave in the next world!" Then the proud Hungarian went smiling to his doom.

It is a romantic tale but, unfortunately, it is the figment of a chronicler's imagination. In reality Conrad, hot from battle and roasting in the August sun, had taken off his helmet to refresh himself with a cup of water when a Magyar arrow pierced his unprotected throat. Possibly the legend arose because the horn, of Roman workmanship with carved battle scenes, has a rather large indentation, perhaps caused by having been smashed against a solid object such as a hard Teutonic head.

The victory was complete. Only seven Magyars survived. After ordering their noses and ears cut off, Otto sent them home to tell their compatriots of their defeat. Called cowards and women, they were promptly sold into slavery after their return.

With the battle of Lechfeld the great Hungarian raids came to an end. Widukind of Corvey likened the victory to that won by Charles Martel over the Moors at Poitier in 732: "So great a triumph has not been the great fortune of any king for the last two centuries!" Otto was hailed as Defender of Christendom and the Father of His Country. "Then ambassadors came to him from the Romans and the Greeks and the Saracens, bearing gifts, namely vessels of gold and silver and bronze, curiously engraved in many patterns; vessels of glass and ivory; rugs of every shape and color; balsam, pigments and paints of endless variety; animals never seen before by Saxon eyes, lions and camels, apes and ostriches, for in Otto all good Christians saw their best hope."

Otto's life was not entirely taken up by battling; it involved a great deal of begetting as well. Besides seven legitimate children, he had a number of illegitimate ones as well, one of whom, William, the fruit of a liaison with a Slavic woman, he made archbishop of Mainz.

In 929, the nineteen-year-old Otto married the saintly Edgitha (Edith) of Wessex, daughter of the English king Edward the Elder and sister of the reigning King Aethelstan. At that time there was already

a good deal of intermarriage between the noble houses of Europe, particularly between the kindred Saxons of England and the continent.
Both countries were still called "Sakslanda," and the language in both
was still nearly identical.

The noble and educated nun Hroswitha of Gandersheim described
in her historic epos, *Gesta Ottonis*, how the royal marriage between Otto
and Edgitha had been arranged: "When, therefore, Henry, the illustrious father and king, decided that, while he himself was still breathing the warm breath of life, he would betroth to Otto, his first born
son and future king, a suitable maiden, he wished to seek her not in
his own dominion, but sent chosen ambassadors to the charming Nation of the English, with splendid gifts, in quest of Edgitha, daughter
of King Edward. She was at that time at the court of her brother
whom an ignoble consort had born to the king. The mother of this
excellent maiden was most noble, but the other woman was of greatly
inferior descent.

"This illustrious daughter of a king was by reputation well
known to all because of her nobility and noble ways. Her calm mien
was one of touching sincerity and she was adorned with a wondrous
calm of queenly bearing. Blessed with extraordinary goodness as with
a radiance, she earned such high praise in her native land that the
people thought her the best among all living women.

"Our king's ambassadors came to the brother of this princess and
related to him the message they bore. He was exceedingly pleased and
in a kind voice explained it all to his sister, urging her to obey the most
excellent king who wished to see her wed to his own son. After having poured into her heart a sweet love for Otto, the royal prince then
gathered countless treasures and when he thought he had heaped up
enough he dispatched the princess together with all these gifts and suitable attendants across the sea, bestowing upon her riches wondrously
precious.

"With her he sent her sister, Adiva, younger in years and inferior
in merit. Thus he honored Otto by sending him two maidens of the
most distinguished birth that he might lawfully wed whom of the two

he wished. But at first sight he loved Edgitha because of her great goodness and deemed her most worthy to be his wife."

Otto's marriage to Edgitha, which lasted for eighteen years until her death in 946, was a happy one. She had a calming influence upon him and a knack for turning his anger away from its intended victim. No matter how much he raged, she always managed to "quiet the stormy waves of his monstrous fury." She was a compassionate woman who once freed a fawn from its trap and restored it to its mother. She gave alms to excess, and the king, so the story goes, forbade her to make any more gifts to the poor, "only to test her." Otto then accosted her, disguised as a beggar. Edgitha lamented, "The king has left me nothing but my clothes." On an impulse, she tore off one of her gold-embroidered, gemstudded sleeves, giving it to the make-believe starveling.

Later, at dinner, the king asked her, "Why do you not wear the fine new dress I gave you?" forcing her to put it on. When he saw that one of the sleeves was missing he smilingly produced it and fastened it to her robe, to the great amusement of all except the embarrassed queen whom the people worshiped like a saint. This English queen bore two children—one son, Ludolf, and one daughter, Liutgard.

After Edgitha's death, Otto took as his second wife the nineteen-year-old Adelaide, daughter of King Rudolf of Lorraine and widow of Duke Lothar of Burgundy, who had also been the ruler of northern Italy. The events leading up to this marriage contain all the elements of cruelty, barbarism, treachery, deceit, and individual courage that were so typical of that brutal age.

Adelaide's young husband, Lothar, "a mere stripling," had a powerful rival in Berengar, margrave of Ivrea, who tried to extend his domain at Lothar's expense. In 950, Berengar managed to have the young man poisoned and to have himself crowned as king of Italy. Having attained his goal, Berengar, who had won the support of the local barons by his seeming friendliness and affability, showed himself to be a despotic monster. His wife, Willa, was even worse—"a revengeful harpie without a single scruple."

By descent more noble than Berengar, and as rightful heir to Lothair's dominions, Adelaide was mistress of northern Italy. The more oppressive Berengar's rule became, the more people of all ranks looked to the young widow for redress. Berengar and Willa saw opportunity in this as well as danger. By a coup de main they seized and imprisoned Adelaide. Once in their power they tried with threats and physical violence to force her to accept their own son and co-regent, Adalbert, as husband, hoping in this way to legitimize their own rule and lawfully to acquire Adelaide's lands.

In the words of Hroswitha, "Engorged with hatred and envy, Berengar directed his fury against Queen Adelaide. Not only did he seize her throne but at the same time forced the doors of her treasury and carried off, with greedy hand, everything he found; gold, jewels, and all kinds of precious things. He even took her royal crown. No single piece of adornment did he pass by. He feared not to deprive her of her attendants and those who waited upon her person. Lastly he also denied her all freedom to come and go as she wished. He kept her shut up in a prison-like cell and put guards around this place, but HE who freed Peter from the chains of Herod released her also."

Adelaide resisted all threats and inducements to marry the ugly, misshapen Adalbert, whom she suspected of complicity in her husband's murder, and she managed somehow to escape, together with the two maidservants her jailers had left her. They did not get far. Recaptured by Berengar's henchmen, Adelaide was punished by the formidable Willa, who tore off her necklaces and bracelets, pulled Adelaide's hair, and scratched her face, beating her with both fists and finally hurling her to the ground, kicking her viciously.

Berengar then imprisoned Adelaide in one of his island castles on Lake Garda, where she languished for four months, closely kept but not forgotten. Warinus, a faithful priest who had once been in the service of her dead husband, started digging a hole into the castle's thick walls. Every night he bored a little deeper into the stone. From the inside, Adelaide and her one remaining maid did their share of countertunneling. At last the wall was broken through and the two women squeezed through the opening to join Warinus, who was waiting with a boat to row them across the lake to the mainland.

> See the good queen
> Fleeing from her pursuers,
> Through night and fog
> On tender feet
> As the sun rose
> They hid in secret places,
> In caves in dark forests,
> Cowering in furrows of plowed fields,
> Hidden by swaying corn.
> See them hurrying on
> As night fell again,
> As fog covered the earth,
> Hurrying on and on
> Among the hooting of owls.

They were pursued and did, in fact, hide themselves in a wheat field. Miraculously, they remained undiscovered, though their pursuers went through the field stabbing to the right and left with their lances. The loyal priest left Adelaide and her maid during the night to make contact with Bishop Adelhard of Reggio, a trusted friend. The queen and her maidservant wandered on and became mired in a bog. Later they encountered a lone fisherman and implored him, for the love of God, to give them something to eat. The man made a fire and roasted a fish for them. Loyal Warinus returned accompanied by some of the bishop's armed retainers who conducted the women to the Castle of Canossa where they put themselves under the protection of its owner, Count Azzo. Berengar promptly arrived to lay siege to the castle. Warinus once more rose to the occasion, making his way through the lines of the besiegers with a letter from Adelaide to Otto, begging him to come to their rescue and offering him her hand together with her kingdom—an offer Otto could not resist. He wanted to become emperor, and this he could not be without becoming master of Italy first.

Not that wedding Adelaide was a hardship. Beautiful and sensual, she was, at twenty, half as old as Otto and attractive not merely because she was wealthy and would bring a crown to her future husband. Rumors later circulated about her entanglements with Otto's younger brother Henry, with his son Liudolf, and with other men. Her personal friend, Abbot Odilo of Cluny, thought that the hardships Adelaide had undergone were decidedly good for her, as they somewhat subdued her lustful hankerings after carnal pleasures.

In any case, Ludolf seems to have thought that he would make a better husband of the youthful queen than his middle-aged father, and he dashed ahead of Otto with a small army of his own to win her hand. For all his pains, Berengar defeated him and scattered his men. In the end, it was Otto who came to her rescue with a sufficient force. The confrontation did not even come to a battle. Berengar never dared to make a stand but fled from castle to castle and town to town together with his shrewish Willa, to become a mere nuisance rather than a decisive factor in history. Otto crossed the Brenner Pass in 951 and met Adelaide at Pavia. They took an immediate liking to one another and promptly celebrated their nuptials with great solemnity. It turned out to be a happy marriage, as such politically inspired unions went, and Adelaide in time bore five children.

The two seem to have loved each other after their own fashion. They might not have been faithful to each other physically, but they were faithful in all other matters. Otto not only restored to Adelaide the lands stolen by Berengar but added to them some choice parcels from his own domains, and he never infringed upon her queenly prerogatives. As for Adelaide, she now wore a double crown, one by inheritance and one by reason of her marriage to Otto.

The pair shored each other up in good days and in bad. She was his Consurs Nostri Regni, the consort of his reign, later Consors Imperii. She had a say in most of his affairs, whether political or cultural, and was hailed as the Literatissima Regina, the most learned queen of her time. She even eclipsed her mother-in-law, the shrewd and formidable Matilda, and, as Mater Regnorum, the reigning mother, she made her influence felt for years after the great Otto's death. Gerbert would come to know her well, and her power would have a direct bearing on the course of his life.

Otto himself had now taken a giant step on the road to Rome and the establishment of his Ottonian Empire. The way was free. On February 2, 962, Otto and Adelaide were crowned and anointed emperor and empress by the Holy Father in the eternal city. Otto was at the same time mystically wedded to Domina Roma, the mistress of the world, and henceforth he was styled the new David, Caesar, and Augustus, ruler of the Holy Roman Empire, triumphator and co-regent of Christ. He promptly fell under the city's magic spell, which from then on kept a whole line of German emperors in its thrall.

The magic of Rome was not necessarily good for either Germany or Italy. Immense effort and blood was wasted by German king after German king in pursuing the chimera of the sacred empire and in adherence to an unattainable mythic ideal. The Italians, on their part, never returned the strange Germanic love-hate for their country, because, though the Germans loved Rome in the abstract, they did not at all love the Romans, or Italians in general. The Germans were fascinated by the mystical aura of the country "where the lemons bloomed." The Romans were not at all fascinated by the uncouth strangers, whom they called barbarian invaders and the New Vandals. The Saxons and Swabians were never at peace among the Romans. The Germans had to fight unceasingly to keep their footholds in a country that rejected them, so that eventually "Italy became the tomb of the German Nation."

But in 972, when Gerbert approached him with temerity, coupled with a determination to pursue his studies, Otto the Great was at the height of his powers. He must have been impressed and grateful for the amount of knowledge Gerbert had imparted to his young son in the brief span of less than a year. Perhaps he intended to recall Gerbert to his service at a later date. At any rate, Otto gave his approval, and Gerbert left with King Lothaire's retinue for Rheims. He was still young—by most accounts in his twenties—but already he was making a name for himself, a friend of counts and abbots, a protégé of the pope, a man befriended by the emperor and his heir.

CHAPTER EIGHT

To Live in France Pleasantly

AFTER WHAT MUST HAVE BEEN a long and arduous journey, the logician Gerannus, with Gerbert in his company, finally reached Rheims—"that most venerable city, cradle of Gaul's Christianity and fortress of learning." Gerbert lost no time installing himself in the famous cathedral school where he was to spend the ten most peaceful years of his life.

Venerable indeed was Rheims, already a city in the days of Caesar, chief town of the friendly Remi tribe, one of the first to accept Christianity. It became a bishopric as early as the fifth century and an archbishop's see in the eighth. The city of St. Remigius was rich in legends, such as the one about the Sainte Ampoule, the vial containing the sacred chrism with which the rulers of France had to be anointed in order to become kings. During a losing battle with the Alemanni, so the legend went, Clovis, the true founder of the Frankish monarchy, vowed that if against all odds he should wrest victory from defeat, he would accept the Christian gospel. He won and went to Rheims where that most holy man, Archbishop Remi himself, instructed him in the way of salvation.

"Preparations were made along the road from the palace to the baptistry. Curtains and rich stuffs were hung up. Houses on either side of the street were decked out, the baptistry sprinkled with balm and perfume. The procession moved from the palace, the clergy leading the way with the Holy Gospels, the cross and banners, singing hymns; then came the bishop leading the king by the hand; after him the queen, lastly the people." As the king bent his head over the baptismal font to be sprinkled with the water of life, St. Remi admonished him "to worship what you have burned, and to burn what you have worshiped."

But where was the oil with which to anoint the king? Alas, there was none. But then out of the heavens descended a dove bearing in its beak the precious vial, La Sainte Ampoule, containing the sacred oil to anoint the newly baptized Clovis. Actually, the legend was invented three hundred years after the event by the pious but not altogether truthful Bishop Hincmar of Rheims. The holy chrism eventually hardened into a dark solid mass, somewhat like amber, from which a tiny bit was scraped with a needle to anoint the many French kings who came to be crowned in the city's cathedral.

In Gerbert's day, the cathedral at Rheims was rather primitive and small. The city had a population of some two thousand people who had become the victims of petty feudal wars. The walls of the episcopal school, to which Gerbert was attached, had fallen into ruins, and even while Gerbert taught there Rheims was taken and retaken by warring factions.

Gerbert was lucky to have as his bishop Adalbero, a famous scholar, builder, and embellisher of his church, as well as an accomplished politician. Adalbero was a born diplomat, easy in the presence of princes, being himself a great noble and cousin of a king. It says much for the spirit of equality within the church that, in spite of the fact that so many of its highest offices were held by nobles, Adalbero quickly accepted Gerbert as a friend.

The bishop himself complained bitterly that Rheims was ravaged, its clergy decadent and walking around in unseemly clothes. The walls and roof of the school were so full of holes that the wind blew hither and thither the parchments on the desks of students who, in winter, scratched away with pens held in frozen fingers.

Most houses in Rheims were made of wood, their roofs thatched, their owners' swine and goats roaming freely in the narrow streets, which were often knee-deep in mud. Human and animal waste, carcasses of beasts, and offal from butchers' shops were indiscriminately dumped into the gutterless streets. One king of France fainted from the stink of the accumulated filth stirred up by his horse's hooves, while another prince was killed falling from his mount when a squeaking pig ran between its legs.

Such conditions and rudimentary knowledge of medicine resulted in many illnesses peculiar to the Dark Ages. Gerbert was all too familiar with the leper's bell announcing the proximity of one suffering from leprosis. This disease was widespread and generally looked upon as punishment for the victim's sins. It began with the destruction of skin tissues and proceeded slowly over a period of years. It was gruesomely disfiguring. Limbs fell off, and faces became unrecognizable. Sufferers became outcasts and nonpersons who lost all rights regardless of former rank. Lepers were expelled from their homes and had to live apart. They had to wear special clothing and announce their approach with rattle or bell. They lived by begging, though the church and some pious nobles built lepers' hospitals in many places in an attempt to ease their lot. In fact, diseases killed half of all children before the age of ten, asking no distinction between the offspring of rulers and serfs.

Finding enough food to eat was a problem. There were long periods, particularly in winter, when no fresh food was available. People gorged themselves whenever they had an opportunity because they never knew when another opportunity might arise.

Preserving food was a matter of survival, because it was hard to keep cattle alive during a hard winter. Salt pork, salted dry beef, and salted herring were the staples. Sometimes meat and fish were simply buried in barrels of salt. Brine-salting with saltwater was widespread. Pounding the lumpy salt until it had the right grainy consistency was hard work. Nobles had their own powderers and salterers to perform this task.

When vegetables were in season, people ate cabbage, carrots, peas, and various garden greens, and from trees they picked apples, pears, and nuts. Bread was made from wheat, rye, or barley, the flour baked without removing the bran and full of impurities. Bread was coarse, and, often, weevilly and moldy. Consequently, teeth were bad and many suffered from foul breath. Pies and pancakes were popular. Horses were eaten with gusto. Some popes tried, in vain, to make people abstain from horseflesh. At the end of the century the monks of the great abbey of St. Gall even treated their guests to a great horse barbecue. Venison was for the nobles who owned the forests and the game in them, the fowl in the air and the fish in the streams. Birds, netted or caught on boards smeared with glue and baited with seeds, were usually roasted on spits. People ate cranes, storks, swans, crows, herons, and loons. Sometimes birds were served in a pastry like the well-known four- and-twenty blackbirds baked in a pie.

Spices were the great rage throughout the Dark Ages, as they not only preserved the food but also killed the taste when it was spoiled. Among those preferred were cloves, mustard, caraway seeds, and pepper. Some of these spices were imported from the East via the Mediterranean and were worth their weight in gold. One medieval poem suggested that all meals should be strongly spiced so that the mouth should emit sweet-smelling clouds.

The great nobles had tablecloths but no plates; in their place one used round flat slabs of bread. When plates came into vogue, they had to be shared with one's neighbor. Bread plates had the advantage in that they were edible, soaked up drippings, and were good for sopping up. Guests had to bring their own knives. Spoons and forks were introduced much later.

Usually people ate two meals a day if sufficient food was available—breakfast upon getting up, and the main meal around three in the afternoon, often a lengthy drawn-out affair. If one could, one ate enormously. Priests especially, were said to be great gluttons, and one can well believe it reading of one feast served up by a bishop celebrating the consecration of a new church. The feast was spread over two days and the menu has been preserved. First day, first course: egg soup with saffron and honey, barley gruel, sheep on skewers with onions, fried chicken with apples. Second course: sterlet with oil and raisins, trout baked in fat, sauteed eel in spices, roast herring with mustard. Third course: cooked sour fish, baked wrasse, hard-baked songbirds in goosefat with horseradish, and ham with cucumber.

On the second day the menu was cooked pork with mustard, egg cake with berries, fish with raisins, spitted swan, stuffed bass, roast goose with red beets, venison with mushrooms, salted pike with parsley, pigeon pie, egg salad, and roasted apples with honey.

Hot, spiced, mulled wine was much in demand, and beer was quaffed in huge quantities in Germany, England, and Scandinavia. One Swedish king chose, among several prospective brides, the one who could brew the best beer. A Swedish queen, St. Brigitte, was rumored to have repeated the miracle performed by Christ at the wedding of Cana, with a slight variation. Brigitte changed water, not into wine, but into beer.

As far as table manners were concerned, a manual of etiquette intended for gentlefolk reminded them not to break wind while at table, neither to hawk and spit on the floor, nor to pick their noses or scratch their heads looking for lice, and, particularly in the case of males, not to fondle the breasts of the women next to them.

All this did not concern the lowly peasants, who ate the same monotonous fare of gruel day after day and called themselves lucky if they could fill their bowls to the brim. In time of famine, an old proverb said, "those men may call themselves rich who have a crust of bread."

From the dawn of history people liked to dress as well as they could. During the second half of the tenth century fashions had a certain charm, even sophistication among the rich. Already Charlemagne's courtiers loved to walk about in Byzantine silks, to the disgust of the Great Charles, who took them on an impromptu hunt and led them through a thick forest during a torrential rain. He then hurried them to dinner without giving them a chance to change their clothes and laughed at them as they sat down in their torn and muddied silks, pointing at his sheepskin coat and saying, "This is much better."

Dandies were always criticized but went on being dandies all the same. Men usually wore a knee-length tunic and a cloak, open on one side and fastened at the left shoulder with a clasp. Below the waist they wore hose, often with legs of different colors. The Ottomans started the so-called *mi-parti* fashion of half-colored clothing: one side of a tunic might be red, the other green. Tunics were also horizontally or vertically striped in various hues. Nobles wore brightly colored outfits, peasants drab shirts of brown or gray on which stains did not show up since they worked and got dirty. Peasants also usually had only one garment. Undershirts came into fashion, and a man was considered a base-born villain if he did not wear one. However, there were no nightshirts as men slept in the buff.

Among great barons fashions were ostentatious. On the occasion of his baptism the Danish king Harald Bluetooth received, as a gift from his godparents, clothes covered with gold and precious gems. In addition, his queen got as presents heavy gold jewelry "for neck, breast, and waist," a gem-studded belt made of chains of interlaced gold, armlets, and massive rings.

In France, at the end of the century, female dress emphasized the shape of the body, particularly of the breasts, "Shapely and slimwaisted like ants should be the lasses."

Long hair was the pride of free men. Serfs and servants had to wear their hair short. The church condemned the use of curling irons by men, but King Alfred the Great made a gift of silver curling irons to his confessor. Bald nobles often wore wigs, with reddish blond being the preferred color. They also braided their hair with silk ribbons or gold threads. Women always had their heads covered in obedience to the words of the apostle Paul: "For if the woman be not covered, let her also be shorn: but if it be a shame for a woman to be shorn or shaven, let her be covered." Covering and hiding the hair was a symbol of the woman's dependence upon the man's will, and theoretically only the husband had a right to look upon his wife's uncovered hair. Virgins, however, had the right to leave their hair uncovered and were not called upon to prove their innocence. Women loved to wear long braids and, if not sufficiently endowed, wore false hair in spite of thunderings from the pulpit that it came from corpses or, even worse, from damned souls in hell. Sometimes women wore several braids, which led Gilles of Orleans to fulminate that women had more tails than the devil. Barbaric luxury went hand in hand with barbaric poverty, crudeness with refinement. In fashions, as in all other things, the tenth century was one of great contrasts.

Attitudes toward sexuality revealed a similar paradox. Intercourse among the unmarried was officially frowned upon by the church but unofficially enjoyed by all, including clerics. In the words of Will Durant, "The promiscuous nature of man overflowed the dikes of secular and ecclesiastical legislation; and some women felt that abdominal gaiety could be atoned for by hebdomadal piety." Orgasms, the church fathers taught, were an invention of the devil, an ecstasy so overpowering "that when it reaches its climax it erases men's mental faculties." If folks had to perform the act for the, alas, indispensable business of begetting, then, the church taught, they should at least not enjoy it, though how this was to be accomplished was not explained.

All through the Middle Ages women were held almost solely responsible for sexual activities. As the saying went, "No woman is good, unless she be a saint." The devil worked his evil through women's bodies. Wives should be thrashed often by their husbands to beat the devil of carnal lust out of them. And, once again, as an example of the tenth-century's innate contradictions, together with derision of women went the cult of the Virgin Mary. But here the church once more had to battle with the fiend, because pilgrims male and female, journeying to shrines sacred to the Virgin (and also to other saints), found many temptations they did not encounter at home and that they could not resist since they were free from being overseen. As a consequence, many female pilgrims returned pregnant or did not return at all, having become prostitutes in a foreign country.

As to prostitution, even St. Augustine admitted that it was necessary because, without it, men's lust would destroy society. Others held that bordellos were sewers and that without them "the filth of lust would overflow cathedral and palace." And so Rheims as well as other cities contained many brothels and streetwalkers. However, men out for dalliance did not have to depend on prostitutes, at least according to their records. "Were there not women in France, high and low, willing and ready?"

Indeed. "Mouth clung to mouth, leg entwined itself with leg. The proud dagger sought its sheath, the cleric's pen its inkwell, the treasurer's key the hole to its treasure chest, while the eager little mouse was not the least afraid of the bushy black cat." Some veiled hints in Gerbert's letters indicate that he was not altogether a stranger to such pleasures. At any rate, some great princes, noblewomen, and even kings were not ashamed to be bastards, nor were they, in France, particularly ostracized or barred from succession.

Homosexuality was seldom mentioned, possibly because those who practiced it were loathe to admit it, as punishment was savage. The Bible held that "if a man also lie with mankind, as he lieth with a woman, both of them have committed an abomination: they shall surely be put to death." The homosexual men of the tenth century therefore risked their heads, or at least their testicles, as castration was one of the milder penalties for homosexuality. But confessors had a lengthy catalogue for meting out suitable penances to sexual transgressors, and the list of a great variety of homosexual acts was long, from which one can infer that they were widely practiced.

As to bestiality, the list of animals that could be used for carnal purposes is truly astounding and, at times, ludicrous. The poor animal was to be held as guilty as the human sinner, and there is at least one mention of a man being burned together with a mare of whom "he had knowledge."

Outside Rheims the countryside was still thickly forested, with here and there a miserable village or rude fortified building trying hard, but unsuccessfully, to deserve the name of castle. Sieges, whether a matter of a few armed men trying to storm a single tower or of an army investing a good-sized city, might take a long time, while besiegers themselves went hungry in a despoiled country or fell prey to the usual sicknesses of medieval soldiers staying too long in the same place. It was therefore the almost universal custom to slaughter not only a garrison that dared to resist, but also the innocent citizens—men, women, children, and even dogs—as punishment for having forced the attackers to mount a cumbersome and time-consuming siege. Such massacres were also meant as a warning to other prospective defenders: "Surrender on demand or take the consequences."

A tragicomic story, related by Bishop Liutprand of Cremona, illustrates the point. Luitprand witnessed the siege of Beneventum by Theobald, duke of Spoleto, whom he constantly called "the great hero." This particular hero habitually castrated all his prisoners and, if they happened to be Greeks, added insult to injury by joking that he had another batch of prime eunuchs to send to his enemy, the Byzantine emperor, who could always use a few more.

During a sally by the besieged, a number of prisoners fell into Theobald's hands and were promptly sentenced to the customary operation. In happy anticipation the duke settled down to watch the proceedings, when out of one town gate burst a disheveled, frantic woman, whose loud cries induced Theobald to listen to her: "Is it true, oh magnanimous hero, that you wage war against women who never did you harm and whose only weapons are the spindle and the loom?"

Puzzled, the magnanimous hero pointed out that he was one of the rare leaders who did not vent his fury upon the female sex.

"But you do war against us," she screamed, "and how can you wound us in a more vital part, than by depriving our husbands of what we most dearly treasure, amputating their proud testicles, the source of our joys and the hope of coming generations? Stealing our sheep and cattle we endured without a murmur, but this grievous injury, this contemplated irretrievable loss, tries my patience and calls to justice in heaven as on earth!"

Theobald was amused, his soldiers guffawed and slapped their thighs, and the captives were released intact. As the woman walked off happily with her even happier charges, the duke sent a messenger after her telling her to come back. "What punishment should be inflicted upon your husband, woman," Theobald inquired, "if he were again caught fighting against me?"

"Should he be guilty of this," was the prompt answer, "he has eyes and a nose and hands and feet. These belong to him and may pay for his misdeed. But let my lord be pleased to spare what his little handmaiden claims as her special and rightful property."

The good bishop, no doubt, was among those roaring with laughter at the prisoners' predicament. He never questioned the duke's right to mutilate men at his whim, a normal procedure in war as in peace.

The castles that dotted the landscape around Rheims hardly deserved the name. The tenth-century castle was merely a small family estate within larger estates of a similar kind, an enclosure made of a wooden palisade with pointed, fire-hardened stakes behind a protective ditch. It was always built around a hill, on top of which stood a tower—the lord's home. Around it, in thatched huts, lived relatives, retainers, hangers-on, servants, cows, pigs, and chicken. Plows and pitchforks lay intermingled with shields and spears. There were also usually sheds and barns for the horses. Sometimes, as insurance, a second inner rampart encircled the tower. One lord, who was called rich and powerful, dwelled in a wooden tower. On the upper floor he took his ease, ate, made love, and slept. The lower story, with an earthen floor, served as storehouse for everything the master needed, including a milch cow.

The typical minor baron neither bought nor sold, nor did he have any ready money. His peasant-serfs furnished his bread, grain, vegetables, and fruits. They provided eggs from their fowls and hams from their swine, which were wild, hairy, and razor-backed, being left to fend for themselves on acorns in nearby woods. Hare, deer, and wild boar the lord hunted for himself, combining sport and manly exercise with putting meat on his table. His serfs hewed the wood and fetched the water. They also made plows, hoes, and shoes for him. A blacksmith, usually a half-free man, lived on the premises as part of the master's entourage. The women of the household spun flax into cloth, made his cloaks, darned his hose, cooked his meal, and warmed his bed.

An extra source of supply came from robbing anybody who was weaker. According to chronicles of the time "if three or four men met two, they robbed or even killed them," and "you will find no man born of woman who is not shut up for safety in a castle or tower."

While a towering castle was a threat to every stranger, a hornet's nest out of which, at any moment, the master's stinging wasps were apt to swoop down upon a likely victim, it was also a welcome refuge to all belonging to the lord's estate. Behind its palisades his peasants and laborers, together with their children and livestock, could find shelter against raids from outsiders. Always a watchman scanned the countryside from the tower, giving timely warning with his far-sounding horn of any approaching danger.

Lords might be powerful, but they were seldom comfortable. The castle's heart was the great feasting hall, its floor covered with straw or rushes. Bones and scraps from the long trestle table were simply thrown upon the floor and eagerly snapped up by the ever-present snarling dogs, who generously supplied fleas to both high- and low-born. Whenever the rushes began to stink of rotting scraps and dog droppings and were so "full of vermin that they seemed to move by themselves," they were thrown out and replaced by fresh ones, on special occasions by sweetsmelling grasses.

The typical castle was dark and dank. Windows were mere slits covered by parchment or small slabs of horn, as glass panes had not yet come into use. Rooms were consequently very drafty, and rheumatism was the common lot of the suffering tenants. In winter, people either fried by roasting their backsides at the fire or shivered if at a distance from the chimney place. Smoke, soot, and cinders found their way into inflamed eyes. Castles were insufficiently lighted by torches or pine slivers dipped in resin. Only the richest barons and prelates could afford candles. It was no wonder that poets waxed ecstatic singing of the coming spring and the fading winter.

People relieved themselves wherever and whenever they could, and crude scatological jokes were part of the table talk. Furnishings were spare. The residents' few possessions were kept in a chest, sometimes covered with a pillow, which also served as a seat. Tables often were just boards laid over trestles. Long benches seated the guests, and always there was a special high seat for the lord and master at the head of the table.

Hospitality was a virtue but also a necessity. Inns were nonexistent, roads bad, nights dark. As castle dwellers lived in isolation and were bored, guests were welcome for the news they brought, especially if they were good storytellers. "Even the dogs rejoice when they see a guest coming. For a good guest the door opens itself." It was considered a great luxury if the lord and lady of the castle had their own private place to sleep; more often they had to share their bed with others. Guests, retainers, and servants slept in the great hall, wherever they could find a place, kicking the dogs aside to make room for themselves. There was no privacy, and such sleeping arrangements led to sexual adventures.

Many tales, some based on fact, relate instances of frightful revenge taken by a wronged husband. A recurring romantic theme was the fiendishly cruel murder of the lover whose heart was cut out, cooked, and served up to the faithless chatelaine with a knife at her throat. Other stories told of ladies wearing *le coeur de ses amants*, cut out by a jealous spouse, as a dried and shriveled relic upon their bosoms. Rich heiresses or widows frequently were raped to force them into marriage—"violated into wedlock," as the saying went.

Finally, there were the scholars spoiling their eyes and lungs hunching over their steeply sloping desks by the flickering light of smoldering torches, their lean buttocks rubbed raw on hard teetering stools. They labored in ill-ventilated, ill-heated chambers, inkhorns in their left hands, the right gripping the goosequill in frozen fingers, scratch-

ing away at the parchment that turned greasy at the slightest touch—
yet for the love of learning, bringing light out of darkness "like dawn
rising out of a somber sea."

Foremost among these was Gerbert. The world he lived in and that
he accepted like the philosopher he was, was politically and physically
insecure. That he and those like him persevered in learning and teaching under the prevailing conditions is, perhaps, their greatest achievement. Gerbert put up with the hardships just as he enjoyed the
advantages of his position. Society, as Adalbero his bishop and patron
laid down, was divided into three parts. "God's house," wrote the
bishop, "which men think to be one, is threefold; some pray in it,
some fight in it, and some work in it."

> For the knight and learned clerk
> Live by him who does the work.

The social order was ordained by God's will, and if Gerbert had
any reservations about it he never mentioned them in his letters. Of
humble and obscure origin he had risen to occupy his place in one of
the two ruling classes, and if this gave him the opportunity to think
and teach for the benefit of all, so much the better.

CHAPTER NINE

A Paradise of Learning

IN RHEIMS, GERBERT LEARNED LOGIC from Gerannus, to whom, in exchange, he taught mathematics and astronomy. Gerbert soon surpassed his instructor, and his rising reputation attracted many students. It was not long before Adalbero placed him in charge of the already renowned cathedral school.

"From far and near came those eager for knowledge and Rheims verily seemed to them a paradise of learning, where in Gerbert they saw a man whose wisdom was so great that all proclaimed that it must come either from God and His angels, or from the devil."

Gerbert revolutionized the medieval system of education. Horace Mann wrote, "The number of his disciples increased every day. It was noised abroad not only throughout the Gauls but throughout Germany and Italy to the Adriatic and the Tyrhennian Seas that there was at Rheims a master who did not think it enough to lecture on the profoundest philosophy of the ancients, but who expounded the natural sciences, and who knew how to brighten one set of studies with the graces of the poet, and enlighten the other by the use of the most wonderful instruments."

He was still under thirty when he began his career at Rheims, and, by his own admission, he was not yet free from the passions of

anger, hatred, and pity. There are hints that he was no stranger to the
love of women. If so, he was very discreet, never letting passions interfere with his work or the pursuit of his ambitions. Ambitious he certainly was, avid for scholarship but also gifted with political acumen.
It would be interesting to know exactly what Gerbert looked like, but
no physical description of him exists. Somehow one pictures him as
tall and lean, thin-lipped, sharp-featured, and pale from studying indoors. Erasmus of Rotterdam comes to mind. But he could just as
easily have been short, fat, and pug-nosed.

As instructor in the seven arts, Gerbert's motto was, "I teach what
I know and learn what I do not know." What he knew best from the
outset was mathematics. Paul Lacroix called him "beyond question
the first mathematician of his time." Some pious men, not wanting to
admit that Gerbert's knowledge of mathematics came from Spain and
therefore, in a roundabout way, from Moors and pagan Greeks, insisted that he had learned his numbers out of the books of Boethius.
Gerbert certainly knew Boethius and valued his works. He called the
sixth-century sage the "Father and Light of His Country" and taught
his theories to the students at Rheims. But Gerbert's mathematics went
far beyond Boethius and were altogether new to the Western world.
As Darlington, a well-known medievalist, put it: "His mathematical
knowledge was different from anything known at the time in Christendom."

Not only had Boethius himself been largely forgotten, but mathematics was looked upon as magic. Instead of teaching the subject
scientifically, scholars busied themselves exploring the mystical properties of numbers and taught that in the arcane numbers three and six
were contained all the secrets of nature, that out of "holy seven" fortune
smiled and luck could be extracted by the wise, that the number twelve
was sacred and pleasing to God, while eleven belonged to the devil.

Gerbert had little patience with such notions. In mathematics he
began by initiating his pupils in the rudiments of arithmetic. He was
the first to introduce them to the Hindu-Arabic numerals 1, 2, 3, 4,
5, 6, 7, 8, 9—but not to the zero, of which he himself knew nothing,

since it became known to Western scholars only much later. Their introduction of numerals by Gerbert made the development of higher mathematics possible in the West. Before Gerbert only Roman characters, which were totally unsuitable for practical calculations, had been used. Formulas in the old Roman style, such as LMCMLXX XV.Xd. "made even the angels weep." The absence of the zero naturally caused problems, which Gerbert solved by replacing it with an empty space. Because of this, 101 was rendered I I but was often mistaken for 11. Still, the introduction of Arabic numerals was a giant step forward. Almost equally important was Gerbert's introduction of the abacus to his students. This instrument, indisputably acquired in Catalonia, caused discomfort among the pious.

Gerbert's pupil said, "He took no less pain instructing them in geometry. To begin with, he had a shield maker construct for him an abacus; that is, a table partitioned into compartments. Its length was divided into twenty-seven parts, on which he arranged nine parts representing the numbers. He fashioned one thousand characters out of horn, which, placed in the twenty-seven compartments of the abacus, enabled one to obtain the multiplication or division of every possible number, dividing and multiplying their infinite numbers with such speed that one could get the answer quicker than one could express it in words."

Equally new and astounding to his students was the subject of astronomy. Though some clerics had recommended its study, and it was recognized as one of the seven arts comprising the quadrivium, it was nevertheless suspect as a close twin to astrology, the accursed, occult, and forbidden art that was, all the same, widely practiced. Astronomy, in the view of some, was "an egg not to be sucked unless cleansed from the nauseous odors of error."

Though malodorous, the astrological egg was sucked by many with relish, an omelet in which astronomy was mixed with astrology and religion. "Since man, like the world, is composed of four elements, reason, as well as faith, persuades us that, under God, human affairs

are regulated by celestial bodies." For many of Gerbert's contemporaries astronomy was the same as astrology—the art of drawing horo-
scopes and predicting a person's fate from the movements and
conjunctions of the stars. A conjunction of Jupiter and Mars was
credited with having ushered in Christianity.

Glaber wrote that comets portended great evils, possibly even the
end of the world. He was fascinated by the cosmic astronomical number four. There are four quarters of the universe and of the earth, four
elements, four virtues, and four Gospels, which are closely linked to
the elements. Matthew, emphasizing Christ's incarnation, stands for
the earth; Mark, stressing baptism, represents water; Luke's Gospel,
being the longest—as wide as the sky—connotes air; John, on account
of his spirituality and frequent mention of apocalyptic flames, stands
for fire.

It was taught that the planet Jupiter represented power, Mars
hostility, Venus desire, and Mercury avarice. Moon was the "moist influence," and moist humors supposedly collected in the heads of those
who slumbered out of doors in the moonlight. It was generally believed that the earth was exactly one million steps around, either
propped up by pillars or "supported by the powers of God." The distance from earth to heaven, as every learned person knew, was 10,000
miles. The Garden of Eden was located somewhere "south of India,"
hell in the center of the earth.

In the face of such a hodgepodge of astronomy, astrology, religion,
and geography, Gerbert taught scientific astronomy. It was a delicate
task, as the purpose of Christian cosmography was "to confute the
impious heresy of those who maintain that the earth is a globe and
not a flat, oblong table as taught by the scriptures." Gerbert not only
taught that the world was a globe but, ever practical, constructed astronomical spheres to demonstrate his theories. He made hollow tubes
to observe the stars, forerunners of the telescope, and "fixed the equa-
tor exactly." His knowledge of astronomy so overawed his students that
they were convinced that he could determine the distance between

points of the earth and in the sky "by just looking." Richer elaborated: "To appreciate fully the sagacity of this great man and to make the reader understand the efficacy of his methods, and what efforts he made to establish the principles of astronomy, I state that he explained this nearly unachievable science, to the astonishment of all, by means of certain instruments. He first presented the shape of the world in the form of a wooden sphere, thus demonstrating something very big through a very small model. Inclining his sphere by its two poles on the horizon, he fixed the northern constellations toward the upper pole and the southern toward the lower. On his sphere he demonstrated the rising and the setting of the stars. He made his students recognize the different heavenly bodies. During the night he pointed out to them the bright stars and made them observe that both at their rising and their setting they moved over the different regions of the universe.

"He constructed another armillary sphere showing how the planets approach and distance themselves from the earth. All the stars of all the constellations were represented under their animal signs. He figured, with wondrous exactitude, the orbits traversed by the planets, whose path and height, as well as their respective distances, he demonstrated faultlessly to his students."

Richer ended his pages on the subject of Gerbert's teachings by saying that it would take him too long to recount all the things Gerbert did to demonstrate his theories, as this would sidetrack him from his main theme—the history of Gaul.

Unique among scholars of the Dark Ages for the scope of his interests, Gerbert was also a serious tinkerer who, with his own hands, put together not only spheres and astrolabes, but also constructed stargazing tubes, a sophisticated sundial, musical instruments, water clocks, abaci, a steam-powered organ, and other marvels.

After becoming a bibliomaniac in later life, Gerbert made spheres in exchange for rare books. He once wrote to a certain Brother Remi of Treves, "We have not sent you a sphere, because at the moment we do not have any. It is not a little work, but one of great labor to make it, particularly now when we are engaged in great affairs. But if you greatly desire to own such an object, copy down for me carefully the 'Achilleid' of Statius, so that by this gift you can get out of me a sphere, which I cannot let you have for nothing, because it is so difficult to make."

There was, consequently, some bickering by letter between Gerbert and Remi, the one complaining that he had not received his book, the other that he never got his sphere.

Important as Gerbert's scientific teachings were, opening his students' minds to the beauty of classic poetry and giving them an illuminating look at ancient philosophy was perhaps his greatest gift to them. Here too, however, he was in dangerous territory. The Cluniac reform was then at its height. Whatever the abbots of Cluny said or wrote was accepted everywhere as gospel truth, and these abbots thundered against tasting of the sweet but forbidden fruit of pagan poetry and philosophy. What Gerbert taught at Rheims "reeked of the stink of heresy." It took great courage on his part to defy Gregory the Great's dictum that "the same mouth singeth not the praises of Jove and the praises of Christ."

In the case of a certain grammarian, Wilgard of Ravenna, rumor had it that he received frequent visits of evil spirits in the shape of Horace, Vergil, and Juvenal, who promised him fame and riches if he espoused their works to the neglect of the Bible. Wilgard was accused of having become so puffed up with pride that he preached one should believe more in the words of ancient poets than in the sermonizing of ignorant, long-winded priests. Consequently Wilgard was burned as a heretic.

To lecture publicly and favorably review the classic authors was looked upon as "leprosy of the soul and spiritual pestilence, as easily spread as sickness." Profane poetry had been condemned by St. Augustine as "the devil's wine." As late as 995, when Gerbert's fame had spread far and wide and when kings and emperors used their powers on his behalf, the papal legate Leo opposed his elevation to the papacy, protesting stridently that "the vicars of Peter and their disciples will not have for their teacher a Plato, a Virgil or any other of that vile herd of philosophers." One prelate hurled at him the accusation "You are not a Christian, you are a Ciceronian!"

But Gerbert was a stubborn man in whom burned a fire, and he knew how to fan the flames of learning. In his assault upon orthodoxy he was staunchly supported by his archbishop Adalbero, himself a friend of the classics. Gerbert threw himself "with a holy fervor" into his teachings. He familiarized his students with the cultural heritage of antiquity, telling them, "Without this, you know nothing. Without allowing these poets to penetrate your brains you allow them to die." He feared that, without mastery of the forms and styles of classic poetry, his students could not acquire the art of oratory which he valued greatly.

"I am not one to separate the useful from the beautiful but always try, like Cicero, to join the one to the other. Since philosophy does not separate moral teachings from the science of speaking, I have always studied to live well and speak well, and though the former is more important than the latter, to a man entangled in public affairs, both are necessary. To be able to persuade and restrain with words of sweet eloquence the violence of lawless men is useful in the highest degree." Thus Gerbert expressed his life philosophy.

In his letters Gerbert constantly alluded to the classics, used their imagery, and cited passages from their words. To Abbot Romualf of Sens he wrote, "Offer the waters of Cicero to one who thirsts."

And Richer once more: "Once having accustomed his pupils to these authors, he made them pass on to rhetoric proper, entrusting them to a sophist so, that disputing against him, they might learn reasoning in a simple, straightforward manner which, for the orator is the height of perfection. Such were his instructions in logic."

Gerbert hated flowery, overblown language. He once wrote to a friend, "He who has business with a wise man does not use many words." With all his enthusiasm for the classics he never forgot that he was a Christian in holy orders and once said, "The art of arts, after all, is the guidance of souls."

Having instilled grammar, mathematics, and rhetoric into his students' heads "as through a funnel," he crowned his labors by also teaching them music. In the words of Richer: "Arithmetic he followed with music, which Gaul, for long, had entirely ignored, making it beloved by all. Arranging the different notes on the monochord, breaking down its consonants or symphonic unions into tones and half-tones, even into third and quarter-tones, and by deftly separating its sounds into tones, he restored a perfect knowledge of music."

What Gerbert actually did was to make a sort of sound box with vibrating strings which, by moving a finger along them at measured distances, produced the notes of a scale, a primitive but effective way to explain his theories of notes. Gerbert's scale consisted of six notes only. As the twentieth-century historian Funk-Brentano said, "Even if Gerbert did not invent the scale, he was, at least, the first to have the idea of drawing staves in which musical notations should be fixed— four lines—and which are still in use in plain chant."

Gerbert is even credited with having given us the familiar *do, re, mi* by bestowing upon his notes their short resounding names, taking as his source the first syllables from the hymn to St. John: "So that the marvels of Thy deeds may resound. . . ."

Ut queant laxis
REsonare fibris
MIragestorum
FAmuli tuorum
SOlve polluti
LAbii reatum
Sancte Johannis.

Later the Italians changed the *ut* at the beginning into *do*.

Gerbert also composed hymns "to the angels and the Holy Spirit." Intoning them he might very well have accompanied himself with still another of his many inventions—a hydraulic organ "in which the air escaping in a surprising manner, by the force of heated water in brazen pipes, emitted melodious tones through multiple openings." He instilled love of music in one of his illustrious students, Robert, son of Hugh Capet, and, later, king of France. One tale has it that the two of them sang hymns together in church.

In view of Gerbert's endless curiosity, it comes as no surprise that he also dabbled in medicine. Western medicine, in his time, was mostly a matter of magic and incantations. Many of the herbalists of the tenth-century were not yet Christian or at least were strongly tinged by paganism. They gathered their plants uttering ancient prayers: "Holy Goddess Earth, parent of Nature, the Great Mother . . . Come to me with thy healing powers and grant favorable issue to whatsoever I shall make from these herbs and plants . . . I beseech thee that thy gifts shall make those who take them, whole." The sick probably fared better in the hands of such a worshiper of the Great Mother, who at least knew her herbs, than in the care of a Christian healer who, instead of herbs, might have used a rabbit's foot to effect a cure after this venerable formula: "Cut off the foot of a live rabbit and pluck a few hairs from its underbelly and then let it go. Of the hairs make a thread and with it tie the rabbit's foot to the diseased limb and you will find it a sovereign remedy. The rabbit's foot will even be more efficacious, if that is possible, if you should add to it a rabbit's anklebone found in the dung of a wolf, provided it has never been touched by a woman's hand. And, as a last bit of advice, after having taken its wool, say to the rabbit three times: 'Flee, flee, little rabbit, and take the sickness away with you!'"

Religion was mixed with medicine. Relics effected cures, and places where reliquaries were kept became the goal of many pilgrims. Water into which the single hair of a dead saint had been dipped became thereby an excellent purgative. Plunging the ring once worn by St. Remi into a brew instantly made the brew into a certain cure for lunacy. Oil from a lamp burning before St. Gall's tomb was a sure remedy for every kind of tumor. A mixture of garlic and holy water, drunk out of a bell, would, it was believed, heal a "fiend-sick" person.

Gerbert thought nature was the best physician. He described his own ailments with philosophical detachment and clinical objectivity. Though he would not treat the sick, he did not mind diagnosing their maladies and giving them advice. Friends confided their symptoms to him, and he told them in writing his opinion of them. To an unknown monk he wrote that he was sure that he suffered from kidney stones; though he would rather have seen him in person, he advised, "Take a small dosage of Antidote Philanthropus and follow my instructions," adding somewhat snappishly, "If you do not follow my regimen, turning what is healing into what is harmful, you have only yourself to blame."

Within Gerbert raged a fervor for books, for reading them, for acquiring them, for having them always by his side—books on all subjects, works on mathematics and astronomy, on medicine and poetry, on philosophy and history. He has been described as a bibliomaniac, as a friend of books (*ami des livres*), as the West's first bibliophile, collector, and owner of a great private library. He himself wrote that "study is for me the greatest remedy against the vagaries of life and I have never regretted an hour wasted upon reading."

To Ebrard, abbot of Tours, he wrote that in order to express himself better and to speak well he must be prepared in advance and for this reason was diligently at work amassing a library. He avidly bought books, copied some for himself, and had others copied for him by monks in the scriptoria of several monasteries throughout Europe. He paid his copyists generously and provided them with expensive parchment and supplies. He was not "one to let his scribes' hands be idle in the scriptorium" and himself corrected a manuscript of Pliny and transcribed a commentary on Terence. He constructed astronomical models in exchange for copies of desired books and promised favors freely to those who would send him manuscripts. Everywhere he had literary spies ferreting out rare books for him. He could not stand to be separated from his precious library, taking it with him wherever he went. He exchanged books and sometimes lent them out so that he himself could borrow.

He jealously guarded his books, his "children," keeping them in strong coffers bound in brass and iron, carrying the keys always on his own person—in the absence of pockets, dangling from his belt. He grew hotly resentful of delay and could not wait to lay his hands on a book that was long in coming. "You abuse our patience," he wrote to the monks of St. Pierre at Ghent. "You come close to stealing from me. You violate laws divine and human"—this for the recipients' slowness in returning one of his books which he wanted them to copy. Though he knew from his own experience how long it took to make a fine copy of one of the larger works, he still goaded his scribes on to be faster and probably ignored the plaintive postscripts of many early monk-copyists who often added to the last page little verses like:

> I wrote and wrote and did my best
> And now my weary hand can rest.

or

> I've calloused my fingers, I'm almost blind,
> I'm weary, so weary in body and mind.

and

> Five hundred pages, all in a row,
> Now please pay me what you owe.

Gerbert's library contained liturgies, precious illuminated Bibles, the lives of the saints, the works of Aristotle and Plato, the writings of Hincmar and John Scotus Erigenus. Probably it included the chronicles of Liutprand besides such authors as Isidore of Seville and the Pseudo-Isidore, Cassiodorus and Boethius, the satires of Juvenal and the history of Lucian. Certainly he owned Ovid, Claudius, Lucretius, and, possibly, Plotinus. One can infer from his writings that he possessed the commentaries of Macrobius, Sallust, Seneca, and Suetonius besides Caesar's *Gallic War*, and other books specifically mentioned in his letters, such as the *Achilleid*. He owned several copies of his favorite author Cicero, whom he called the "Father of Roman Eloquence."

He never mentioned how many books he owned. We know, however, that his library was unique for the times in which he lived, and that it was probably greater than that of his friend the emperor Otto and of many of the great monasteries.

Gerbert's writing was strongly influenced by his reading. In his many letters he bared his heart, expressed ideas, speculated, theorized, mused, flattered, criticized, stormed, enthused, laughed, and lamented. At times he conducted politics by letter, voiced his rage and indignation, and, now and then, even slipped in one of his own poems. Always his style was spiced with a dash of the classics. He was a master of words who always expressed himself with lucidity, elegance, and a certain rhythm in his flowing sentences. In the opinion of many, he wrote the most elegant Latin, but like almost all Western scholars of his time, outside of Byzantium, he knew no Greek. As the saying went: *Graecum est: non legitur*—it was "all Greek" to him. But given his passion for books, a strange fact emerges: in all his many surviving letters, some two hundred of them, Gerbert—monk, abbot, bishop, and, finally, pope—never once asked any of his friends for a book on religion. All of his requests were for secular works.

CHAPTER TEN

Surpassing All
in Wealth and Vice

FOR CENTURIES CONSTANTINOPLE, the ancient Byzantium, was
the most dazzling city of Christendom—half mud and half gold,
surpassing all in wealth and vice, the heir of Greek culture now sunk
into Oriental despotism. Constantinople's influence made itself felt
in distant lands. German emperors wore Byzantine crowns and built
themselves Byzantine-style palaces. In Aix-la-Chapelle, Byzantine
traders displayed their silks and brocades on the market. Swabian and
Thuringian women adopted Greek loose-sleeved fashions, while a
bishop of Cologne read the *Iliad* in its original Greek version.

The Viking ruler Harald Hardraada came back from Miklågard
(Constantinople) clad in a Byzantine gold-embroidered robe and drank
his mead from iridescent glass cups made in Galata, instead of from
curved cattle horns. Byzantine mosaics adorned Italian cathedrals while
Greek artisans helped to build Abd-er-Rahman's palace at Cordova.
All through Gerbert's lifetime the West was touched and ensplendored
by the flow of goods and ideas emanating from Constantinople, the
Golden City, "the only place worthy to be called CITY."

As early as 968, Otto the Great had sent an embassy under his gruff and caustic bishop Liutprand to the Byzantine emperor Nicephorus Phocas, to sue on behalf of his nine-year-old son for the hand of one of the daughters of the deceased *basileus* Romanus II.

Byzantium was then at its zenith, the shield of Christendom against Islam, the largest and most populous of all Christian cities. It was said that two-thirds of all the wealth on earth was concentrated in Constantinople, the other third scattered throughout the world. An Arab visitor proclaimed that at one end of the inhabited world stood Cordova and at the other Byzantium, and that nothing in between was worth mentioning.

As the first millennium approached, Byzantium had regained the power and magnificence of the days of Justinian. The city reigned as the head of a large empire, much of it reconquered from Slavs and Muslims, wealthy not only through its trade and heaped-up treasure, but also through the competence of its soldier-emperors, the imagination of its artists, and the learning of its scholars. During Gerbert's lifetime, Byzantium reached a population of almost one million, of whom only the families of a small ruling class were Greek. More people lived in Byzantium than in all the other European cities combined. Constantinople, in the words of Will Durant, "was at the crest of its curve, surpassing ancient Rome and Alexandria, contemporary Baghdad and Cordova, in trade, wealth, luxury, refinement, and art."

Byzantium was "as old as the hills and the rocks," having been founded by a certain Byzas in 657 B.C. According to an ancient legend, Byzas had asked the oracle at Delphi where to build his new city. After having chewed the sacred laurel leaves, sipped water from the prophecy-inducing spring Cassotis, and inhaled the intoxicating mystic vapors rising from a fissure in the ground, the Pythian virgin, famous for her obscure, puzzling pronouncements, had finally delivered herself of this answer: "Build opposite the Blind!"

Somewhat dazed, he sailed on, through the Dardanelles, until he arrived at the city of Chalcedon on the Asian side of the strait. At once everything became clear to him. Those who built Chalcedon had been blind indeed to ignore a vastly better site less than one mile away on the opposite, European shore. The town that he promptly founded there Byzas named after himself—Byzantium, while Chalcedon became known henceforth as the City of the Blind.

In A.D. 330 the Roman emperor Constantine made the city his seat of government and, following Byzas's example, renamed it Constantinople after himself. Constantine had his city patterned after Rome, built on seven hills, divided into fourteen districts, ruled by the emperor with the help of wise senators. To it he had brought the Palladium, the city-protecting, age-old wooden statue of Pallas Athena, carried from burning Troy to Latium and Rome by the hero Aeneas, beloved of Venus. In spite of such heathen marvels, Constantinople was dedicated to Christos Pantocrator, to Christ the All-Ruler.

The city's wealthy were rich beyond imagination. One traveler remarked that Constantinople's upper-class Greeks all seemed to him like the sons and daughters of kings. Byzantine women kept an army of perfumers and scent mixers busy creating ever new fragrances "required to deodorize queens and princesses." One noblewoman visited the *basileus* being carried on a sumptuous, oversized litter borne by three hundred slaves and surrounded by a train of pretty boy eunuchs. The rich owned both town houses and country villas, with a fine view of the straits—of blue waters filled with leaping dolphins. Interiors were splendidly furnished in an oriental profusion of ornament, silk curtains, and doors inlaid with silver and ivory.

Such homes and owners stood in stark contrast to the ragged, disease-ridden paupers and beggars in their huts and tenements. Wealth was concentrated in the hands of a few families of oligarchs. During the many famines, starving peasants sold their holdings for a pittance, sometimes for just a month's supply of food, to speculators and landowners. A few emperors enacted laws against the crasser forms of exploitation, stipulating that those who had received less than half of the fair price for their homes or fields should be reimbursed. The emperors asked not necessarily out of pity or piety, but because too much wealth in a few private hands led to social unrest, excessive power for the very rich, and, consequently, danger to the throne.

And yet Byzantium was far ahead of western Europe in its sense of social responsibility. Eighty thousand loaves of bread were distributed daily to the hungry, continuing the Roman institution of *panem et circenses* which guaranteed the poorest citizens their dole and free entertainment. The same emperors who plucked out the eyes of potential rivals and ordered captured pirates skinned alive lavished fortunes on hospitals, poorhouses, orphanages, homes for the elderly, and free accommodations for destitute travelers. One *basileus* burst into tears viewing a crowd of starving peasants and then busied himself condemning men to death and torture. Byzantine cruelty was frequently wedded to benevolence.

This metropolis of mud and stink, as well as of gold and silk, surpassed all other cities in wealth and vices, vigor and weakness, piety and prostitution, luxury and wretchedness. Byzantine women were accused of being extremely wanton as well as extraordinarily pious, spending their youth in fornication and their old age in prayer, and sometimes doing both at the same time. Prostitutes could be seen standing outside church doors, soliciting men who had just finished their devotions. People were very devout, but even more superstitious, keeping scores of soothsayers, astrologers, and necromancers busy and enriching the makers of magic amulets and counterfeit relics.

Constantinople called itself the New Rome, head of the East Roman Empire. Its laws, government, and other institutions were patterned after those of Caesar's city on the Tiber, but Latin speech had all but disappeared, replaced by Greek and a babble of mixed barbarian dialects. Civic virtue, administrative zeal, and competence went hand in hand with bribery, corruption, and cabals of every sort.

Brawny generals preaching ancient martial virtues kept young boys to warm their beds. Foreigners were astounded to learn that not a few victorious army commanders were in fact eunuchs. No shame was attached to having been castrated. Being a eunuch was often an advantage, because one could neither become emperor nor beget future successors to the throne, and therefore one was no threat if appointed to a high position. Noblemen sometimes had their sons emasculated to further their careers. The emperor Romanus I had both his legitimate and illegitimate sons' testicles removed to fit them for the great offices of state. At the same time he ensured for them a long life, as they were not worthy to be blinded or assassinated, being no danger to possible rivals for the crown. Doctors aspiring to become specialists in gynecological diseases sometimes voluntarily underwent castration, since uncut men were not allowed to attend female patients. Manufacture of eunuchs was a thriving business, performed by "crushing the testicles of young boys in a hot bath"—a somewhat dubious form of anesthesia. Constantinople thus was indeed a city of great contradictions in which eunuchs were envied, prostitutes were pious, emperors cruel and kind, and squalor the poor twin of splendor.

Splendid the city was, full of architectural marvels. It boasted of containing within its walls the Seven Wonders of the Universe, as many as the whole ancient world had known in an earlier day, "and with these wonders she adorned herself as with so many stars." These were the Hagia Sophia, the Hippodrome, the Sacred Palace, the Augustaeum, the Thermae of Zeuxippus, the equestrian Statue of Justinian, and the Column of the Three Serpents.

Foremost among all these was the Hagia Sophia, the Basilica of Sacred Wisdom dedicated to the divine Logos. "Words failed to describe it. Mute stood the most eloquent before her majesty." The first St. Sophia had been built by Constantine in the fourth-century but had been destroyed in 532 during a devastating riot, the so-called Nika Rebellion. The mob that burned it down, together with nearly half of the old city, had no premonition that it acted as the involuntary vanguard of an army of architects, builders, sculptors, and artists who would make Constantinople the most beautiful city of the early Middle Ages.

The riot started in characteristic fashion inside the Hippodrome with a fight between rival groups of racing fans—the blues and the greens. When the emperor sent troops to suppress the rioters, both parties turned against them. They were joined by a huge mob incited by real or fancied grievances. Running through the streets with lighted torches and crying "Nika, nika!" ("Conquer, conquer!") the rebels soon had the city in flames. Seeing that the mob's purpose was to forcibly replace him with an emperor of their own choice, Justinian contemplated flight. His empress, Theodora, a former prostitute, coolly told him, "If you wish to run away, my emperor, there is the sea, there are the ships; but as for me, I shall stay. Those wearing the purple do not flee. The purple makes a fine death shroud!" Justinian did not flee. The rebels were subdued with great slaughter. More than thirty thousand died.

Like Nero before him, Justinian saw that the charred, flattened city would make a magnificent building site. On the rubble marking the spot where Constantine's church had stood, Justinian was determined to erect a new Hagia Sophia, an edifice "the like of which the world had not seen since the days of Adam." Ten thousand workers toiled for five years before the basilica was finished. On the 27th of December, in 537, the new Hagia Sophia was dedicated. To celebrate the event the people of Constantinople were treated to an enormous barbecue of six thousand spitted sheep, one thousand oxen and an equal num ber of pigs, and five hundred deer together with myriad fowl.

The building truly seemed the work of angels. Praising its beauty in a lengthy poetic paean, Paulus Silentiarius stated that there was really no way for mortals to describe its grandeur and beauty: "Who shall describe the fields of marble gathered on the pavement and lofty walls of the church? Light green stone from Carystus, and many-colored Phrygian stone of rose and white, deep red and silver; porphyry powdered with bright spots, emerald green mineral from Sparta, and Iassian marble with undulating veins of blood-red and white; streaked purple rock from Lydia, crocus-colored marble from the land of the Saracens; celtic stone like milk poured over shining black; the precious onyx with gold shining through it, and moss-green marble from the country of Atrax. Words worthy of it are not to be found. After we have spoken of it, we cannot speak of anything else."

While the work was going on, the emperor, dressed in immaculate white robes, haunted the building site "like an avenging angel or goading demon" spurring on the masons, clambering over scaffolds, agonizing or enthusing. When the last stone and the last mosaic tile were finally in place, he is said to have exclaimed, "Glory be to God, who has considered me worthy to finish this work, Solomon, I have surpassed thee!" While Gerbert was teaching at Rheims, the basilica's dome, which was showing signs of decay, was rebuilt and adorned with the great mosaic of Christ seated on a rainbow.

After the Hagia Sophia, the Hippodrome was considered Constantinople's most magnificent edifice. Built by Septimus Severus and enlarged by Constantine, it was over four hundred yards long with seats for sixty thousand spectators and a special royal box from which the emperor could watch the races and other sports, fights of wild beasts, the contortions of acrobats, the antics of clowns, and, last but not least, public executions. The Hippodrome was adorned with many magnificent statues and an obelisk carved from a single block of porphyry.

Of the several imperial residences, the Sacred Palace was a city within a city, a grandiose rabbit warren of audience halls, chapels, baths, pleasure gardens, pavilions, libraries, and barracks. It contained the so-called Triconchos, or Three-Shell Room, named after its scalloped arches; the emperor's private apartment, the Kamilas, with columns of emerald green marble; mosaic-covered walls; and a golden ceiling. The Sacred Palace also enclosed the marble Hall of the Pearl and several Heliaka, or sun rooms. The palace was constantly extended by emperor after emperor, though its most luxurious and eye-dazzling parts were inspired by the ninth-century ruler Theophilus.

Theophilus also let his fantasy run wild building another palace, the Magnaura. This baroque whimsy contained the raised Golden Throne of Solomon, which was flanked by golden lions and griffins and shaded by a golden tree with golden branches decorated with golden birds. On special occasions, such as visits by foreign dignitaries, the griffins stood up, the lions wagged their tails, and the golden birds began to twitter. Still other palaces were the New Palace of Basil I and the Bucoleon of Nicephorus Phocus, whose wide marble stairs led down to a colonnaded pier on the Sea of Marmara. Most royal residences commanded magnificent panoramic views of harbor and hillside.

The city's main square was the Forum Augustaeum, a large rectangle bordered by colonnades. It was Constantinople's hub and heart, surrounded on all sides by the Hagia Sophia, the imperial palace, the Hippodrome, the Senate building, and the Milion arch. From the Augustaeum, the city's main avenue, called Mese, led to the beautiful oval Forum of Constantine, encircled by loggias containing masterworks of ancient Greek sculpture. Further on, the Mese led through a triumphal arch into the Forum of Taurus, from whose center rose the lofty column of Theodosius. On and on it stretched, past monasteries, loggias, mansions, aqueducts, shaded porticos, and gigantic sculptures, past the churches of the Holy Apostles and St. George, all the way to the northern walls and the Gate of Charisius.

Wonderful also were the Thermae of Zeuxippus, restored by Justinian, the largest and most sumptuous of more than one hundred public baths, surpassing in size and luxury the Baths of Caracalla in Rome. Other sights for the visitor to gaze at were the Column of the Three Serpents, said to have been taken from the site of the Delphic Oracle and the equestrian Statue of Justinian portraying the emperor as the reincarnation of Achilles, in Greek armor and horsehair-crested helmet, holding in his hand the orb as symbol that all the world was subject to him.

Constantinople was viewed with awe by the barbaric nations. It was the fabled Miklågard of the Vikings and Tsarigrad (Caesar's City) of the people called Rus. Besides its treasures of art and architecture, Constantinople was famous for having nearly as many sacred relics as the rest of Christendom combined. Foremost among the relics was the Virgin's robe, the most holy garment of God's mother, which was brought out in solemn procession at times of great danger and which was said to have protected the city on many occasions against barbarian onslaughts. All these marvels were ringed by thirteen miles of walls, encompassing within them the greatest living museum in the world.

On a less exalted level, Constantinople was the Purple City, purpled by imperial splendor but also by blood and vice, the Womb of Nations, a place where hetaera embraced skin-clad barbarian Norsemen, where Muslim infidels impregnated Bulgar women, and sailors from Amalfi begat dusky children with Nubian slave girls. The city swarmed with foreigners speaking a patois that was deemed, by the better sort of people, an insult to Hellenic speech. In its busy streets Armenians, Venetians, Pisans, and Cappadocians rubbed shoulders with Syrians, bearded Jews, close-cropped Bulgarians, blond, shaggy Norwegians, Anglo-Saxons, Russians, members of the emperor's ax-carrying Varingian guardsmen, and strange folk of the steppes whose language no one could understand.

Above all, Constantinople was a city of commerce. The Mese was lined with shops of every variety; the workbenches of goldsmiths, leather workers, and tailors; the stalls of the sellers of fruit, bread, olive oil, and honey; fishmongers, soothsayers, amulet makers, perfumers, and money changers. The many bazaars had a distinctly oriental flavor. Banking, the invention of which has been generally credited to the Florentines, Venetians, and Genoese, had its roots in Byzantium.

Craftspeople were organized into guilds of specialists. A leatherworker was not allowed to do any tanning. A minter of coins could not also be a jeweler. This division of labor resulted in products of high quality. Trade was strictly regulated. The government raised taxes, controlled loans and interest rates, supervised exports and imports, fixed duties on foreign goods, and suppressed piracy that interfered with commerce. The Byzantine *byzant* was the most stable and readily accepted currency of the early Middle Ages.

Byzantium imposed on the world its own absolute monopoly on silk and purple. Other nations might manufacture their own wool and linen, but their nobles also had to have silk and purple. For emperors, kings, and dukes, the wearing of silken gowns and purple cloaks was a symbol of royalty and legitimacy, for bishops and prelates a sign of God-willed spiritual rule. In Constantinople there existed a certain hierarchy of the cloth. A very few distinct articles of clothing, such as the imperial cape, called *chalmys*, and purple boots, were forbidden cloth reserved for the emperor alone. But the people at large were allowed to dress themselves in the richest and most showy stuffs if they could afford them, and the city's dandies were known to impoverish themselves in order to cut a fine figure.

The secrets of silk manufacture had once been as jealously guarded in China as in Constantinople, but, according to one story, some Byzantine monks, possibly sent out as missionaries, managed to smuggle silkworm eggs back to their country in hollowed out canes. At any rate, sericulture flourished in the Eastern empire during the tenth century, and the quantity of silk and purple cloth to be exported was strictly limited in order to keep the price high. Internally, the government had a monopoly on grain. The income of all state monopolies enabled some emperors to amass gold reserves of up to three hundred thousand pounds—riches unimaginable to other Christian monarchs. Last, but not least, ever since the emperor Justinian, it was a maxim of state that the foremost duty of the citizen was to pay taxes "because the government is always in need of more money."

The empire's wealth supported not only the raising of splendid edifices and the pomp and circumstance of the court, but also education. Teachers were paid by the state, and tuition was free to talented students. Byzantium prided itself on being the guardian of Hellenic heritage. It was taken for granted that educated persons knew Homer and were familiar with the plays of Euripides, Sophocles, Aeschylus, and Aristophanes. The odes of Pindar and Sappho were widely quoted; the works of historians such as Thucydides, Herodotus, Xenophon, Plutarch, and Polybius were ardently studied. At the university the Consuls Among Philosophers and the Great Masters of Rhetoric transmitted to their students the glories of Greek philosophy, literature, and science. While Byzantium had great teachers, philosophers, and very good historians, its literature was thriving but superficial. Polished and polite, it lacked profundity; often it was an artistic and elegant rehashing of ancient paganism mixed with a great dose of Orthodox bigotry and more than a dash of superstition. Still it had grandeur—a gilded galley sailing under multicolored banners on shallow waters.

At the head of this glittering, far-flung empire stood, as undisputed ruler, the emperor, *autocrator* and *basileus*, responsible only to God and to himself, the *isapostolos*—the equal of the apostles, nearer by far to the deity than to his subjects. He was despot, the oriental king of Kings. As God was invisible, the emperor became his visible living substitute, the Creator's champion on earth and the center around which, if one believed his courtier's flatteries, the whole universe revolved. King and priest in one, he was the head of the church, determining doctrines, nominating and consecrating bishops. Like the Japanese *tenno*, only he could perform certain religious rituals, a living link between God and the people. As the *basileus* was also the supreme judge and lawgiver, logic dictated that he was above the law and could do no wrong. To rebel against the emperor was to rebel against God. The great Justinian himself, offspring of upstart Illyrian peasants, had once proclaimed, "What is there greater, what more sacred than imperial majesty?"

The courtiers of a Byzantine emperor agreed with such concepts, at least outwardly, hailing their *basileus* with such traditionally expected flatteries as "We have no duty but to look toward thee, our sun, oh supreme master of the universe," or "Venerated lord, we are your slaves, and God will make all peoples on this earth your slaves so that they might bring gifts, as the Magi did to the newborn Christ. You are the shining lodestar, the light and glory of mankind."

The emperor appeared to the people like the manifestation of a higher being, clothed in gold, a living, breathing holy icon. Regulations for approaching the divine majesty decreed that from imperial princes and chief ministers down, all entering the exalted presence had to prostrate themselves three times, devoutly kissing the *basileus*'s hands and feet.

Edward Gibbon wrote, "The most lofty titles, and the most humble postures, which devotion has applied to the Supreme Being, have been prostituted by flattery and fear to creatures with the same nature as ourselves. The mode of adoration, of falling prostrate on the ground and kissing the feet of the emperor, was borrowed by Diocletian from Persian servitude; but was continued and aggravated till the last age of the Greek monarchy. Excepting only on Sundays, when it was waived, from a motive of religious pride, this humiliating reverence was exacted from all who entered the royal presence, from the princes invested with the diadem and purple, and from the ambassadors who represented their independent sovereigns, the caliphs of Asia, Egypt, or Spain, the kings of France and Italy, and the Latin emperors of ancient Rome."

Among those who were compelled to kneel before the emperor in self-abasement was Otto I's ambassador, Liutprand, bishop of Cremona. He made his obeisance most unwillingly, muttering under his breath, before the golden throne with the golden roaring lions and the golden warbling birds. When, after touching the ground three times with his forehead, the bishop looked up, he beheld on the throne, hoisted by an engine from the floor to the ceiling, God's representative on earth floating high above the kowtowing dignitaries, concluding the audience in "haughty and majestic silence."

While such magic tricks had impressed Asiatic and Scandinavian chieftains, they left Liutprand merely fuming, furtively nursing his rheumatic knees. Byzantine emperors, like awe-inspiring semigods, moved "amid chants, rhythmic acclamations, processions and solemnities . . . But beneath this dazzling exterior one glimpses an extraordinary emptiness." And not merely emptiness, but crime and debasement. Neither outward magnificence nor the flattery of court eunuchs nor the blessings of religion could guarantee an emperor long life and a peaceful death in the royal bedchamber. No fewer than twenty-nine Byzantine rulers were assassinated—poisoned, starved, stabbed, mutilated, blinded, strangled, pole-axed, hacked to pieces, drowned in their baths, or tortured to death. One wonders that so many men conspired, dissembled, and committed murder to occupy the throne of their victims, only to become, in their turn, instant targets for a rival's dagger or the redhot blinding iron. To be *basileus* was to live dangerously.

In 968 when Liutprand traveled to Constantinople to sue, on behalf of Otto the Great's young son, for the hand of a Byzantine princess, it was Nicephorus Phocas who occupied the hazardous Byzantine throne. Liutprand was first made to wait before the Golden Gate for hours. He was then made to walk on foot because he was not considered important enough to ride and was housed with his retinue in the ruin of a roofless palace. Not even a sack of straw was provided for a bed; he lay on cold marble with only a stone for his pillow. He and his men were not allowed to leave, were insufficiently fed, and could not even get water though they offered to pay for it: "The wine of the Greeks we could not drink, finding it unpalatable as being mixed with pitch and resin. But our greatest plague was the keeper of the building, who was supposed to take care of our daily needs, such a villainous man that one could hardly find his like in hell; what he could invent in the way of doing us harm, of blackmail, of making us miserable and suffer, he never got tired of inflicting upon our persons and of all the 120 days we remained there, not a single one passed without lamenting and sighing."

After four long months, Liutprand was finally given an audience.

"On the day of Holy Epiphany I was led to the throne room, which the Greeks call 'Stephana,' and brought before Nicephorus. I found him looking like a monster—a dwarf with an oversized fat head, little moles' eyes, a broad, thick, and partially gray beard, a short neck and unkempt hair, the color of his face as dark as that of a Negro."

The audience went badly. Nicephorus opened matters by saying that he would have received Liutprand more honorably if Liutprand's master, Otto, had not invaded Rome, causing the execution of many noble Romans by sword and rope. Otto's pretensions of peace were false, Nicephorus said, and Luitprand had come as a spy rather than as an ambassador.

Then followed a procession: "The parade was not all that grand. A great crowd of peddlers and common folk stood in solemn rows to acclaim Nicephorus on his way from the palace to the Basilica of St. Sophia. The guards were armed with little shields and puny throwing spears. Most of them were barefoot. The courtiers, accompanying the emperor, wore ankle-length robes of state, old and full of holes. They would have done better to come in their everyday clothes. These robes must already have been bought second hand by their grandfathers. Only the emperor was decked out with golden jewels and precious stones. His ornate clothes, made to fit his father's body, only made him look more ridiculous. I was led into the church to watch the procession and found a place in the choir amid the singers. As this abomination of a dwarf crept closer, the singers intoned: 'Behold, the morning star cometh, Eos arises and with his radiance darkens the rays of the sun; the one who is death to the Saracens, Nicephorus, the ruler, appears. Honored is he before all nations. Bend, bend your knees and necks before the mighty prince.' Thus acclaimed by the fawning lickspittles, puffed up like a toad, he entered the Hagia Sophia." This puffed-up dwarf had seized the throne because he was an outstanding field commander, but reading Liutprand's description of Nicephorus, one is tempted to forgive his adulterous wife, Anastasia-Theophano, and her lover, John Tsimisces, for doing away with him.

After the procession came the feast: "Nicephorus invited me, but not a single one of my companions, to share his meal. He did not deem me worthy to be seated before his courtiers but put me in the fifteenth place. Table and plates were filthy and some of the guests seemed drunk. Everything dripped with oil and the stink of a disgusting fish sauce spoiled my appetite.

"Oh, the smell of garlic and onion! Oh, the bad wine, or rather brine, mixed with pitch, resin, and plaster! Oh, the courtiers' kisses, sweet and cloying, of idle creatures, soft effeminate, lying, neutered! Oh, the capon Greek bishops sipping wine, tasting like bath water, from tiny glasses!"

Liutprand concluded that Nicephorus was "one whom it would not be pleasant to meet in the middle of the night." He advised travelers to guard their wallets well while walking in Constantinople's streets. Finally, Liutprand complained that the abominable food had given him a frightful case of diarrhea.

Nicephorus asked Liutprand about Otto and his realm. Liutprand did a good public relations job, which made the *basileus* angry. "He shouted, 'You lie! The knights of your army neither know how to do battle on horseback, nor to fight on foot. Their big shields, heavy armor, long swords and weighty helmets hinder them during battle. They are also impaired—and here he laughed—by their gluttony, because the belly is their god, drunkenness their courage, intoxication their bravery. Fasting is their downfall, sobriety their greatest horror.'" Thus the evening ended amid mutual insults and recriminations.

In the end, Liutprand was told, "It is unheard of that a daughter, born to the purple from the loins of a purple-wearing father, should be given to a stranger." Even offering much of southern Italy in return for bringing away a Byzantine princess had availed nothing, and, after answering Eastern ridicule with some choice Teuton invectives of his own, Liutprand had been obliged to depart empty-handed.

But after the haughty Nicephorus had been murdered by his nephew, friend, and one-time ally, John Tsimisces, the atmosphere changed. John, having treacherously killed a strong ruler, found himself in a precarious situation. He needed peace in the West, and, just as Otto wished to legitimize his own rule as emperor of the Romans by way of a Byzantine marriage, so John, or Little Slippers, as he was known, wanted to strengthen his own position by improving relations with the Saxon. Therefore when Gero of Cologne, much more suave and diplomatic than Liutprand, went to Constantinople in 971, he not only was given Theophano, but he did not even have to give up land and cities for her. On the contrary, he was promised some Byzantine towns in southern Italy as her dowry, though the wily Greeks later reneged on that promise.

Nevertheless, Little Slippers might have gotten the better of Gero. Theophano was something of a skeleton in the Byzantine closet. Officially the daughter of Emperor Romanus II, she was, unofficially, nothing of the kind. Theophano's mother, some said, was Theophano I, who had charmed young Romanus by her "radiant, superhuman and divine beauty." John's courtiers spread the word that the bridegroom's parents had been overjoyed to find such a highborn, well-bred wife for their son, but it soon became apparent that Theophano I was not quite that highborn. Her father had been a tavern keeper in the slums of the capital. Her name, originally, had been Anastasia, and she had reputedly been a high-class prostitute. Sexual attraction overcame all objections to the woman's past, however. When she was widowed at twenty-two, the former courtesan went looking for a new powerful protector, and settled upon the grizzled and rather repellent soldier Nicephorus Phocas, some thirty years her senior, and subsequently married him. But then Nicephotos's nephew, the much younger and already famous general John Tsimisces, appeared. Thinking that it was better to ally herself with a young rising sun rather than being tied to an older sinking one, Anastasia-Theophano I became John's mistress.

Old ugly Nicephorus clearly had become superfluous. On December 1, 969, Nicephorus Phocas retired for a good night's steep. His empress told him that she would join him later and that he should leave the door to his bedchamber open. She reappeared soon in company with her lover and his hired assassins. They found Nicephorus sleeping, soldier fashion, on a panther skin, his body covered with a red felt blanket. John Tsimisces woke him up by pulling on his beard while one of the conspirators stabbed him. In vain the old commander cried out for help. Laughing, John Tsimisces clove in this skull with a sword. The guilty pair then endeavored to rule Constantinople, but when public opinion turned against his paramour, John banished her to a convent in faraway Armenia, where she in fact languished at the time of her daughter's marriage to Otto. It must be said, however, that according to some accounts, the younger Theophano was not Anastasia-Theophano's daughter at all, but merely the niece of Little Slippers.

Being the niece of a man like Little Slippers and the target of so many ugly rumors hardly made the teenage Theophano a bargain on the royal marriage market. It was soon said at the Ottonian court that Gero had bought a pig in a poke, that the scoundrel Tsimisces had fobbed him off, in the words of Thietmar of Merseburg, "with not at all the desired maiden." In the opinion of Hroswitha of Gandersheim, she was not worthy of being Otto's wife. Some said that she was not even Little Slippers' niece but merely a distant relation. Byzantine annals do not mention the Theophano-Otto II marriage at all—a silence that speaks volumes. It is also surmised that by giving away a young woman with no real rights of succession to the Byzantine throne, Tsimisces made sure that no Saxon influence could ever be exerted in this respect upon the court of Constantinople.

When all this became known at the court of Otto I, some of his counselors advised him to send Theophano back, to remit her. The old emperor rejected their suggestions. For him, he declared, she was a legitimate princess, an emperor's daughter who was, de facto if not de jure, Byzantium's acknowledgment of Saxon emperorship. Besides, he liked the high-spirited young woman.

It was a wise choice. Theophano was good for Otto II and the Ottonians. As Thietmar put it, "Though not entirely free from the frailties of her sex, she was firm in action and, what was rare among the Greeks, led an unblemished life, free from scandals. She guarded the empire well. . . ."

Meanwhile, under the reigns of John Tsimisces and his successor, Basil II, nicknamed Bulgar-Killer, the Byzantine empire reached the height of its power. Whatever else one might think of John Little Slippers, he was a superb soldier and administrator.

After throwing Russian hordes under Tsar Svjatoslav out of the Balkans, John Tsimisces, in 974-975, proceeded to fight his main campaign against the Saracens of Syria. In a succession of brilliant actions and sieges, he took Damascus, Tiberias, Nazareth, Caesarea, Beirut, and Sidon, though Jerusalem remained beyond his grasp. In the words of a chronicler, "And the people feared the wrath of Tsimisces, and the sword of the Christians mowed down the infidels as with a scythe."

In a short time John Tsimisces consolidated the gains of Nicephorus, pushing back the barbarians everywhere while extending the empire's borders in the Balkans and the Middle East. He died of typhoid at Constantinople during the month of January 976, after a short reign of only six years.

On April 14, 972, as Gerbert was leaving to study at Rheims, young Otto II married the princess from Constantinople. Theophano was, at the time of her nuptials, still an adolescent. A deep-bellied trireme had brought her and her retinue from Byzantium to Bari where Bishop Gero of Cologne awaited her in festive procession. Two archbishops and many German dukes and counts conducted her to Benevento and hence to Rome. There the sixteen-year-old for the first time set eyes upon her seventeen-year-old bridegroom. She was described as thin-lipped, pale-skinned, and blue-veined, dark-eyed and raven-haired, delicate as murrhenian glass and most elegant—*vultu elegantissima.* Her only likeness is a stereotype ivory carving copied from many similar others. She was certainly not the ideal beauty from the point of view of the average Saxon baron, who preferred his wife to be hefty, earthy, not too well-educated, and submissive.

Theophano, who later became Gerbert's close friend, was a "fair blossom from the luxuriously poisonous garden of Constantinople," brought up by eunuchs and slavish courtiers, her uncle and warden an assassin, her mother a murderer. No doubt Theophano had been told that she had to sacrifice herself for the good of her country in marrying a ruddy half-savage and uncouth Saxon. We do not know how these two teenagers felt when they first met, total strangers to each other still in the marriage bed, but we can be sure of the feelings of Otto the Great as he watched Pope John XIII crown and bless them with trembling old man's hands. To unite the family of the emperor of the West with that of the *basileus* of the East had been one of his oldest and fondest dreams.

In 973 Otto had reached the age of sixty-one and had lived longer than a tenth-century man had a right to expect. He celebrated Easter at his favorite *Pfaltz* of Quedlinburg, feasting with his friends. He went on to Merseburg to attend the funeral of a faithful vassal. True to his habit, he continued on to Memleben in the Harz Mountains, the place where his own father had died. On May 7 he got up as usual, before sunrise, remarking that he felt a little weak. He heard early mass in his chapel, went back to bed, got up again, and took the host for a second time. Then he went out to distribute alms to the poor, as was his custom, and rested again. He dined with his nobles "right merrily and gladsome" and went at vesper once more to chapel. His companions noted that he was feverish and unsteady on his feet. They brought him a chair and he sat down, slumped in his seat, and "seemed to have passed away." He came to, however, demanded and received the consecrated body of Christ amid pious songs, and calmly recommended his soul to his Savior. Then his head dropped to his chest and he was dead.

He died in his thirty-seventh year as king, his twelfth as emperor. His eulogists praised him because he had rid the realm of barbaric enemies, ended the wars among his own nobles, brought peace to all, subdued the wild Magyars, vanquished Danes and Slavs, fought the Greeks with success, made Rome and Italy his, united all Christendom, built churches on the sites of pagan temples, and sent the message of the *evangelium* to many lands.

CHAPTER ELEVEN

He Rose like a Meteor

THE LIFE OF OTTO II, called Rufus or The Red on account of his ruddy hair and complexion, was Alexanderlike in its intensity and brevity. Crowned king of Germany and Italy at the age of three, taken on campaign to witness his first battle at six, reigning king at fourteen, emperor as well as master of Rome and the papacy at sixteen, married to a Byzantine princess and soon to be a father at seventeen, he was called Augustus, Imperator, and Lord of the Universe at twenty, and he was dead at twenty-eight. "He rose like a meteor and fell like a shooting star." History grew out of breath trying to keep up with him. His contemporaries described his life as strange, unbelievable, and astounding.

He was finely built, not rugged like his father, pleasant and often smiling, well educated in contrast to the first Otto, short and unimposing in stature but strong and brave even to rashness. He was courteous and polite but also hot tempered, flaring up at the slightest provocation. Quick witted, he was good at getting at the heart of a matter, but also obstinate over unimportant details and apt to change his mind often. He acted imperiously, thinking himself above the law, and appeared lordly and commanding. "Small in body, but great in virtue," one chronicler described him, "as Augustus better than his father and, in the memory of all, the most Christian of all Caesars."

This was a matter of opinion. Bruno of Querfurt criticized him severely: "Swiftly after his father, he climbed the realm's summit, but did not know how to reign in the proper spirit or with mature wisdom, and while he unwisely thought that all men should humbly serve him, he lost the empire and killed the peace which fear of his father had created. Now Germany learned to mourn the death of his father, the great helmsman on stormy seas, missed him who, like a good wagon driver, had known how to steer the world. The helmsman, blessed with God's favor, was dead now, he who had done so much for the Christian faith. Only lost battles opened at last the eyes of the son and shame overcame him for having listened to women's advice. Too late he rued having taken childish counsel from childish friends instead of from wise elders. He worked for his own honor, not for your victory, Oh Christ!" The criticism was valid, though chauvinistic in some respects. However, the bad advice came not from Otto's mother Adelaide or from his wife Theophano—shrewd, cultured, and worldly-wise women—but from the young emperor's peers.

Up to the time of his marriage to Theophano, Otto II had been under the influence of his mother Adelaide, and, for two years, he benefited from the tutelage of Gerbert. But after Gerbert left for Rheims he listened more and more to the advice of his wife. Theophano was a superb politician, being, as a Greek, used to gynecocracy—the political rule of women. Both she and Adelaide were imperious, strong willed, well educated, pious, and proud of their ancestry, whether Burgundian or Byzantine. It was only natural that these two would not take to each other. Adelaide became estranged from her son for a while and withdrew to her brother's court in Burgundy. Mother and son were eventually reconciled, and, after Otto's death, both empresses worked closely together defending the interests of the three-year-old Otto III.

Otto I, Magnus et Maximus, had been feared. Otto II was still untried, and his youth encouraged many old enemies to fall upon the empire from all quarters. His relative, Henry the Quarrelsome, duke of Bavaria, lived up to his nickname and, allying himself with Henry of Carinthia and Henry, bishop of Augsburg, started the so-called War of the Three Henrys, which gave the imperial forces much trouble before it was finally brought to a satisfactory conclusion. Later, one of the rebels, Bishop Henry of Augsburg, fell fighting bravely at Otto's side against the Sicilian Arabs.

In 974 the Danes under Harald Bluetooth crossed the frontier wall and raided deep into Germany. Otto marched against them and drove them back to the wall but could not pursue his success further. A tenuous truce was the best he could achieve, having his hands full with so many other enemies. Of all the pagan invaders his father seemed to have tamed, only the Magyars kept the peace.

Otto also became entangled in a war with King Lothaire of France, which had a curious beginning. Lothaire had a trouble-making brother named Charles, who spread rumors that the king's wife, Emma, was committing adultery with Bishop Ascelin of Laon. To complicate matters, Emma, the queen of France, was Adelaide's daughter by her first husband, Lothar of Italy. Fleeing from Lothaire's wrath, Charles sought a refuge with Otto, who, inexplicably, gave him a dukedom. Understandably angered, Lothaire invaded Germany and took Aix-la-Chapelle Charlemagne's ancient *Pfaltz*, turning the great bronze eagle of the dome of its cathedral around so that it faced backward, as a sign of his disdain for Otto. It was now the young emperor's turn to become enraged and to march into France. In 979, he took Rheims, Laon, and Soisson, plundering far and wide though "generously sparing those churches and abbeys previously robbed of their treasures by Norsemen and Hungarians." Otto advanced as far as Paris, planting his banner on the heights of Montmartre. As a fresh army was gathering to resist him, he contented himself with ravaging the countryside and withdrew to Germany. In the first seven years of his reign, Otto was so continuously on the warpath that he received a new nickname; Otto the Ruddy became Otto the Bloody—Sanguinarius.

During the years of Otto's campaigns and long absences, matters in Rome had returned to normal—that is, back to the usual rebellions of local patricians against Ottonian officials, and to the usual vicious fights between popes and antipopes, who resumed their old pastime of murdering each other. As early as 974, when Otto's rule was only in its second year, a Roman noble named Crescentius decided to depose the young emperor, to get rid of all Saxons, and to rule the Eternal City as self-appointed exarch. He stormed the Lateran, seized Pope Benedict VI, installed by Otto I, dragging the pontiff through the "low black entrance of Sant' Angelo into the bowels of the forbidding fortress" where the unfortunate victim was cast into a noisome dungeon. Crescentius then set upon the throne one of his own creatures, a certain Deacon Franco, under the name of Boniface VII. The new pope promptly ordered one of his hirelings, a priest called Stephen, to strangle Benedict in his cell. Boniface was so outrageously evil that he was called Maleficius. The bishop of Orleans referred to him as "that horrid monster, surpassing all other mortals in wrongdoing, a criminal steeped in the blood of the Holy Father who ruled before him."

Otto, busy campaigning north of the Alps, sent one of his commanders, Count Sicco, to put things right. Boniface-Maleficius lost little time getting away, but not before stealing and taking with him the sacred, gem-encrusted treasures of the Vatican. "Paving his way with gold, he found protection at the court of Constantinople." Crescentius also escaped punishment, dying peacefully in his bed. His tomb bore the inscription "Here lies the body of Cresentius, the illustrious, the honorable citizen of Rome, the great descendant of a great family." Count Sicco then managed to have Bishop Sutri of Viterbo enthroned as Pope Benedict VII, who ruled quietly and largely undisturbed until 983.

Otto still had to contend with the Arabs of Sicily and southern Italy. Saracen forces had driven the Byzantines from Sicily and, in

976, had crossed the Strait of Messina to gain a foothold in Calabria, from where they made devastating forays. As Roman emperor, Otto had little choice but to accept the challenge. It was his duty to dislodge the invaders and rout them—if he could.

The Muslims took one city after another, and when they stormed ancient Tarento, a shudder went through all Christendom. Many remembered the days when the cities of France and Italy had trembled before the warriors of Islam. All looked to the Saxon emperor for succor.

CHAPTER TWELVE

A Fateful Debate

IN THE YEAR 980, Gerbert accompanied Archbishop Adalbero to Rome on a mission whose exact nature is unknown, but that undoubtedly had to do with church politics. At Pavia their paths crossed that of the young emperor Otto II, who was at the time gathering an army to drive the Saracens from Italy. There the old bond between Gerbert and Ottonian emperors was renewed, and both parties traveled on to Ravenna. There Gerbert had a famous and fateful debate with a rival German scholar named Othric and became "the emperor's man."

This Othric had been hailed as the most learned and accomplished teacher in Europe. To the school he headed were sent the sons and nephews of the great German nobles and prelates. He was called the Saxon Cicero and had become adviser to the young Otto II who, so Othric hoped, would make him an archbishop. Stirred to envy by rumors of Gerbert's fame, Othric sent one of his own students to Rheims to spy on Gerbert and to report back to him any mistakes his French rival might make in lecturing and theorizing. Report back the informer did, wrongly as it turned out, and a triumphant Othric soon confronted the new young emperor with voluminous notes on Gerbert's "errors."

As Horace Mann wrote, "Success, unfortunately, besides engendering respect, provokes jealousy. While a strong light illumines many objects, it throws others into shadow. And Othric of Saxony, head of the palace school of Magdeburg, imagined that his fame was dimmed by the rising reputation of Gerbert. He determined to prick the gallic bubble."

Thus it was not surprising that when Archbishop Adalbero and Gerbert arrived at Pavia, Otto was accompanied by his Saxon Cicero Othric. Otto graciously invited his two prominent guests to accompany him by boat to Ravenna, where he informed his former teacher, Gerbert, that it might be best to settle the scholastic dispute with Othric by way of a great public debate that would decide the issue.

Otto himself was "accounted the most skilled in philosophic disputes" and something of a scholar in his own right. He loved to discuss the finer points of philosophy and "all that was obscure and ought to be made clear." He was particularly fond of mental combat between intellectual equals, which, as he said, "whetted and honed minds growing dull."

In a way, such disputations had their parallels in the judicious combats and ordeals through which, with God's help, one might discover during a trial who was wrong and who was right, who spoke the truth and who did not. Among common folk a male defendant could prove his innocence by carrying a heated plowshare or red-hot iron in his bare hands for a certain distance or a specific time. If his wounds healed within a fixed number of days he was innocent. Women accused of a crime had their hands and feet tied together and were then thrown into a lake or stream. If they floated they were judged guilty "because water will not accept anything evil." If a woman sank, she was most certainly innocent. If she drowned because the bystanders could not fish her out in time her relatives could console themselves with the thought that, proven guiltless, she would probably attain paradise.

Between nobles, the matter of truth or falsehood was often decided by judicial combat. God surely would grant victory to him who spoke the truth, though he was a physical weakling. Kings and dukes could hire a champion to do the fighting for them. Saxon law even provided for legal combat between a husband and wife. Allowance was made for the fact that women were not as tall or as muscular as men. Therefore the husband was placed at a disadvantage by having to fight from a hip-deep hole. He was given a club, his wife a shift with an extra-long sleeve into whose end a heavy stone had been sown. If, circling hole and husband carefully, the good wife managed to brain her spouse, then obviously she had God on her side. On the other hand, if the man managed to get hold of his wife's sleeve, dragging her into his pit and dispatching her with his club, it was made manifest that he had been right all along. Similarly, in a scholastic dispute, it was expected that divine justice would endow with a special portion of eloquence the disputant with the better cause.

The famous Gerbert-Othric debate was held before a great assembly of courtiers and *scholastici* who attended the affair as partisans—some for Gerbert, many more for Othric. The emperor opened proceedings with a speech praising the learned disputes which sharpened mental faculties while at the same time revealing divine truth. The main point debated that day, namely the subdivisions of philosophy and which of them should have precedence over the other, seems of little importance now. As the old Saxon proverb had it: "'Much loud squeaking and little wool,' said the peasant shearing a pig." Gerbert gave physics precedence over mathematics. He defended his views in the most elegant Latin and with the greatest eloquence, quoting Boethius and Victorinus. He proved that his method of dividing and subdividing gave to the mind the habit of analysis and to the tongue cleanness and precision. Both rivals enlarged upon their subject, discussing the nature of philosophy.

The debate turned upon questions of metaphysics, the foundation of the world, the cause and properties of shadows. It lasted all day, testing the endurance of debaters and listeners alike, but while Othric began to wilt, Gerbert grew stronger and sharper as the day progressed. The totally exhausted Otto finally ended the great mental duel with a wave of his hand. For Gerbert, the whole discussion might have been merely an exercise in rhetoric, a fine art which he practiced with particular zest. He was acclaimed the winner and became even more famous than before. More important was the favorable impression he had made upon Otto and the recementing of his ties to the imperial house. Rewards were tangible. He was sent back to Rheims loaded with presents and, in due time, was named by the young Saxon ruler abbot of Bobbio, near Pavia, which housed within its walls the foremost library of western Europe. This abbacy was one of the highest positions an ambitious scholar and ecclesiastic could obtain. Gerbert would have had ample reason to exclaim, "Otto I is dead, long live Otto II!"

CHAPTER THIRTEEN

Triumph of the Saracens

OTTO GATHERED A SMALL but well-equipped army and, in 981, marched south, taking Theophano and his little son with him. Over mountains and hills they rode, through fertile and arid valleys, through oak and pine forests, olive groves, and vineyards. He joined up with the sons of tough old Duke Pandolf Ironhead, a longtime supporter of the Ottonian cause. Around Christmas Otto conquered the sea fortress of Salerno and, after that, the port and city of Tarento, founded by the Spartans in the eighth century B.C. King Pyrrhus of Epirus and Hannibal had once fought for it. The Saracens had utterly destroyed it in 927. Nicephorus Phocas had rebuilt it in 967, and, until now, the Saracens' banner had once again waved over its ancient walls.

On the army marched, through dry brush country where once Romans had cultivated fields worked by plantation slaves, always tramping along the coast and in sight of the sea. Otto's men skirmished with Greeks allied to the Saracens, soldiers of the Byzantine emperor, who was withholding certain Apulian lands and cities from Otto Theophano's dowry.

At the castle of Rossano he left the bishop of Metz with his war chest, without which, even in the tenth century, no campaign could be undertaken. There also he left Theophano and their little boy. It was a sad parting with many angry words. In a minor battle the Greeks had beaten a handful of Germans and Otto's Byzantine wife had mocked him, saying with a malicious smile, "See how my countrymen have frightened you!" Thoughtless banter, perhaps, from a sharp-tongued woman who, in spite of her mocking ways, had always stuck by him through thick and thin, but it hurt all the same. Thus Otto rode off in a dark mood.

At last the Christians met up with the elusive Saracens, little swarthy men on small dancing horses, lightly armed, so it seemed. Spurring on their big chargers, the heavily armored Christians carried the day. The Saracen emir, Abdul Qasim, fell a martyr to his faith, ascending, his men were sure, straight to his Islamic heaven and the arms of the houris of paradise awaiting him with cups of snow-cooled sherbet.

In high spirits Otto's army marched on, but the emperor over-estimated his victory. These Arabs, he remarked, were but gnats; their arrows, flea bites. Already he had styled himself Pallida Mor Saracenorum—The Pale Death of the Saracens. But on the thirteenth of July, 982, between the sea and steep hills, he stumbled upon more Arabs. The Christians chased these infidels along the seashore, many not even putting on their helmets and chain mail, seeing that their enemies were few and fleeing, and also because the day was very hot. But in the hills, hidden from view until it was too late, waited the Saracens' main force. Otto had fallen into a trap. "Then many lifted up their hands in prayer calling aloud unto God for help, but help there was none." Hemmed in on all sides, the Germans and Italians were slaughtered. Those not cut down by the sword were driven into the sea and drowned. Those few who escaped had little cause to rejoice. Many died of their wounds or of thirst in the waterless country. Some were caught and sold as slaves in Egypt and Syria. Few of these ever returned. Only night brought the massacre to an end. Among the slain was Otto's swordbearer, Richari; the two sons of Pandulf Ironhead; Bishop Henry of Augsburg; the abbot of Fulda, and margraves, barons, and "nobles without numbers whose names are known only to God."

Otto had fought with his usual reckless courage. His horse had been killed under him. A good Jew named Kalonymus saw it and offered the emperor his own mount. Otto galloped off the field together with a small handful of followers, making for the shore. A ship was anchored there, a Byzantine salandrine. The crew had wind of Otto's defeat and refused to take them aboard. They found a second Greek vessel. Otto spurred his horse into the sea toward the ship. The horse foundered. Otto swam the last stretch. The captain eyed him with suspicion. A Slav sailor recognized the emperor and persuaded the master to take the fugitive on. He whispered in Otto's ear to hide his identity, saying that the Greeks were not his friends now that he had been beaten.

Otto, pretending that he was the emperor's treasurer, persuaded the captain that they must sail to Rossano for the treasure chest. He promised the captain and his crew great riches if only they would do what he asked of them. They agreed. When their salandrine landed near Rossano, Otto and his men quickly jumped overboard and made for the castle. Seeing themselves duped, one of the sailors grabbed hold of Otto's cloak trying to pull him back. The emperor plunged his dagger into the man's side and hurried on. Panting, they reached the castle and safety. They gathered up Theophano, the boy, the bishop, and the war chest. Then they fled north as fast as their horses would carry them. But the army was lost.

"Cut down by the sword fell the purple flower of the country, the blond-haired ornament of Germany, men dear above all others to the emperor who was forced to watch the People of God delivered into the hands of Saracens, trampled beneath the feet of heathens."

To avenge his defeat, Otto assembled a fleet to invade Arab Sicily. It was sunk by the Muslims off Cape Calonna and its crews drowned. Victorious elsewhere, the self-styled unconquerable Imperator Invictissimus had no luck with Saracens, and darkness and terror once again descended on his domains.

Encouraged by news of the emperor's defeat at the hands of Italian Saracens, the Wends again crossed the border into Germany, ravaging the sees of Magdeburg, Havelburg, and Brandenburg. Thietmar of Merseburg vividly described this great raid. On July 2, they got over the walls of Brandenburg, committing many atrocities, "because this had been once their own chief town and they had never forgotten it." Bishop Folkmar managed to escape by the skin of his teeth, but the remains of his predecessor Odilo, himself a victim of these same Wends, were dug up and thrown to the dogs. Further north, the Obotrite Chief Mistislav burned Hamburg and did so thorough a job of looting that he left the survivors not enough to feed a sparrow. Everywhere the Slavs carried away men and women to be held for ransom. Sometimes those who had escaped capture still had to surrender themselves voluntarily as hostages to free members of their family. Thietmar himself was once on the way to give himself up to "those greedy dogs" in exchange for an uncle who, luckily for the chronicler, managed to get his captors drunk and escape before Thietmar could surrender himself.

Recently Christianized tribes returned to the ways of their ancient gods, to Thor, Isten, and Swantepolk. Nations, swallowed up by the SaxoRoman empire, reasserted their identity and rose in revolt. A "fauna of human wildcats and highway robbers with noble names" thought that good times had come again. The empire seemed to be on the verge of breaking up. "What will become of this vast fragile structure?" asked Henry Focillon.

History does not record why, in the midst of assembling a great force to avenge himself against the Saracens and to beat back the barbarians crossing his borders, Otto sent for Gerbert. Certainly he wished to attach Gerbert to his cause, and by naming him abbot of the monastery of St. Columban at Bobbio, he gained not only a spiritual and intellectual counselor but a loyal feudal vassal, but it took some courage on Otto's part to name a foreigner, not an Italian, to this important abbacy.

CHAPTER FOURTEEN

Big Crown
on a Tiny Head

BEGINNING WITH THE YEAR 983, Gerbert entered a labyrinthine twilight world of danger, coups de main, intrigues, politics, treachery, and civil wars. At times he appeared as a broker of crowns, at others as undercover agent. Often his head was at stake. Frequently he found himself between two fires—his loyalty to the German emperors, whose liegeman he considered himself to be, and loyalty to the rulers of the land of his birth, France.

The abbacy of Bobbio was one of the most important positions Otto II had the power to bestow, Bobbio's abbot being not only a spiritual leader but also a great feudal vassal. In 982 Otto gave the position to Gerbert. Attached to Bobbio were a number of fiefs, and Gerbert as abbot was expected to maintain and command a body of knights in the emperor's service.

Gerbert's new position was at the same time a trial and a delight, a trial because of the difficulties he encountered there, a delight because of the opportunity to forget his troubles in Bobbio's famous library and scriptorium. From Bobbio he asked his friend Adalbero in faraway Rheims to send him the *Astrology* of Boethius, and other things no less admirable, and he offered to present Adalbero in return with copies of manuscripts in the Bobbio library.

The abbey was situated in the Apennines, close to Pavia and near the River Trebbia, scene of one of Hannibal's great victories over the Romans. Beautifully situated and encircled by fertile lands, the abbey owned properties in a hundred places. The countryside around Bobbio was sprinkled with the monastery's fields, vineyards, saltworks, forests, and gardens. Hundreds of men and women worked under the monks' direction—shepherds, armorers, smiths, weavers, potters, carpenters, millers, shoemakers, saddlers, and peasants. As Gerbert wrote, "What part of Italy does not contain possessions of St. Columban of Bobbio?" And yet he found its fields devastated or lying fallow, the abbey's buildings in disrepair, its treasury empty.

Bobbio's riches had also been its undoing. As the old proverb says, "Where there is carrion, there will be flies." Flies in the shape of powerful local nobles intent upon getting their hands on the abbey's lands and estates were many, and one particularly big fly—Gerbert's predecessor, Petroald—had seen his opportunity to steal and had stolen. Petroald had leased out monastery land at nominal rents to some of his noble cronies and received kickbacks. He had borrowed money on St. Columban's most valuable properties and failed to repay the loans, forfeiting the pledges to his favorite partners in these transactions. He took bribes. He had relaxed the discipline of his monks so that they grew "lascivious and unruly." The brothers themselves rose up against him in disgust. He was deposed and reduced to the rank of a simple monk to be replaced by Gerbert, but even from his plain monk's cell, Petroald continued to intrigue against his hated successor.

In Gerbert's letters he lamented that his monks were shrunken with hunger and pinched with cold for want of warm clothes. "The sanctuary of God," he complained, "is up for sale. The lease money has disappeared, granaries and wine cellars are empty and there is not a single coin to be found in the money chest." When he tried to restore the abbey's property he ran up against the local nobles and prelates who had profited from Petroald's misdeeds. They ganged up on Gerbert to the point of open violence.

To add to his troubles, the former empress Adelaide, widow of Otto I, demanded that he give church lands to some of her favorites and, when he refused, turned against him. His enemies slandered him. Because he had brought some of his relatives with him to Bobbio, the emperor was told that he had a wife and children "and even worse things." With some justice Gerbert wrote, "What part of Italy is there which does not contain my enemies?" The sudden death of Otto II, his protector, pulled the last props out from under him.

Otto had managed to restore the situation in Italy to the neglect of his northern dominions. In 983 he was in Rome, brooding and in a melancholy humor, according to Richer. He had succeeded in making his adherent Pietro Canepova pope under the name of John XIV, but still he complained of Roman faithlessness and plotting vassals. It was whispered that Otto had incurred the anger of St. Laurentius because of his dissolving of the bishopric of Merseburg, founded in the saint's memory by Otto the First, his illustrious father, after his great victory over the Magyars. A pious visionary had come to ruddy Otto the Younger, telling him that St. Laurentius had appeared to him in a dream. The visionary had seen the emperor seated upon his golden throne, surrounded by his lords temporal and spiritual, when the saint had entered the assembly, advancing with knitted brows and angry mien upon Otto, pulling the silver footstool from beneath his feet. One of the vassals had challenged St. Laurentius, exclaiming, "Who offers insult to the Augustus?" The saint then had revealed his identity, thundering, "If Otto does not repent and make good the damage he has done to me, I shall tumble him from his throne!"

This vision, vouched for by the holy mystic, troubled Otto when he heard of it, and he attributed many of his misfortunes to the saint's wrath. Overworked and depressed, he fell ill. At first, the sickness seemed to be light, mere digestive troubles—"an intestinal constipation." To cure himself, and with his usual haste and impatience, he took four drachmas of aloes: "ingesting large overdoses of prescribed medicine and thus making himself worse rather than better." The result was a "derangement of entrails, fever, hemorrhoids and hemorrhages." He got up too early, against his physician's advice, and sepsis set in, which led to death within a few days.

As Otto felt his end drawing near he divided his treasures into four parts. The first he willed to St. Peter's Church, the second to his mother and sole sister, "in token of the love he bore them," the third to his knights and soldiers, "which esteemed their love and obedience to him higher than their love for life and home." The fourth part he bequeathed to the poor. Then, in the presence of his wife and members of his family, the pope, many bishops, and a host of loyal men, he proclaimed in a loud voice his faith, confessed himself, and received absolution. In such a God-pleasing manner he died on the seventh of December, 983, "being put to rest with many tears and lamentations" in the "Paradise," that is, the portico of St. Peter's. His body was enclosed by an antique marble sarcophagus and covered with a great slab of red porphyry that had once sealed the tomb of the Roman emperor Hadrian. Otto was called fortunate to have been laid to rest so near to the last abode and the bones of St. Peter.

"It was a wild world upon which the young man of twenty-eight took his last look, with a heart perhaps broken by the contrast between the great ideal and the impossibility of fulfilling it." His son and successor, Otto III, was just three years old.

Adelaide and Theophano tried to protect the rights of the child emperor against a wolf pack of powerful nobles intent to seize the boy in order to rule in his name. In Rome, the Ottonian cause seemed lost. The Saxon borderlands were in danger of being overwhelmed by Norse and Slavs who saw in Otto's death and his son's minority their last chance to regain what they had lost. Everything was in a flux, shifting, stirring, aboil with suspicion and terror, and no one knew what the next day might hold.

The soldiers Gerbert had raised for Otto II mutinied upon the emperor's death. According to some writers, part of St. Columban was pillaged and Gerbert was taken prisoner, though he mentions nothing of this in his letters. At any rate, he fled from Bobbio, to Pavia, where the former empress Adelaide maintained her court. He found her still angry with him for not having enriched her friends. Theophano, still in shock after her husband's death and with the three-year-old boy king to safeguard, had little time for him. Gerbert was glad to go back to Rheims, as he said, "to drown the memories of his troubles in philosophy." Upon arrival, he wrote to his friend, the monk Raymond, at Aurillac, "Since matters in Italy were such that we had to submit shamefully to the yoke of tyrants . . . or attempt to use force, which would have meant gathering followers, fortifying camps, employing robbery and murder, we have chosen the peaceful leisure of studies rather than the doubtful business of war."

He still thought of himself as a teacher and happily immersed himself once more in his beloved books, but, in reality, he had merely jumped from the frying pan into the fire. Great events were at hand involving kings and nations. In France, the last of the Carolingians tried feebly to save Charlemagne's heritage, and the fate of Gaul was at stake. Like it or not, Gerbert would have to play his part in an avalanche of swiftly changing situations.

In retrospect, the troubles he had been forced to deal with at Bobbio might have been a good training ground to confront the tasks before him. The nineteenth-century German historian Giesebrecht thought him well equipped for whatever problems he might have to solve: "Gerbert belonged to those rare scholars who are at home in the business of the world as well as in the empire of ideas, who can master the darkest and most opaque conditions, whose intellectual flow never runs dry and who can stay on top of a number of tasks at the same time." All these qualities now came to the fore.

At the time of his father's death, little Otto III happened to be in the care of Bishop Warin of Cologne, who promptly and wisely had him crowned at Aix-la-Chapelle on Christmas Day 983 with the help of Willigis, bishop of Mayence, and John, bishop of Ravenna, symbolizing the child's dual elevation as king of Germany and Roman emperor. The big crown rested uneasily upon a tiny head. Restless in exile, his vaulting ambitions unfulfilled, lived Duke Henry the Quarrelsome. Already he had twice rebelled against Otto II and for this reason had been deprived of his dukedom of Bavaria and banished to Utrecht.

Henry was a nephew of Otto the Great and cousin to Otto II. All his life he had dreamed of becoming emperor as, theoretically, the Germany crown was obtained by election and not necessarily by descent. Henry felt that he had a better right to rule than two women—one old and one Greek—and for this reason he should be Otto's guardian. With the young king in his power, what wonderful things might not happen! Counting on the many disaffected nobles, unwilling to endure a government by women, Henry persuaded his jailer Poppo to join him and marched upon Cologne. Bishop Warin, either intimidated by threats or enticed by promises, surrendered the child. Henry immediately proclaimed himself king and held an assembly at Quedlinburg with great pomp and ceremony. He was joined by dukes, counts, and bishops who saw a champion in him. No doubt they also hoped to regain their old independence, restricted by Otto I. Under a new ruler of their own making, they saw in the coming struggle for power an opportunity for looting and land grabbing as well as a chance to sell themselves to the highest bidder.

In this crisis Adelaide and Theophano turned to Gerbert, begging him to use his influence and connections to bring together a coalition against Henry, to encourage the loyal barons and prelates, to persuade the waverers, and to oppose those who had abandoned Otto III. It was a task calling for great acumen and finesse, both of which, luckily, Gerbert had in abundance. He found his greatest ally in his old master, Archbishop Adalbero of Rheims, himself a master politician. The two friends busied themselves organizing the resistance to the usurper—"two bodies having but a single heart and soul" ("*qu'un coeur et qu'une âme*").

Gerbert's zeal in the Ottonian cause is easy to understand, having been attached to it by old ties of affection and gratitude as well as the oath of fealty he had sworn to Otto on the occasion of his investiture as abbot of Bobbio. But Adalbero owed nothing to the Ottonians and, as a Frenchman, might have been expected to work in the interests of his own country rather than the Saxon monarchy. The English historian A. S. Allen asked, "Is it not natural to suppose that love for the country of his birth (Lorraine) would lead him to desire its annexation to the country of his adoption (France) rather than its continued annexation to the Germany throne?" The clue, some thought, was in his loyalty to the house of Lorraine. He was, after all, a part of the family.

One has to keep in mind that nationalism and love for a particular homeland was an idea whose time had not yet come. For men like Adalbero and Gerbert, Christendom was one's homeland, Latin its universal language. Loyalty was to one's liege lord and to one's self-interest.

Accordingly, the two began hectic and delicate negotiations to undercut Henry and safeguard Lorraine for Theophano. Much can be learned from Gerbert's letters. First of all, he strove to win over to his cause the Carolingian king Lothaire as a counterweight to Henry. Lothaire stood in the same relationship to Otto as did Henry through his descent from Gerberga, sister of Otto I, and by his marriage to Emma, half-sister to Otto II. Not surprisingly, Lothaire thought that he himself should have the advantage of being the boy king's guardian. Gerbert skillfully played off Lothaire as his trump card against Henry and also recruited to his cause several important men: Charles, duke of Lower Lorraine; Duke Conrad of Swabia; and the influential bishops Notker of Liège, Dietrich of Metz, and Willigis of Mayence. The latter needed little persuasion being, like Gerbert, a tutor of Otto III. Willigis was a formidable character, immensely learned, opinionated, and strong willed. He was a born fighter whose love for a good brawl often got the better of his wisdom. For years he was the most powerful man in Saxony. Otto I had discovered Willigis's talents, making him archbishop of Mayence and chancellor of the empire. During her pregnancy, his mother had experienced a vision dreaming that out of her womb the sun was sending its rays and lighting up the world. His father had been a wheelwright, and the Mayence prelates, resenting rule by a non-noble, drew with chalk a wagon wheel on the church wall and underneath the legend:

Willigis, Willigis, Willigis,
Consider who your mother and father are!

Not in the least disturbed by this and other similar graffiti, Willigis adopted a white wheel on a red ground as his own as well as Mayence's coat of arms. Gerbert acknowledged the great debt the Ottonians owed this archbishop, writing, "It was Willigis who snatched the tender lamb (Otto III) from the jaws of the wolf and gave it back to its mother."

The great coalition Gerbert and his friends got together proved too much for the quarrelsome Henry. Already the two empresses were in Germany, and a meeting between the parties was arranged. All lords temporal and spiritual took part in the deliberations, during which they saw a star rise in broad daylight, a sign, all believed, in favor of Otto. Among hallelujahs and hosannahs the nobles surrounded Henry, crying, "Give up, give up, God wills it!"

Barely six months after the death of Otto II, The Quarreler was forced to give up the child king to his mother, Theophano, releasing his followers from the oaths they had sworn to him. Otto the Third's accession was assured, and Gerbert had played a major role in enthroning his first king.

CHAPTER FIFTEEN

He Makes and Unmakes Kings

THE PRICE FOR HENRY THE QUARRELER'S capitulation had been the return of his dukedom of Bavaria, and it was not long before he was dreaming anew his dream of orb and scepter. He offered to the French king Lothaire, his erstwhile rival, the duchy of Lorraine. Lothaire, for his part, was more than willing to accept the bribe. Henry was by then merely a pawn swept off the board but was still capable of doing mischief. His actions at once placed Adalbero and Gerbert in a most awkward and dangerous position.

Adalbero was the primate as well as the chancellor of France. Lothaire, his liege lord, had been Otto's ally but was now his enemy. Gerbert and Adalbero had, up to this time, worked harmoniously with both Lothaire and Otto; now they had to make a choice. For Gerbert this was easy. For Adalbero it was not, yet he decided to throw in his lot with Otto and the German cause. Some French historians have condemned Adalbero as a traitor to his country, but *France* was merely a word, not a reality. Most contemporary chroniclers still referred to it as Gaul. One historian pointed out, "If he betrayed his king, it was to preserve his country; if there was a fault, it lay in preferring his country to his lord, his country's safety to the preservation of a dynasty."

Gerbert and Adalbero now plunged into a snakepit of intrigue. While pretending to work for Lothaire—Adalbero even collected soldiers for him—they secretly labored on behalf of his enemies. While Adalbero wrote letters to influential nobles, exhorting them to be steadfast in Lothaire's cause, Gerbert wrote a second set of letters to the same recipients, telling them to disregard the earlier ones and rally to Otto. They played a dangerous and deceitful game that, at any moment, could have cost them their heads. Fortunately, theirs were cool heads, capable of concealing intricate schemes and counterschemes.

Even so, Lothaire became suspicious and, after having seized Verdun, took Adalbero's brother Godfrey, together with one uncle and one nephew, prisoner as a pledge for the archbishop's good behavior. He even hailed Adalbero before his court at Compiègne on a charge of high treason, and one can only speculate on what the outcome would have been had not Duke Hugh Capet come up with six hundred men to disperse the assembly.

This Hugh Capet, duke of the Franks and son of Hugh the Great, was a secular abbot himself. His abbatial charge encompassed nearly all the rich abbeys in his dominions, and it was from this that he derived his surname Capet ("wearer of the cope").

Hugh had secretly become Gerbert and Adalbero's ally, and the both had come to the conclusion that in the scramble for the French throne, Hugh would prevail, particularly as, in 980, he had gone to Rome to conclude an alliance with Otto II. On March 2, 986, Lothaire's sudden death seemed to end their troubles.

The new and last Carolingian king was Lothaire's son Louis V. Nicknamed the Sluggard, or King-Do-Nothing, Louis was only nineteen years old and very much under the influence of his mother Emma, a German and the former empress Adelaide's daughter. Emma recalled Adalbero to the court, released most of his relatives from captivity, and made Gerbert her secretary. Being aware of Hugh's rising power, a great threat to her and her son, she was playing the German card. Louis was not too sluggish to see that his mother was pursuing a Saxon, not a French, policy. He expelled her and her counselors from his court and at a large assembly of notables called Adalbero "of all men on earth the most guilty." He then went to besiege Rheims, within whose walls Adalbero and Gerbert had taken their refuge. Adalbero was forced to give hostages as token that he would appear before Louis to be tried for his offenses against the house of Charlemagne. He also had to agree that, as added surety, he would demolish the strong castles that he held in fief from the German emperor. He further was told to swear a solemn oath of fealty to Louis or quit France forever.

Before the trial could take place, however, the two friends were rescued by fate. Louis fell from his horse while hunting and, following massive hemorrhages, died. Some said that the hemorrhaging was helped along with poison administered by Emma. At any rate, Hugh Capet's hour had come. One day after Louis's funeral, the lords who had assembled to try Adalbero were instead called upon to elect a new king. Lothaire's brother Charles, duke of Lower Lorraine, and a certain prelate Arnulf, who was Lothaire's illegitimate son, were the only Carolingians left, and, as a bastard, Arnulf was disqualified from the beginning. Of course, whether illegitimacy disqualified a man from becoming a ruler depended on which party happened to be in power. This left Charles, described as a weak and stupid intriguer.

Adalbero now came forward as Hugh's champion with Gerbert working behind the scenes and masterminding Hugh's election. Already men were referring to him as the monk "who makes and unmakes kings." The first order of business was the squashing of accusations against Adalbero. To this end, Hugh himself came forward first to address the crowd of notables: "Give up every suspicion you harbor against Bishop Adalbero and render honor to him as the first and foremost bishop of the realm. Acknowledge his righteousness, his wisdom and nobility, honor him as he deserves."

After Hugh had spoken, it was Adalbero's turn: "I well know that Charles has many followers who would give him the crown by right of inheritance, but the French throne is not to be won thus, but through being chosen, not by being of illustrious birth but by being worthy.

History teaches us that rulers of the most noble descent, through incapacity, lost their crown to make room for those better fitted, who have honor for their shield and liberality for their ramparts, though somewhat less noble.

"Shall we confer the highest dignity upon Charles, unheeding of honor, benumbed by indolence, one who did not blush to serve foreign princes and who took himself a low born woman to make our queen? No, Charles has forfeited the throne by his own faults, not by those of others. If you want your country's ruin, vote for Charles, but if you care for its welfare, put the crown upon the head of our most excellent Duke Hugh. Let none of you be blinded by affection for Charles, nor let any former aversion to Hugh stand in the way of declaring for him.

"Choose the duke, who recommends himself to you by his deeds, his nobility and his armed might. You will find in him not only his country's defender, but also the defender of your own private interests. In him you see a father. Who among you has ever asked a favor from him in vain?"

Shrewdly appealing to the nobles' honor as well as their self-interest, the persuasive Adalbero had the satisfaction of seeing Hugh become their unanimous choice. His speech, abbreviated here, was taken down by Richer, Gerbert's pupil and friend, who most probably heard it with his own ears. Adalbero had contributed the voice, Gerbert the strategy. It was more to Gerbert than to Adalbero that Hugh owed his crown. To quote Jules Michelet, the famous nineteenth-century French historian: "It is a great thing for the Capets to have such a man attached to their interest: if they help him to become archbishop, he helps them to become kings." In obtaining the throne for Hugh, Gerbert and Adalbero had helped France to become a nation, and it was Adalbero who, on December 30, 987, consecrated Hugh king at Rheims.

Though Hugh was now the "Eldest Son of the Church and a most Christian King," his powers were still very limited. His kingdom as yet merely consisted of the Ile de France. This was the heart of the country, but its body was still in the hands of great feudatories, many of whom had more land, more men, and considerably more power than he. Hugh could not even travel from Paris to Orleans without permission of the lord of Puiset, whose great castle at Etampes lay athwart the road between the two cities.

Hugh, however, did something of the greatest consequence for the developing nation. The nobles who had chosen Hugh over Charles, a king's son with a better right to the throne, did not intend to found a dynasty. They liked much better keeping the central authority weak by electing a king from among several families as their interests dictated. But Hugh was set on passing his crown in an unbroken line to his descendants and, following the example of the Ottonians, had his son Robert crowned and anointed while he himself was still alive. This became a tradition among the Capetians, depriving the great nobles of their right to choose kings at their whim. Robert was duly enthroned by Adalbero on December 30, 987, at Orleans, the last occasion also when Gerbert's old benefactor, Count Borrel, appeared in the forefront of history. Borrel had appealed to Hugh for help against Al-Mansur, whose Arabs had once again stormed and taken the count's capital, Barcelona. Hugh used the event to announce his determination to lead a crusade against the infidels in Spain, a promise never fulfilled as the king was soon involved in a struggle against Charles, the rejected candidate for the crown.

Gerbert now thought himself at the summit of his ambitions. He had become Hugh's secretary as well as the tutor of the king's son. He handled Hugh's important diplomatic correspondence, for instance by asking the Byzantine emperor Basil II, on behalf of young Robert, for the hand of a Greek princess. But, as Gerbert was soon to find out, king making was not so grand as it had seemed. On January 25, 989, his great friend Archbishop Adalbero died. Gerbert took it for granted that he would be appointed his successor and thought that all the bishops and most of the nobles would support his claim. Most of all, he counted on the king's gratitude, but, true to historical priorities, gratitude lost out to the exigencies of politics. As it turned out, Gerbert had very few supporters. Archbishoprics had always been reserved for the highborn, and most nobles hated to watch the See of Rheims awarded to an upstart.

Many abbots had always resented his teaching of pagan authors, while prelates and monks alike feared his reforms, which would impose upon them discipline and austerity.

Hugh favored instead Arnulf, Lothaire's son, a bastard, to be sure, described as a young, rough, ill-mannered man, but very clever and sly as a fox. What mattered was his royal lineage and that installing him as archbishop would split, and at the same time placate, the Carolingian faction. Hugh thought that if he could win over Lothaire's son he would thereby neutralize his uncle Charles. The young man seemed overjoyed, heaping upon Hugh fervent thanks, fulsome declarations of loyalty, and vows of eternal gratitude.

Hugh was not altogether fooled. He made Arnulf swear terrific oaths of fidelity and made him sign a paper calling down on Arnulf's head horrendous curses should he prove false. He even forced him, while taking the holy sacrament, to pray aloud that it should turn into his eternal damnation if he ever violated his oath. Hugh seemed to have forgotten that even the most solemn oaths existed only to be broken.

Arnulf had hardly been installed at Rheims when he began plotting to surrender the city to Charles and also to help him replace Hugh as king. Charles at that time was at Laon, which he had taken by a coup de main. He marched from there to Rheims, whose gates were opened to him. The town was pillaged, and Gerbert and Arnulf were carried off to Laon as prisoners. The latter, as insurance in case Charles should wind up the loser, played the role of captive of his uncle and even excommunicated the looters. This fooled nobody. At a council subsequently held at Verzy, Bishop Gautier of Autun shouted scornfully, "Is this bishop [Arnulf] mad, who for the theft of a few sticks of furniture excommunicates his poor fellows, yet is silent about his own captivity and that of his clergy and people?" Of course, excommunicating his captors would have meant including Uncle Charles, his co-conspirator, which Arnulf could not afford to do.

Gerbert's life was in danger, so he also pretended to join Charles's cause. He even wrote letters on behalf of the pretender, describing the Carolingian as the legitimate heir to the throne, unlawfully deprived of it by Hugh. He went so far as to compose Arnulf's condemnation of Charles's robber-soldiers. In return he was permitted to accompany Arnulf to Rheims as his secretary. He would later reproach himself bitterly for his weakness, referring to himself as "the Devil's instrument" and "Prince of Crimes." However, after his escape, Hugh never held it against him that he had to do these things in order to save his life. In the end Arnulf the betrayer was betrayed.

Like Gerbert, bishop Adalbero of Laon—not to be confused with Gerbert's departed friend—had been forced to pretend joining forces with Charles and Arnulf, promising to trick Hugh into a compromise favorable to the Carolingian party. At a time when both Arnulf and his uncle were back in Laon, Adalbero struck. On Palm Sunday, 991, some suspicious-looking fellows were seen in the inns and taverns of Laon, and several faithful followers warned both uncle and nephew, that something was afoot. But they were blinded by the advantages to be derived from Adalbero's friendship. On the fateful evening, Charles and Arnulf sat together at table with Adalbero. Charles placed white bread in a golden bowl, poured wine over it, and said, "My Lord Bishop, you have today blessed the people and given me communion. Therefore I won't believe those who whisper in my ears that you mean us harm, especially when the day of our Lord Jesus' suffering and death is so near. I offer you this cup filled with bread and wine so that you should empty it as a sign of your new friendship with me."

Adalbero answered, "Without the least hesitation do I accept this cup and drink."

"And keep the faith with me," added Charles.

"And keep the faith," repeated Adalbero, "and should I break it, may I perish like Judas."

The meal ended amid mutual oaths of everlasting friendship and fidelity. Then Charles and Arnulf went to bed in the bishop's castle. In the small hours of the morning, while the Carolingians slept, Adalbero, under some pretext, sent away the porter keeping guard before the door. He then crept into their bedchamber and removed their weapons. He opened a sally port to let his own well-armed men in.

Then Adalbero took a sword from under his bishop's cape and, together with his hirelings, went once more into the room where his enemies rested. Startled from their sleep by the clanking of arms, Arnulf and Charles saw themselves surrounded, Adalbero hovering over them with a naked sword in his hand. They groped for their own weapons only to find that they were gone. Charles reminded Adalbero of the oaths of friendship sworn in the Savior's name. Adalbero coolly remarked that he was only doing to them what they had done to him.

Thus Arnulf and Charles, together with his wife and children, were taken prisoner. Their supporters, lodged throughout the city, tried to retake the castle but failed and took to their heels. Adalbero sent word of his success to Hugh, waiting at Senlis, and the king lost no time joining him at Laon. The crowd, which had just cried itself hoarse hailing Charles, now outdid itself cheering the Capetians. Charles died soon after in prison, and with him died the great dynasty founded by Charlemagne.

At the monastery of St. Basle of Verzy, near Rheims, Arnulf was tried on a charge of high treason. On his knees he had to beg for his life, was shorn of all his honors, and had to surrender his bishop's ring. He also had to sign his abdication as primate of France. In his stead the bishops elected "the Abbot Gerbert, a man of mature years, in character prudent, amiable and merciful. Nor do we prefer to him flighty youth, unbridled ambition and rash deeds. Hence we elect Gerbert, whose life and character have been known to us from the days of his youth, and whose knowledge of things, both of God and man, we have ourselves for long been aware of."

At the time of Gerbert's elevation to the See of Rheims, many parts of France were swarming with heretics. One group was the Cathari or

Pure Ones, who preached that an evil principle was responsible for the writing of the Old Testament. The evil principle was opposed to the principle of light and goodness represented by the New Testament. These sectarians also maintained that no priests were necessary to stand between humanity and God and that the seven sacraments were not divinely ordained but superfluous. They condemned private ownership of any kind as well as the eating of meat. They particularly forbade coitus and marriage as the works of the evil principle.

Hence Gerbert, at the time of his consecration, had to make a profession of faith that has been preserved in one of his own letters written in June 991. In part Gerbert vowed: "I, Gerbert, by the overwhelming grace of God soon to be Archbishop of Rheims, in plain words affirm these articles of faith. I maintain that there is one God, the Father, the Son, and the Holy Spirit, and all three persons to be One God. He who was the Son of God the Father in his divine nature, became the Son of the Mother in his human nature.

"And I confess that He assumed flesh in His Mother's womb, having a human, sentient mind, possessing at the same time both natures of God and man, one Person, one Son, one Christ, one Lord of all creatures, of whom He is the Creator. I affirm that He suffered the real Passion of the flesh, that He died a real bodily death, and that He was resurrected by the real resurrection of the flesh and the spirit, by which He shall come to judge the quick and the dead. I believe the Author of the Old and the New Testament to be one and the same—the Lord God. I maintain that the devil became evil not by nature but through his own free will.

"I do not prohibit marriage, nor forbid any second marriages. I do not forbid the eating of meat. I affirm that reconciled penitents ought to be permitted to receive communion. I believe that through baptism all sins are forgiven, and I profess that outside the Catholic Church there is no salvation." And thus he became primate of all Gaul.

Gerbert was very different from other prelates. Because of his many achievements, both spiritual and secular, some called him a sorcerer, and others even thought that he was the Antichrist. He read the ancient pagan authors more often than sacred religious tomes, but in his heart he never strayed from what he believed to be the true faith. He had no use for bigots or heretics, and he became the first bishop of France to administer his see with wisdom and compassion.

An old medieval sword was once found whose blade bore the inscription "Nulla Crux—Nulla Corona." The meaning was that the crown of glory was won only by also wearing the crown of thorns and pain. Gerbert was soon to find out that his own crowns of glory, his bishop's miter, and, later, his papal tiara were also full of thorns.

From the church's point of view Anrulf's deposition—for political reasons, not for any transgressions against canonical law—was illegal, as was Gerbert's election. An archbishop, in the view of Rome, could be tried and deposed only by the pope. Arnulf's only fault was being Lothaire's son. His conspiracies on behalf of Charles were of no concern or interest to the pontiff, who jealously watched over the prerogatives of his holy office. The French bishops, on their part, maintained their own rights vis-à-vis Rome with equal determination. Gerbert found himself not only caught between two fires, but excommunicated by Pope John XV as a usurper, while all who had taken part in depriving Arnulf of his see were suspended from office. Gerbert was forced to argue his case before John's successor, Gregory V, a grandson of Otto I and cousin of Otto III. Gerbert's ties to the Saxon emperor availed him nothing. Gregory, as pope, was more interested in maintaining the rights of St. Peter's see than in accommodating the young emperor's friend and tutor. He called Gerbert an "invader of the See of Rheims" and insisted that Arnulf must first be reinstated before the pope could consider the charges against him and render a final judgment. Little did Gregory dream that he was dealing with his own successor when he sent Gerbert back to France with empty hands. As long as Gerbert had the king's support, he was able to maintain himself, but Hugh Capet died on October 24, 996, shortly after Gerbert's return from pleading his cause in Rome.

Robert, the new king and Gerbert's former pupil, was of little help, having done the unforgivable: he had married out of love. His wife, Berta, was his cousin, too closely related in the eyes of the church, which condemned the marriage as incestuous. Robert hoped that the pope might be induced to sanction it and therefore dared not oppose him in the matter of the Rheims archbishopric. Rome eventually ruled against Robert and even excommunicated him, but this did not help Gerbert in his hour of need. As he was under the ban, his own clerics and even his own relatives shunned him, his servants refused to obey him, and his soldiers mutinied. He had been reduced to an outcast, forced to eat his meals alone, and could not even find one single man to assist him at mass. In vain did he complain of the "undeserved persecution by his brethren."

The young prodigy had become middle-aged, worn out by political battles and personal problems. From the year 995 on he began to suffer from painful ailments common in his time. One of his main troubles was rheumatism, the result of long years spent in badly heated stone buildings. To the former empress Adelaide he wrote, "I am nearing the end of my days. Old age threatens me with death. My lungs are inflamed and oppress me. My ears ring and my body seems to be pierced by needles. I have been in bed all year, never without pain. I rise from my couch only to be consumed by fever." He longed to be back with young Otto, his pupil who loved and understood him. In 997 he left France, never to return. His king-making days were over.

CHAPTER SIXTEEN

Götterdämmerung

AS THE CENTURY NEARED ITS END, portents and prodigies, meteors, dragons seen in the sky, and freakish births signified to many that the end of the world was near, that the millennium was at hand. Amid war, pestilence, and volcanic eruptions the earth seemed to be on the verge of giving birth, but nobody knew what she would bring forth.

Opposed to fear and trembling was a feeling of hope and euphoria. The fatal day was about to break, for sure; the trumpet would sound and the dead rise from their graves amid howling and the gnashing of teeth but God's loving-kindness would not allow humankind to perish. Things would be bad, very bad; but when the Day of Wrath was over, everything would be better than before, and peace would reign eternally.

"The only thing certain was that after the advent of the Great Champion, whoever he had been or might be, the great tribulations would begin. But they would endure only for the appointed time. Just as the Passion of Christ was as a darkness between two days, so the last assault of evil on good would meet with its defeat. Soon would open the seventh age of humanity, like the seventh day of creation, a prelude to the eternal repose of a day that should have no end."

The church itself, at the highest level, frowned upon those who preached the end of the world on a specific day. It held with St. Augustine that the church was the kingdom of Christ and that the millennium began with Christ's birth and appearance on earth and was therefore an accomplished fact. "When will the Last Judgment take place? 1000 years after Christ? No, but tomorrow morning, because tonight I may die, and from that moment on my fate is sealed." The notion of a specific date was rooted, however, in the vast lower strata of Christian society.

A hundred times more people belonged to the lower strata than high clerics or scholars, people who could not read or understand the Latin of the prelates, who got their faith from grandmothers' tales. As Felix Dahn, a nineteenth-century author put it, "The belief, that with the winter solstice of the year 1000 the world would perish and the Last Judgment befall was accepted in the West as gospel truth." There were some equally sure that it would happen on Christmas Day.

For most people the fear of impending doom intruded only vaguely into their daily lives, a nebulous idea that momentarily made them shudder and break out in goose pimples, only to be shrugged off quickly so that the toiling for survival or the chase after pleasure could go on. Many simply laughed at the notion that there was any magic in the number 1000. Others trembled at the mere sight of the mystical figure M. Some, smug in their righteousness, knew not only the day and the hour of the coming cataclysm, but also its exact duration— three and a half years. These good Christians, taking their inspiration from an ancient saying that "the blessed rejoice in the sight of the damned," gloated in anticipation of the scoffers, soon to be souls in torment, tortured by devils amid screams of never-ending agony, crushed like grapes, grasped with hooks of red-hot iron to be plunged alternately into fire or ice. With pleasurable thrill they contemplated sinners hung by their tongues, their genitals gnawed by venomous snakes; others beaten together on an anvil into a dripping mass, boiled and strained through a cloth. Virtuous women rapturously imagined those who had succumbed to lust being embraced by glowing, flaming, stinking fiends and, after being sexually abused by devils with yard-long, spiked phalluses, cast into the bottomless pit.

Pagan kings and chieftains were uneasy too. Shortly before 1000, the kings of Sweden, Norway, and Denmark accepted baptism. During one great sea battle in this year of wonders, Jarl Erik Haakonson replaced his "stem dweller," an image of Thor, with the cross. It was during these last years of the tenth century that the Vikings gave up on their old gods, Odin, Thor, and Freia. While Christians expected the millennium, Scandinavians awaited Ragnarök, the Twilight of the Gods, the all-consuming Götterdämmerung:

> An axe age, a sword age,
> Shields are cleft;
> A wind age, a wolf age,
> Ere the world sinks;
> No man spares another man.
> The sun blackens,
> Sea swallows the earth,
> Bright stars fall from heaven.
> Life-feeding fire
> And hissing steams rage;
> A great heat rises
> Towards heaven itself.

Just as in Revelation the angels blow their trumpets, so in the *Völuspa Saga* the god Heimdall blows his horn as the forces of good and evil meet in a last battle. On the Field of Vigrid, the Norse Armageddon, the slaughter ends in mutual destruction. Dying, the Aesir—Thor, Odin, Heimdall, Thyr, and Frigg—have slain the evil ones: Loki, Lord of the Underworld; Fenris, the monster wolf; Gram, the Hound of Hel; and the hideous giant Surt. There are no winners, only losers. The Aesir, the great gods, lie dead. The earth is afire. Flames spurt from cracks in a charred earth. The rivers boil. The world is swallowed up by foaming waters. A black sun turns to ice. Nothing is left. All is finished. Yet, as in Christian beliefs, a new sun will rise upon a new earth. The Muspilli—a partially Nordic, partially Christian, partially Germanic Armageddon—is related in a mid-ninth-century poem:

> This is what the wise men have told:
> The Antichrist shall fight with Elijah.
> The Evil One is well-armed, they will fight it out.
> The warriors so mighty, the stakes so great.
> Elijah fights for eternal life.
> Antichrist stands by the side of Satan.
> He will fall wounded on the field of battle,
> And will be the loser on the killing ground.
> But wise men think Elijah will be wounded also,
> So that his blood will drench the earth.
> The mountains catch fire,
> No tree is left standing.
> The seas will dry up, the sky catch fire;
> The moon will fall, the earth burn up,
> No stone will be left standing
> On the day of Judgment.
> Fire rages, people consuming.
> Kin cannot save kin,
> In the Face of the MUSPILLI.
> A red hot rain burns up everything
> Fire and hot steam will purge all.
> Where then the place where brother fought brother?

All the world's mythology contains passages resembling those in the Bible: "And the fourth angel poured out his vial upon the sun; and power was given unto him to scorch men with fire. . . . And men were scorched with great heat and blasphemed the name of God."

For the idol-worshiping people of the North, their world, the world of Thor and Odin, did indeed come to an end. For Scandinavians the great twilight became a reality, accompanied by unspeakable cruelties.

As elsewhere during the tenth century, warfare was fiendishly cruel, but the Scandinavians had their own specialties. It was the custom to burn the house of an enemy with every living creature inside, though often the attacking party would exempt women and children. A war leader might call out, "So-and-so come out. You are only a guest in there and not involved. Save yourself." But the uninvolved bystander might feel that hospitality received obligated him to let himself be burned together with his host. Faithful bondsmen also often chose to die with their masters rather than be spared.

A hated enemy, such as the slayer of one's father, was sacrificed by being made into a Blód-örn, or blood-eagle, by having his ribs chopped off along the spine and spread apart like bird wings so that the quivering lungs could be torn from the living body and pulled out through the open back: "The jarl found Half-dan on Ranar's hill and had a blood-eagle cut on his back with a sword."

Also in northern Europe lived warrior societies such as the Jomsvikings in their famous burg on the Baltic Sea under their leader Palnatoki. They were pagan warrior-monks rather than typical Vikings, living under a strict discipline. No man under eighteen or over fifty could be admitted to their ranks, nor one who had run from an enemy. Booty was held in common, private property frowned upon. Women were not allowed among the Jomsvikings, and no man could leave the burg for longer than three days and nights without special permission. Their religion was war, their pastime fighting. "Every summer they went out and made war in different countries, got high renown, and were looked upon as the greatest warriors; hardly any others were thought their equals."

Men who scorned death and were good at wielding ax, spear, and sword dreamed of becoming champions or *kappi* and having *skalds* make up fine songs about them, but the bravest of the brave were the Berserks, so named because they fought half-naked, without *serk* (shirt) or armor. War-mad, they worked themselves up into such a fury that they uttered frightful wolf and bear growls, gnawed their shields, and gnashed their teeth until they snapped. In a veritable intoxication of blood they sometimes discarded their weapons to rush at the enemy with their bare fists.

Norse poetry was devoted to war. Bards waxed lyrical when speaking of arms. A sword was called the Ice of Battle, Terror of Ringmail, or Wolf of the Wound. Axes were Shield-biters or Itch of the Helmet. Spears were referred to as Long Adders of Battle or Shooting Serpents, arrows as Venom Teeth or Wound Thorns. Of defensive weapons, shields were described as Odin's Moon or the Sun of Thor, while *brynyas*, that is ring-mail armor, was called Odin's Shirt or the Warrior's Tent.

Death or life, victory or defeat in battle was decided by the Norns, or Weird Sisters, a female trinity of the Fates, who rode through the sky in blood-spattered armor on steeds with hailstorm-dripping nostrils and dew-foaming mouths. Sagas glorified them as Blood Maidens, She-graspers of Spears, or Blood-ale Bringers. Sometimes they rode down from the sky to help a favorite warrior, blowing their horns, their spears shedding rays of light, getting into the midst of mortal men's fights if necessary. Not infrequently they gave their bodies to a favorite champion. Then the Valkyries rode to the battlefield to choose among the corpses whom they would bear to Valhalla.

Valhalla was the Norse paradise, tailor-made for red-blooded Vikings. Only those who died in battle were admitted. Those unlucky enough to die of natural causes went to Niflheim, the land of mists, cold, damp—a boring place. How different Valhalla, Gladsheim, the Merry Land! There the weapon-dead men, the happy *einherjar*, did what they liked best: fight and drink. Every day they got up to put on their armor and helmets and hurried to Odin's Meadow, properly enhazeled, where they smote, pierced, and poleaxed each other with gusto until the grass was covered with gore. At dinner time, all wounds closed up and the dead rose again as the *einherjar* sat down in merry fellowship to quaff and gorge themselves, waited on by Odin's Maidens. They appreciated their food and drink.

"Then said Gangleri: 'Thou sayest that all men who have fallen in battle have now come to Odin in Valhalla. What has he to give them to eat? It seems to me that there must now be a great multitude?' Har replied: 'Thou sayest true that there are very great hosts of men there; but there are never such hosts in Valhalla that there is not more than enough of the flesh of the boar called Saehrimnir. He is boiled every day, and every night he is whole again.'

"Then Gangleri said: 'What have the Einherjar to drink which may last as long as the food? Is water drunk there?' Har answered: 'Strangely dost thou ask; as if Allfather Odin would invite to him kings and jarls and other powerful men and give them water to drink; and, by my troth, many comers to Valhalla would think the drink of water dearly bought if no better cheer were to be had there, and they may have suffered pains and wounds unto death. The Goat Heidrun stands on the roof of Valhalla and from her teats flows a mead which fills a large vessel every day; the vessel is so large that all the Einherjar may get quite drunk out of it.' Gangleri said: 'That is an extremely useful goat for them.'"

It was dangerous to be a Norse king and even more dangerous to be a king's son. The sagas are full of tales in which kings and jarls sacrificed their own children. Jarl Hakon the Great, who died in 995, thinking that he was about to lose a battle against the Jomsvikings, prayed to his favorite goddess, Thorgerd Hordatroll, "but she was angry and would not listen." He offered horses and cattle, but she rejected them all. She scorned thralls and other human victims. Hakon increased his offers until she finally accepted his seven-year-old son Erling, a "handsome and promising boy," which the jarl gave to a slave to be put to death after "Hakon's usual manner." The saga does not tell how Hakon knew that the goddess would accept only his son or how he was sacrificed. Victims were hanged or drowned in bogs, thrown down hallowed springs or had their backs broken on sacred dome-shaped rocks. All prisoners of war were considered slaves suitable to be sacrificed.

The burial of great chieftains was often accompanied by the slaughter of wives, bedmates, or favorite thralls to administer to their needs in Valhalla. Grave gifts were sometimes "killed," that is damaged, holed, or, in the case of swords, bent double, as otherwise they would be of no use in Gladsheim. It was a grim world, but there was also a gentler side to life—hospitality, openhandedness, gift giving, the songs of bards, and poetry. There was also a lot of lovemaking. As the proverbs had it:

> A ship is made for sailing,
> A shield for sheltering,
> A sword for striking.
> A girl for bedding.

Many other sayings also dealt with this aspect of life: "In the same bed with that maiden, I feel like a king, even like Odin himself," or "take not another man's wife for your ear-whisperer," that is, mistress, and "Be wary always, but most wary when at ale with another man's wife." The life philosophy of the Norseman was summed up in this five-liner:

> Faith for faith,
> Gift for gift,
> Laughter for laughter,
> And blow for blow
> Should men return.

The story of late tenth-century Scandinavia can be summed up in the person of Olaf Trygvesson, first Christian ruler of Norway and last of the great sea kings. Olaf was born a typical pagan Viking, and after his conversion he wielded arms against the enemies of Christ as cruelly as he had against the enemies of Odin.

He was born the son of one Trygve, a minor Norwegian chieftain who was murdered by rivals at the time of Olaf's birth. His father's enemies were looking for the newborn, as it was not wise to let live the son of a man one had killed. His mother, Astrid, fled with the child to Sweden, but their pursuers followed them. Astrid had a brother named Eric at the court of King Waldimar at Gardariki (Vladimir at Novgorod) in the Land of Rus (Russia). She decided to seek his protection. Accompanied by only a few relatives, bondswomen, and little Olaf, Astrid in 971 persuaded a group of merchants to take them on their ship. As they sailed out on the Baltic, their longboat was captured by Esthonian Vikings, who enslaved all on board. Together with a foster brother, little Olaf became part of a certain Klerkon's share of the booty. Klerkon promptly sold Olaf to another party in exchange for a fat ram. A third man then bought Olaf by giving a warm cloak for him.

Olaf's true identity was accidentally discovered by Sigurd, a cousin, who was collecting taxes for Vladimir in Esthonia. He bought the then nine-year-old boy and took him to Novgorod. The ruling class in the Land of Rus was at the time made up entirely of Waringians, or Varyags, that is, Scandinavian Vikings. A few years later the teenage Olaf chanced upon Klerkon in the market place and promptly clove his erstwhile owner's skull down to the brain with a little ax he carried in his belt. This high-spirited deed brought him to the attention of Queen Ilgard (Olga), who liked the handsome boy and paid the murder fine for him.

When Olaf was eighteen years old he was already a captain of note in Vladimir's bodyguard and a veteran of many fights. But some ill-wishers told Vladimir, "We do not, indeed, know what it is Olaf can have to talk so often with the queen." The king grew jealous, probably with good reason, and Olaf, wisely, got himself a ship and a few men and abruptly left the Land of Rus, never to return.

Olaf then began his career as sea rover, plundering Wendland and the island of Bornholm. Because of his prowess and luck in raiding he attracted many Vikings and ships, also many women, both queens and slave girls. He married the daughter of the Slav king Burislav. Her name was Geyra, and "she liked Olaf exceedingly well." This was the first of his many marriages.

From 991 to 994 he ravaged Northumberland, Scotland, the Hebrides, the Orkneys, Wales, Ireland, and part of the French coast from the Seine to the Loire, spreading fear far and wide. In the Scilly Islands, Olaf met a soothsayer who foretold him things that came true. So impressed was Olaf that, when the man told him to embrace Christianity, he complied. Immediately, he became a fanatic promoter of the new faith, gathering souls by making all he met an offer they could not refuse: "Get yourself baptized and receive gifts, or get yourselves killed."

In England, Olaf chanced upon Gyda, daughter of the Viking ruler of Dublin. Olaf was wearing his rough, bad-weather clothes, and he was bespattered with mud. Gyda asked him what kind of man he was. He answered, "I am just Ole, a stranger."

Gyda said, "Wilt thou have me for a wife if I choose thee?"

"I will not say no to that," he answered. She was young, good-looking, and they were married. They lived for some time together in Ireland with her father, King Olaf Kvaran. At that time Jarl Hakon, the slayer of Olaf's father, was all-powerful in Norway. Olaf thought the time was ripe to avenge his father and to make himself king of Norway. His Dublin father-in-law helped him to man five dragon ships, and Olaf set sail for the land of his birth. He was in luck because the *bondi*, Norway's freeholders, had risen against Hakon and had put the jarl to flight. The country was up for grabs. Olaf went before the rebels and, standing on a rock beside a reeking pigsty, offered himself as their king and was accepted. He also promised to make rich anybody who would bring him Hakon's head. It so happened that Hakon and a slave were hiding in a root cellar within earshot. When Hakon fell asleep the thrall cut his throat, chopped off his head, and brought it to Olaf. The new, self-made king gave a golden armlet to the killer as a reward and then had him hanged for his faithlessness.

Olaf went up and down Norway, smashing idols, robbing and burning temples, baptizing his people with fire and sword. "Those who opposed him he punished severely, killing some, mutilating others, and driving some into banishment." Olaf cut down the image of Frey, the Norse god of sun and rain, fruitfulness and peace, and patron of marriage. First he said, "'Now I will try, Frey, if thou canst talk and answer me." Frey was silent. 'If thou,' said the king, 'canst not or wilt not, then may the one who is in thee, and has long strengthened thee, answer me.' Frey was silent. The king said: 'Still I speak to thee, Frey; if thou canst give to men strength and power, then spare it not, and do what you are able to do, and if thou sleepest, awake and defend thee, for now I will attack thee.' He raised his axe and cut off Frey's hand, but he did not move. Then he struck blow after blow until he had cut asunder the whole idol."

Olaf vowed to bring all the Northland under the cross or die. To those who resisted he showed no mercy. A certain stubborn and proud man called Raud refused to be baptized, though the king offered him friendship and continued ownership of property if he submitted. When Raud refused to accept the "faith of cowards, women, and thralls," the enraged king swore that the man should die the worst of all deaths. He had Raud spread-eagled, face up, prying his mouth open with a piece of wood, trying to force a poisonous adder head-first down his throat. But Raud breathed on it and the snake recoiled. Olaf then put the adder into a funnel made of horn and, putting a fire to it, drove the snake down Raud's gullet so that he died. He then slaughtered or tortured to death all of Raud's men.

A certain man named Iron Beard refused to be baptized and Olaf had him beheaded. Oddly enough, he then proceeded to marry Iron Beard's daughter Gudrun. "When the wedding day came King Olaf and Gudrun went to bed together. The first night they lay together, as soon as Gudrun thought the king was asleep, she drew a knife with which she intended to cut his throat; but the king saw it, took the knife from her, got out of bed, and went to his men and told them what had happened. Gudrun also took her clothes and went away with all her men. Gudrun never came to the king's bed again."

In 998, Olaf proposed marriage to Sigrid the Haughty, daughter of the Swedish king. When he insisted that, first of all, she must accept Christianity, Sigrid told him, "I will not part from the faith which my forefathers have kept before me. You may believe in whatever pleases you." Olaf boxed her ears and called her a faded heathen whore. Without changing her expression Sigrid said calmly, "This may some day be thy death," and from that moment she worked with her father to create a coalition to bring about Olaf's downfall.

In 999, Olaf married for the last time. King Svein Forkbeard of Denmark had promised his sister, Thyre, to King Burislav of Wendland, Olaf's erstwhile father-in-law, but the high-spirited young woman refused to marry the aged heathen and ran away to Norway where Olaf, seeing that she was beautiful, married her.

In Rome, Gerbert, now Pope Sylvester, kept abreast of developments in Scandinavia and sent a letter to Olaf to replace the runic with the Latin alphabet if he wanted his country to be recognized as a Christian nation. Olaf, who obeyed no man, obeyed Gerbert.

Olaf was hated for his high-handedness by Christians and pagans alike. He had despoiled so many kings and jarls that he was called King Subduer. Sigrid the Haughty had meanwhile married Svein Forkbeard of Denmark and, remembering Olaf's fist in her face, kept after her husband to get together a great force against Olaf Trygvesson. The alliance thus formed consisted of Svein Forkbeard of Denmark, Skautkonung of Sweden, and Jarl Sigvald Stallari, Olaf's Master of the Horse and pretended friend. But the most formidable among the members of the alliance was a Norwegian exile, Jarl Eirik, eager to avenge the death of his father Hakon. On September 9, 1000, the allies trapped Olaf's fleet at Svolder, near the Baltic island of Rügen. Before battle was joined Sigvald Stallari went over to the enemy with the bulk of Olaf's fleet, leaving the king with only eleven long ships. But Olaf's own dragon, the famous *Long Serpent*, was the biggest Viking ship ever; it was 180 feet long, 32 feet wide, with 34 rowing benches—and Olaf stood on the *lypting* (quarterdeck) for all to see.

His chiefs pointed out to him that he faced overwhelming odds and advised him to row as fast as possible while there was still a chance to avoid battle. The king shouted that he had never yet run from a fight. He ordered the war horns to be blown, the sails lowered, and the ships tied together as was the custom in defending a fleet so that his dragons could support each other as the need arose. The *Long Serpent* (*Long-Orm*) was so long that its stem stuck out some ten yards from among his other ships.

Ulf the Red, the king's standard bearer and stem defender, said, "If the Serpent shall be put as much forward as it is larger and longer than other ships, the men in the bow will have a hard time of it." The king answered, "I had the Serpent made longer than all other ships, so that it should be put forward in battle and be well known, but I did not know that I had a stem defender who was both red and faint-hearted."

Ulf replied, "Turn thou, king, no more back in defending the lypting than I will in defending the stem."

The king had a bow in his hand and laid an arrow on the string and aimed at Ulf. Then Ulf said, "Do not shoot me, my lord, but rather where it is more needed, that is at our foes, for what I win I win for thee. Maybe you will think your men not over many, before the evening comes." The king took off the arrow and did not shoot.

Svein Forkbeard with the Dana host attacked first and was beaten off without too much trouble. Then Skaut-konung came up with the Svia fleet. Olaf said that these heathen Swedes would soon wish themselves at home, licking their sacrificial bowls, and that these horse eaters would cause little trouble. And they too were forced to retire. Then Olaf asked what kind of men were rowing up on the left and was told that it was Jarl Eirik with his Norwegians. Then Olaf grew thoughtful, saying these were high-hearted folk with a just cause against him.

Jarl Eirik had been busy. His flagship, *Ironsides* (*Jarn-Bardi*), had iron beaks on both stem and stern and was iron plated along its whole length down to the water. Eirik had worked his way into the mass of Olaf's ships, concentrating on one at a time, methodically cutting it loose from its fastenings as soon as he had cleared it. Olaf's men began to jump from the smaller ships to defend the bigger ones, but always Eirik managed to reinforce his *Ironsides* faster with more men, drawing for support also on the Danish and Swedish crews, saving his best men for the *Long Serpent*. At last, all of Olaf's ships had been cleared, and all of his men still able to fight had come aboard the *Long Serpent*. Jarl Eirik laid his ship alongside the *Long Serpent*, and a fierce hand-to-hand struggle erupted.

Olaf stood out from among his men in his gold helmet, gilded armor, and scarlet cloak. "The king stood on the *lypting* of the *Long Serpent*, and chiefly used during the day his bow and javelins; and always two javelins at a time. It was agreed by all, both friends and foes, that they had known no man fight more valiantly than King Olaf. . . . The king showed the bravery of his mind and the pride of his heart, so that all men might see that he shunned no danger."

Olaf noticed that his men's swords no longer cut through their enemies armor, and he shouted to them, "Why do you swing your swords so slowly? Do they no longer bite?" They told him that their weapons had become blunt and their arms tired. The king opened his weapon chest and took from it many swords, both bright and sharp, distributing them among his warriors who fought on with redoubled fury.

Eirik ordered his men to throw heavy timbers on board the Serpent so that it would lean over, lose its advantage of height, and be easier to board. The jarl spared neither himself nor his men and soon was aboard the *Long Serpent*.

When Olaf saw that Eirik was on the *Long Serpent* he hurled three throwing spears at him, but they all missed. Olaf said, "Never before did I thus miss a man. Great is the jarl's luck. I think he has substituted the image of Christ for the image of Thor as his stem dweller."

Then a brave Viking, Thorstein, fighting near the king, said, "Lord, each man must now do what he can." "Why not?" answered Olaf. Then Thorstein seized a huge sail-yard and with it laid about him killing many enemies. Soon the king's shield was so thickly covered with arrows that he could hardly lift it. All the great sea fighters aboard the *Long Serpent* had fallen. The end had come. The king jumped overboard. The jarl's men surrounded the *Long Serpent* with many small boats and they tried to take the king alive, but Olaf Trygvesson threw his shield over his head and sank beneath the waters.

So ended the last epic Viking battle, and when it was over even the victors accepted the Christian faith. The Icelanders and the folk in far distant Greenland had also taken up the cross. Christ instead of Thor now dwelled in all the ships' stems. The old gods were dead and the bards sang sad songs, being no longer allowed to praise the once mighty Aesir:

Sacrifices are forbidden now
And we must shun them,
Throwing old gods to the wind,
And pray to Christ.
Once I made songs
to win Odin's love,
And I remember them well,
Those rhymes of old.
Now I must serve Christ
And must hate and deride,
Against my will,
Odin, whose power I liked well.
Frey and the strong Thor
Now are angry with me,
As I call on Christ
Whose anger I fear.

CHAPTER SEVENTEEN

A People Called Rus

TO THE EAST OF THE VIKINGS stretched a vast empty land of seemingly endless plains and steppes, monotonously flat, windswept, and divided by mighty rivers. Five months out of twelve it was covered with snow, in the grip of icy, bone-chilling frosts that made trees crack apart with the sound of thunderclaps. For another three months it was an ocean of mud, while the rest of the time it was dry, dusty, and hot.

This was the land of the Rus. They came from a country of ruddy, red-bearded, ax-swinging, bloody-handed men and therefore were given their name meaning Reds, though some say it came from *Rothmen*, that is, seafarers, or from *Ruotsi*, Finnish for Rowing Folk, or even from the River Russ, a tributary of the Dnieper. Liutprand, who had met them, wrote that these *Rusios* were the same as the *Nordmannos*—Vikings.

They had come from Sweden and Norway to lord it over the great mass of Slavs who inhabited the land and outnumbered them—slowmoving, towheaded folk of whom nothing is known except what some Arabic and Byzantine travelers have written about them, namely that they were "tall as palm trees," deep-chested, rosy-cheeked, and handsome in a barbaric way. These Slavs were good-natured and hospitable, fond of music and poetry. They were fierce and cruel in war, but not treacherous. On the attack they were clumsy but in defense stubborn and unyielding. At one time, during the ninth century, they managed to expel their Nordic masters but then fell into such disorder that they asked the Rus to come back to rule over them again.

A Greek who came to know the Slavs wrote that "fear and presents were the way to deal with them," adding that treaties meant nothing to them, particularly as they could not read them. They got drunk often because "these people rejoice in drinking and cannot do without it." Their settlements were made up of huts of one extended family descended from a common father. Out of these grew the town, *gorod*, a jumble of wooden shacks surrounded by a wooden palisade.

The Slavs lived by hunting, trapping, fishing, and beekeeping, developing agriculture only late in the tenth century. They loved to trade, though money did not exist among them. Instead they used the pelts of sable and marten in lieu of cash. Instead of small change they used the snouts and tails of animals. Their main articles of export were furs, beeswax, linen, and, above all, those pale-skinned, ample-bosomed, and pink-nippled maidens so avidly sought by wealthy Greeks and Saracens. Slaves, traded for or captured at birth, were considered the best of merchandise because they could walk themselves to market.

They liked to swap them for Byzantine silk, enameled jewelry, and beads. One Greek trader wrote of the enormous profits he made by exchanging a single green glass bead for a valuable pelt. Slav traders sold their wares at the great fairs at Kiev and Novgorod, leaving the long and dangerous journey by boat down the great rivers to the Black Sea and thence to Constantinople to the more experienced Scandinavians, though some of them also dealt directly with the Byzantines and Arabs.

The chief deity of the Slavs was Perun, God of Thunder, depicted with an eagle hovering over his head. Other gods were Dazhdbog, Lord of the Sun, and Volos, God of Cattle. Some of the lesser gods were thought to be merely emanations of Perun. Great rituals were performed in honor of the sun and rain gods, the creative and regenerative powers. On the day of the summer solstice men and women, wearing wreaths of leaves and flowers, frolicked around huge fires. On this day humans were supposed to understand the language of animals. The night was propitious for lovemaking, as life was being renewed. The Slavs also believed in nymphs and wood sprites, called *vilas*, who lived in springs and lakes. They had great respect for seers who could predict the future. Life after death was conceived as merely a prolongation of life on earth, but much better. Of the finer things in life, in the opinion of both Greeks and Arabs, they knew nothing.

A certain Fadhlan, or Ahmed ibn Fazlan, who lived in the ninth century during the reign of the Caliph Muqtadir, as whose ambassador he traveled to the king of the Slavs, wrote down a description of the Rus. At the end of the ninth century, the word *Rus* was used by foreign travelers to describe both Scandinavians and Slavs. Ibn Fazlan used it mainly when he spoke of Slavs: "Of all the people Allah created, they are the filthiest. They neither clean themselves after answering a call of nature, nor after having polluted themselves during the night with coitus, just as if they were wild-running asses rather than human beings.

"They come from a distant land down the Itil [Volga], which is a big river, and anchor their ships on the river bank. On the heights above they build large wooden dwellings. In such a house ten or twenty of them live together. Every one of them has a long bench and on it he whiles away the time with his girls and little beauties which he wants to trade. Upon such a bench he takes his pleasure with one of these women while his friend watches. Verily, at times, any number of them are busily at it in the presence of each other. It often happens that a trader walks into the house to buy a girl which is just then pleasured by one of these Rus, and he goes on with what he is doing until he has satisfied his lust and then, straight out of his arms, sells her to the merchant.

"Every day they wash themselves a little—hair, face and hands only—with the filthiest, dirtiest water they can find. Each morning one of these girls comes to such a fellow with a big bowl of water and sets it before him. He washes his face, combs his hair into the bowl, spits out his phlegm, and blows snot from his nostrils into it. As soon as he is done, the girl carries the same bowl with the same water to the one next in line, and so she goes along from one to the other.

"As soon as their ships reach the main anchorage, every one of these fellows goes on land, well-provided with bread, meat, onions, milk, and intoxicating drinks. He walks over to a huge pole the top of which is carved in the likeness of a human face. This big image is surrounded by a number of smaller idols. He walks up to the big one, bows down and addresses it:

"'O, my Lord! I have come from a far country and have so and so many girls with me, and so and so many sable or marten pelts.' And he goes on listing all the merchandise he carries. He continues: 'I have brought thee, my Lord, a gift,' and he lays his presents at the foot of the pole and says: 'I want thee to send me a buyer with many coins of gold and silver, who takes all my goods without haggling.' Then he walks away. If business is bad, and he has to tarry longer than he wants, he goes back, bringing more presents to the big pole, and if this doesn't help, he gives presents to the smaller idols, saying: 'These are my Lord's sons and daughters whom I ask to come to my aid.'

"But if business is good and he sells all his merchandise at a great profit, he says: 'My Lord has fulfilled all that I asked for, it is my duty to repay him.' He then takes a number of oxen and sheep, slaughters them, gives some of the meat to the poor, hanging the head and some meat of the oxen around the neck of the big pole, and the head of the sheep and some mutton meat on the smaller ones. During the night come the dogs and eat it all. Then the fellow says happily: 'My Lord loves me. He has consumed my gifts.'

"They keep a good watch on their stuff. If they catch a thief, they lead him to a tall, thick tree, put a sturdy rope around his neck and hang him from the stoutest branch, leaving him dangling there until wind and rain have done their business. They burn up their dead, but in the case of a slave, they just leave him to the dogs and the crows.

"When a great chief dies they divide his riches into three parts. The first is for his family, the second to pay for his rich funeral clothes, and the third to buy a great quantity of an intoxicating drink called nabis. Before the funeral they abandon themselves to the guzzling of wine [*chamr*] to the point of madness, keeping on quaffing day and night. Often one of them dies of overindulgence with the drinking cup still in his hand.

"Now, if all is ready to burn the dead man, his kinfolk ask of his followers and women: 'Who among you wants to die with him?' They do not have to volunteer, but if one of them says 'yes,' he or she cannot go back on their word. Usually it is his favorite woman who assents. It is expected of her. They adorn her and wash her hands and feet during the days before the funeral; and she is merry and smiles and sings and even cohabits with one of the dead man's chief warriors.

"I watched such a funeral. They had drawn the deceased lord's biggest ship on shore and put on board his long bench [*serir*] covering it with Greek gold brocade [*didbadsh*]. Then appeared an old hag whom they called 'The Angel of Death.' It is she who will kill the girl who agreed to die with her master, and truly she did not look like an angel but like the devil. They put into the ship also much intoxicating drink and his harp, fruit, basil, meat, and onions. They took his favorite dog, cut him in two, and threw the parts into the ship. They also killed two horses and two oxen, cut them to pieces and threw these also into the ship.

"They had made a thing looking like a gate with protruding eaves. To this they led the girl and lifted her up three times. The third time they handed her a hen and she cut its head off and threw it away. The rest of the bird they also threw into the ship. The first time they lifted her up, she said: 'Behold, I see my father and mother'; the second time: 'Behold, I see all my dead kinfolk;' and the third time: 'Behold, I see my master awaiting me. He is calling me.'

"Then they led her to the ship. She took off her two armlets, giving them to the death-angel who was about to murder her. She took off her ankle rings and gave them to the two maidservants of the old hag. Then came the men with shields and sticks handing her a cup of numbing drink. She took it, sang, and emptied it, taking leave of life.

They gave her another, larger bowl to drink. She took it, intoning a lengthy song. The old she-devil told her to hurry up and go where her master was lying dead, but the girl hesitated. Quick as lightning, the old hag grabbed the girl by the hair, dragging her to the corpse. At once, all the men began to beat their shields with the sticks, making a loud noise so that one should not hear the screams of the girl which might discourage others to follow her example.

"The old woman quickly put a rope around the girl's neck, handing the ends to two men who began pulling with all their might. At the same time the death-angel plunged her broad-bladed knife between the girl's ribs. And so she died.

"Then the nearest relative of the dead chief came, stark naked, with a burning torch in one hand, the other between his buttocks, and he hurled the brand on the funeral pyre. Then came the rest of the kinfolk and also set fire to the wood, and soon the ship, the chief, the girl, and all the grave goods were burning. Next to me stood one of the Rus, saying: 'You Arabs are foolish people. You take him who is the most beloved and respected and bury him in the earth to feed the worms. But we burn him up so that, in the twinkling of an eye, he ascends to paradise.' Then he burst into laughter, telling me: 'You see how our gods love us, making such a big wind so that all is rendered into ashes in no time at all.'" It seems a good description of a Viking funeral.

Another Arab traveler said of the Norsemen, "If a son is born to one of them, he puts a sword beside the infant, exclaiming: 'That belongs to you what you can seize with your sword.' If their king has to judge between two men and cannot decide the case, he tells them: 'Judge between yourselves with the swords,' and he who has the sharpest weapon wins."

Wherever the Rus settled they established their own laws, similar to those of the Vikings. If a man knocked out the front teeth of a free man, he was punished by a fine equal to that imposed for stealing a dog or killing a slave. Manslaughter and physical injury could be atoned for by a payment of *viry* (*wergild*). Debtors could be sold as slaves. A man could kill his own slave without paying a fine, provided he reported the deed. Women had property rights, could inherit, and could bequeath.

The first Rus apparently arrived in the interior of Russia as early as the eighth century, and the settling of the Swedes in Kiev, around the year 850, is looked upon as the beginning of Russian history. The first of these Nordic invaders we know of was a man called Rurik (Hrörekr), said to have been invited to rule over some Slav folk dwelling near the Baltic, as they "had some trouble governing themselves." Rurik arrived with two brothers and a band of sturdy followers, carrying long shields slung over their shoulders. They had already made a name for themselves throughout Europe as brawlers and plunderers. Starting out from Sweden, they had sailed across the Gulf of Finland and rowed their boats up the Neva River until they came to a big lake near which they founded a city called Ladoga. They went on to conquer Novgorod (Nye Gard), the chief trading center of the northern Slavs. Here they settled down for a while.

What these Rus had in their minds from the beginning was to control the overland route to Constantinople, golden Miklågard, where all the riches of the world could be gotten by guile, swapping, or, a most pleasant thought, by storm. It was a watery road down the great rivers to the Black Sea or the Caspian, made to order for these rowing men. The Rus loved the rivers and their ships even more, referring to them poetically as "reindeer of breezes" or "snakes of winding waters."

Rurik sent two of his chieftains, Askold and Dir (Höskulder and D″ril) to reconnoiter in the direction of Byzantium. On the way they conquered the Slav's biggest town, Kiev, by treachery and surprise. They eventually reached Constantinople and attempted to storm it, entering the Bosporus with some two hundred boats, but they were repulsed, it is said, with the help of the Sacred Robe of the Virgin, carried by the patriarch at the head of the city's defenders. On their way back these Rus were set upon by a Slavic tribe, the much-feared Pechenegs. According to their custom, when facing overwhelming odds, Askold's men formed a circle, warriors in their ring-mailed *brynyas* behind their huge, interlocking shields making a living fortress around the women and merchandise in the center. This was their famous *skjald borg* or shield burg, and it stopped the attackers.

Most of the time these northerners came to Constantinople in peace, welcomed for the goods they brought in trade. They were fed and housed at public expense and entitled to visit the steam baths free of charge because the Greeks thought that they were in great need of them. They could enter the city only by way of the Golden Gate, without arms, as the Greeks never quite trusted these warlike strangers. On the other hand, they trusted their own subjects even less and therefore established for their own protection the famous Varangian Guard, made up mostly by Norsemen from Russia, but also by Danes, Norwegians, and Anglo-Saxons. Armed with battle-axes, these formidable fighters were lavishly paid to ensure their loyalty.

Rurik died in 879. As his son, Igor (Ingvar), was a mere infant, a kinsman named Oleg (Helge) ruled in his name. This Oleg was bold and crafty, planning to extend his sway over the various independent Rus chiefs. His own city, Novgorod, did not satisfy him. His imagination had been fired by tales of the beauty of Kiev and the glory of Byzantium. Kiev, however, was in the hands of Askold and Dir. These two chiefs had been ruling harmoniously together. They had made treaties as equals with the Byzantine emperor. Arabs called them "chiefs among Slav kings and rulers over great cities full of people."

Oleg set out for Kiev with his *druzhina*, his bodyguards, taking the boy Igor with him. He anchored his ship on the Dnieper River below Kiev. The town rose above him on a high bank, and the longer Oleg looked at it, the less he liked the idea of having to take it by storm. Crafty and deceitful, he sent some of his men up into the city, telling everybody that rich merchants had arrived on their way to Constantinople, their ship full of fabulous goods, asking Askold and Dir to come down and see for themselves. The two jarls were enticed to come on board where Oleg, hoisting little Igor on his shield, called out to them, "This is your lord, Igor Rurikson, whom you have neglected in your pride!" Before they knew what was happening, the two men were cut down with ax and sword. Thus Kiev was taken without a fight.

Oleg lost no time shifting his residence from Novgorod to Kiev, consolidating his swiftly expanding realm. The capture of Kiev in no way satisfied him, and in 907 he set out to conquer Constantinople. On the way, according to a saga, Oleg met a soothsayer who foretold that he would reign long and victoriously, but that the fine horse he was riding would be the cause of his death. Oleg promptly gave the horse away, took another, and rode on. When he arrived before the walls of great Miklågard he found that the Greeks had strung heavy chains across the Bosporus to prevent his ships from entering the straits. Undaunted, so the legend has it, Oleg had his boats dragged ashore, had wheels put beneath them, and, under full sail, drove into battle. Oleg also waged psychological warfare by flying huge kites with monstrous faces to terrify his enemies. The Byzantines, for their part, used their secret weapon, the Greek Fire, an early forerunner of napalm.

It is doubtful whether Oleg ever thought himself strong enough to take the city. It is far more likely that he used his men and ships as bargaining chips to get what he wanted—a favorable trade agreement. The Greeks were happy to buy him off. A treaty, satisfactory to both parties, was quickly concluded, and Oleg went home laden with rich gifts and a great quantity of sweet wine. In 911, Oleg sent an embassy of fourteen men to Constantinople to ratify the treaty. Their names have been preserved, all Norse, with not a single Slav name among them—Injald, Farulf, Gunnar, Frithleif, Angantyr, Throand, Leithulf, Hrolf, Vermund, Harald, Karm, Karl, Fast, and Steinvith—proving that at that time the Russian upper class was still entirely composed of Scandinavians.

Years later, the tale goes, it occurred to Oleg to inquire what had become of the horse that had been prophesied would be cause of his death. He was told that it had long been dead and buried. One man offered to show him where. Wind and rain had laid bare the animal's skeleton, and Oleg addressed the skull: "There you are, dead and gone, while I am alive and well." Idly he stirred up the scattered bones with his foot, and out of one of the skull's eye sockets crept a poisonous adder that stung him in the ankle, and so he died. One suspects that it was a human snake that laid him low. This happened in 912, and "the people wept with a great weeping."

Oleg was succeeded by Igor who, in the meantime, had married Olga (Helga), a shrewd and strong-willed princess from Pskov. After making two fruitless raids upon Byzantium, Igor busied himself with raising tribute from various Slav tribes, a process that usually degenerated into plain and simple looting. "In this year, 945, Igor's men said to him: 'the men of Dereva are adorned with weapons and fine raiments, but we are naked. Go forth with us, Oh prince, after tribute, that both you and we may enrich ourselves thereby.' Igor sacked Dereva and collected much 'tribute.'" Not satisfied, he marched upon Korosten, the chief settlement of the Drevlyans. Led by their chief, Malu, they ambushed the Rus party and took Igor prisoner. They tied his hands and feet to the inward bent tops of two tall trees and then let them snap back so that Igor was torn asunder. Out of the prince's skull Malu made his drinking cup, on which were engraved the words: "You came to take what was another's, and did lose what was yours."

Igor was survived by his son Svyatoslav, whose original name had been Svend. He was the first Rus prince to adopt a Slavic name. As he was still a child, his mother Olga ruled in his stead from 945 until 955. According to the saga, the Drevlyans, fearing that she would seek revenge for Igor's death, sent word to her that the trouble between their tribe and the Rus could be settled by Olga's marriage to Malu, her husband's slayer. Olga pretended to be flattered. A large Drevlyan embassy arrived. Olga had a big ditch dug, covered with branches and leaves, and the Drevlyans were enticed to tumble down into it to their deaths. Olga sent a message to Korosten: "Send more envoys, for the people of Kiev will not let me go." The Drevlyans promptly sent many of their most eminent men. Olga lured them into a huge sauna, "to purify them for a great feast," and then scalded them with hot steam until they died. A third embassy was invited into the great feasting hall, plied with drinks until they became senseless, and then killed with ease. Olga then burned Korosten to the ground, revenging herself in great style.

In 955, Olga made her celebrated journey to Byzantium accompanied by a great retinue. She was received with great pomp and admitted into the presence of Emperor Leo, the Philosopher. At a state dinner Olga was given a large, gem-encrusted bowl filled to the brim with gold bezants, while her ladies received gifts of precious perfumes. During this visit Olga had herself instructed in the Christian faith by the patriarch himself, "absorbing his teachings like a sponge." Upon becoming a Christian she adopted the name of Helena and, eventually, was made a saint. She tried to convert her son Svyatoslav, but he rejected the new faith, saying that his men would laugh at him if he accepted a religion fit only for women and cowards. Olga died shortly after her visit to Constantinople at the age of seventy, eulogized as the Morning Star Before Sunrise and the Dawn Before Daylight.

Olga was succeeded by her son Svyatoslav, who reigned from 958 to 973 and was the first to admit Slavs into his bodyguard. Following tradition, Svyatoslav led sixty thousand men into the Byzantine provinces, entered Thrace, stormed Philoppopolis, massacred some twenty thousand of the country's inhabitants, and marched upon Constantinople. He met his match in Emperor Tsimisces, a thoroughly bad man but most able commander. John Tsimisces attacked the Rus prince, cutting off his communications with the help of a large fleet of two hundred ships. Tsimisces quickly won a number of battles. The Rus were still relying on their long shields and battle axes, ineffective against Little Slippers's heavily armored cavalry and mounted archers. After inflicting heavy losses upon each other the opponents, sensibly, ended hostilities in the traditional way—by concluding a commercial treaty. To be rid of him the emperor even provided Svyatoslav with money and provisions for his return journey, but on the way, in 972, Svyatoslav found his road blocked by a huge army of Pechenegs and was killed fighting, his skull winding up as the Pecheneg chief's drinking cup.

For a future saint, Svyatoslav's successor, Vladimir, nicknamed the Fair Sun, had a decidedly inauspicious early life. Though he was born the youngest son of Svyatoslav and one of his wife's maidservants, Vladimir's father treated him in no way different from his legitimate sons, giving him Novgorod as his fief and putting him under the guardianship of an uncle named Dobrinya. At the death of Svyatoslav, his oldest son, Yaropolk, was a mere stripling and ward of the strongman Sveneld, who stirred him up to take his brother Oleg's town and land. After Oleg had been disposed of, Yaropolk marched upon Novgorod and forced Vladimir and uncle Dobrinya to flee for their lives to Sweden. For the next seven years, Yaropolk held undisputed sway over the land of Rus, but then Vladimir returned with long ships full of hardy Vikings who had joined him upon the promise of rich rewards. The people of Novgorod rallied to him, and soon it was Yaropolk's turn to flee, while Vladimir marched upon Kiev.

On the way he stopped at Polotsk, sueing for the hand of Rogneda (Ragnhild), daughter of Prince Rogvolod (Ragnwald), already promised to Yaropolk. The haughty girl refused him indignantly, saying, "Never will I unloose the shoe-clasps of a bond-slave's son." Enraged, Vladimir stormed Polotsk, slew Ragnwald and his brothers, and took Ragnhild by force. Then he sent word to Yaropolk: "I am coming, beware!" Soon Vladimir stood before the walls of Kiev. Seeing which way the wind was blowing, one Blud, advisor to Yaropolk, betrayed his master into the hands of Vladimir, who had him killed. One of the first things Vladimir did was to take for himself his half-brother's young widow, a lovely Greek woman whom his father had brought back from one of his raids.

Vladimir's life was exceedingly barbaric. At his succession he was a zealous heathen, savagely suppressing Christians, Jews, and Muslims, sizable numbers of whom lived in Kiev. He put in front of his wooden Kreml the image of Svarog, the Father of Gods; Dazhd-Bog, Master of the Sun; Stribog, the Wind God; and, or course, Perun-Thor, the God of Thunder, with a head of silver and huge, golden mustaches. He celebrated his victories with human sacrifices, nearly one thousand in all. Sometimes he chose a youth or maiden by lot to be hanged in a sacred grove to propitiate Perun, who needed human victims for his food. On one such occasion the lot fell upon the son of a Christian Varangian, "beautiful in soul and body." His father refused to give him up, berating Vladimir: "You say 'the gods want your son'; well, these are no gods but just pieces of wood who do not speak, eat, or drink and who will rot away." The enraged crowd fell upon father and son, slaying them on the spot, and they became Russia's first Christian martyrs: St. Theodore and St. Ivan.

Vladimir was a human satyr with superhuman sexual appetites. To his wives, Ragnhild and his brother's widow, he swiftly added two more, one Bulgarian and one Bohemian. These he might have wedded for reasons of foreign policy, but a monk-chronicler reported that he was "overcome with lust for women, had seven great wives and kept eight hundred concubines or lesser wives—three hundred at Vyshgorod, three hundred at Belgorod, and two hundred at Berestovo." Even in distant Saxony, Thietmar of Merseburg had heard similar stories and recorded them in his chronicles.

Besides women, his other great passions were hunting, hawking, feasting, and drinking, but he was a strong, robust man who, in spite of his less laudable activities, had more than enough energy left to administer his country with a firm hand and embark on victorious wars of conquest. He captured Wolhynia, Galicia, northern Lithuania, and a large stretch of the Baltic coast, he retook Russian land from the Poles and extended his rule all the way down to the Carpathians.

As the Twilight of the Gods approached near the end of the tenth century, Vladimir too, like the kings of Denmark, Norway, Sweden, Poland, and Hungary, accepted the Christian faith. Before making his decision, however, Vladimir made a survey of available religions. According to the saga, he sent out envoys to sample a number of different beliefs or invite priests of various persuasions to come to him at Kiev. The Bulgarians were quickly disposed of as being stinking, filthy people whose gods were the same way.

Muslim mullas traveled to Kiev. Their leader exhorted Vladimir, "Prince, you are wise and powerful, but you have no religion. Take ours. Pray to Allah."

Vladimir asked them, "What is your faith?"

They told him, "We believe in one God, and our prophet, Muhammad, taught us not to eat pork, nor drink, but after death be happy with women. In our paradise seventy beautiful women will be given to you."

Vladimir liked the part about the women but not the one about abstinence. He roared, "Drink is the delight of the Rus and we cannot live without it. Go away!"

Then came some Nyemetsi (Germans). They said, "We have been sent by the pope in Rome. We adore our Savior, Jesus Christ, but your gods are made of wood."

Vladimir inquired, "What are your commandments?"

"To fast according to one's strength, to mortify the flesh, to foreswear fornication, and to eat and drink moderately to the glory of God only."

"Begone," cried Vladimir, "Begone! Our ancestors taught us no such thing."

Then arrived some Khazar Jews, who said to Vladimir, "We believe only in the God of Abraham, Isaac, and Jacob."

"And what are your observances?" Vladimir asked them.

"Circumcision, abstaining from the flesh of swine and hare, celebrating the Sabbath."

"And where does your God dwell?"

"He used to dwell in his temple at Jerusalem before the Romans destroyed it and we Jews were driven out of Palestine."

"Begone!" Vladimir told them also, "Begone! How can you teach others when your God and yourselves have been driven from your home?"

But at last came the Byzantines, who showed to Vladimir a painting of the Last Judgment, depicting on the right hand the righteous ascending to heaven and eternal bliss, and on the left the damned souls being swallowed up by hell. Vladimir was impressed and exclaimed, "How happy are those on the right, but woe to those on the left!" Then he sent ambassadors to Constantinople to learn more of the Greek faith.

The ambassadors were led into the basilica of St. Sophia to witness a solemn service amid clouds of sweet incense and even sweeter songs. The ambassadors returned to Kiev and reported to the prince, "We were taken to the place where the Greeks worship their God, and we almost thought we were already in heaven, for nowhere on earth have we beheld such beauty, and we have no words to describe it."

On the spot Vladimir decided to accept Greek Christianity, particularly as he was about to be wedded to Anna, the Greek emperor's sister. But before he could marry her, he had to get rid of his other wives. Predslava, the Varingian, he sent to Novgorod. Ragnhild of Polotsk, renamed Glorislava, he sent to a newly founded nunnery. The Bohemian, Malfreda, simply died of grief at the prospect of parting. This left his most recent wives: Adela, a Czech, and Milolika, a Bulgarian, besides his eight hundred concubines in various places. These he gave in marriage to his chiefs, *boyars*, and favorite warriors.

Vladimir was duly baptized, celebrating his nuptials with Anna at Kherson in 989.

Back in Kiev, Vladimir summoned all the people to be baptized. The great image of Perun with its golden mustaches was pulled down, tied to a horse's tail, and dragged down the hill while the crowd beat it with sticks. Finally, it was thrown into the river. "Then the people entered the river to be baptized—some joyfully and some out of fear." Many took to the woods in order to escape having the new religion forced upon them.

In Novgorod, the people rose in arms against Dobrinya, who once had sacrificed Christians to pagan idols and who now was just as ready to kill pagans in the name of the Savior. His attempts to impose the new religion by force led to riots, resulting in many deaths and the burning down of a good part of Novgorod. Here, too, the statue of

Peron was dragged to the river and beaten, while the idol, so some said, cried pitifully, "Woe is me! They are smiting me without mercy!" But after hurling Peron into the stream, the people watched in horror as Perun swam back to the shore and tried to climb up the river bank. Then the people pelted the idol with stones and pushed it back into the water, crying, "Peron, you have been given more than your share of food and drink and blood. Swim away and bother us no more!"

For a long time to come, paganism and even human sacrifices persisted in the more remote areas, while Christianity, in order to make it palatable, was served up mixed with heathen rites. Vladimir built his Byzantine-style cathedral, which became known as the Church of the Tenth because he assigned to its support one-tenth of all his revenues, whether in furs, corn, wax, or honey.

It was said that after his conversion Vladimir became an exemplary ruler, gentle where before he had been cruel, chaste and decorous instead of insatiably lecherous. He was so full of the milk of human kindness that he did not even want to punish robbers and murderers with death. It was up to his bishops to admonish him that even for the most saintly Christian rulers it was often necessary to cut off diseased limbs lest the whole body of the people sicken and die. After Vladimir's death, the country's Norse element was quickly swallowed up by the non-Scandinavian majority. Nordic speech and custom disappeared as Varangians and Slavs intermingled, no longer Rus but Russians. Holy Mother Russia was born.

CHAPTER EIGHTEEN

A Zest for Martyrdom

IT MUST HAVE GALLED GERBERT to see Russia fall under the domination of the Greek instead of the Roman church, but he could console himself with the Western Slavs receiving the Gospels from the pope in Rome instead of the patriarch of Constantinople.

Christianizing the Slavic tribes between the Elbe and the Bug rivers—the Wends, Sorbs, Obotrites, Kashubes, Havellers, Prussians, Poles, and Bohemians—took considerably longer than converting the Magyars and distant Russians. Throughout Gerbert's lifetime, war raged between Christian Germans and heathen Slavs, and many churches and cloisters went up in flames. Many Christians were martyred, some of them Gerbert's friends, and many non-Christians also, as the German methods of converting them were carried out according to an ancient verse, freely translated:

> And wilt thou not a Christian be,
> I'll smash thy skull, just wait and see.

Some tribes clung to their own gods for centuries longer. As late as 1314, at the funeral of a Lithuanian duke who had been considered a Christian, his horse, his favorite servant, and three German prisoners of war were burned on his funeral pyre to serve him in the afterlife.

Generation after generation the Saxon kings advanced into Wendland, while the Slavs retaliated by raiding deep into Germany. Both sides took turns at being defenders or aggressors. No victory was ever permanent, no peace of long duration.

Otto I had to defend his borderlands against an alliance of tribes, sending his best commanders, Hermann Billing and Count Gero, to deal with them. The Slavs planned to murder Gero in his tent, but the count forestalled them by creeping into their camp during a moonless night when the Slavs, as not infrequently happened, were besotted with drink. With his own hands Gero killed some thirty of them and got back to his men without a scratch. From 947 to 949 the fight raged between the Elbe and Oder. In 955, while Otto had his hands full with the Hungarians, the Slavs seized their opportunity to set the whole border area aflame.

Widukind of Corvey described the Slavs as a rugged, durable folk "used to living on almost nothing. What to us Germans is hardship they look upon as a lark. They rather wage war than live in peace and will endure anything to remain free." Even after Otto had defeated the Magyars on the Lechfeld, the Wends persisted, laying waste to the eastern mark under their chieftains, Stoinev and Nacko, pillaging their way through Mecklenburg and Pomerania. Otto's border captains tried to persuade them to desist and during a meeting told Stoinev that if he would only give back the lands he had overrun, "you will find Otto a friend, not an enemy." Stoinev laughed in their faces, intimating that he might be inclined to make peace provided he could keep what he had already taken. Otto resolved to take his chances. Covered by his archers he managed to cross the Recknitz River, behind which the Wends had taken up position. In the meantime Count Gero threw three bridges across the Recknitz further downstream, unobserved by the enemy, who found themselves suddenly attacked from the rear. Again the Wends fought with desperate courage but were beaten with great losses.

Neither was there any peace under Otto II. At his death the Wends took advantage of the fact that Otto III was only three years old by raiding along the Saale River. Thietmar of Merseburg vividly described this great raid of 983. His own father, Sigfrid, had been forewarned of the dire calamities to come by a vision from heaven. The Slavic Havellers first stormed Havelberg on June 29, burning down its cathedral. On July 2, they got over the walls of Brandenburg, committing many atrocities. Everywhere the Slavs carried away men and women to be held for ransom. Sometimes those who had escaped capture still had to surrender themselves voluntarily as hostages to free members of their family. Thietmar himself was once on the way to give himself up to "those greedy dogs" in exchange for an uncle who, luckily for the chronicler, managed to get his captors drunk and escape before Thietmar could surrender himself.

The Saxon army engaged the same enemies in 985 and 986, the six-year-old Otto III riding with his men. The Polish prince Mieszko, himself a Slav, but also a victim of the Wends' fury, helped the boy king and even gave him a camel for a present. Whence the animal came and what happened to it later is not known.

The year 993 was one of blistering heat and bone-chilling cold. There were droughts and epidemics, during which Otto's army had to conduct no fewer than three full-scale campaigns against the Wends without, so the victims of ongoing raids complained, accomplishing anything. The years 994 and 995 saw Otto allied with Boleslav of Bohemia trying to stem the onslaught of the ubiquitous Obotrites. At the end of the century the Bishop of Schleswig lamented, "My see has been devastated by Slavonic barbarians, my city made into a desert, my church an empty shell. I no longer have a bishop's see." And still no end was in sight.

Saintly martyrs abounded. Foremost among them was St. Adalbert, the Apostle of the Prussians, a trusted friend of Gerbert, Theophano, and her son, the emperor Otto III, "one of the most lyrical and most heroic figures of the Church." A man of the Czech nation and born in Bohemia, he was at first given the name of Woytiech, meaning Helper of Hosts. His father, Slavnik, was a nobleman—"outwardly a Christian but a heathen inwardly." To make up for it, his mother was pious to the point of bigotry. In spite of his warlike name, the boy Woytiech was sickly and subject to frequent seizures. His mother placed him upon an altar of the Blessed Virgin and vowed to give him to the church if he got well. He did and was sent to Magdeburg, where one of his teachers was Gerbert's old rival Othric. Woytiech was confirmed and renamed Adalbert, after the first bishop of Magdeburg. He was subsequently consecrated as a priest, but he still persisted being "an imp of hell, eager to taste the lures of the world."

He returned to Prague in 981 and became deacon to the revered Bishop Dethmar, still "a giddy youth bent upon worldly pleasures." Standing at the deathbed of his bishop and hearing this saintly man bemoaning his sinful past brought about Adalbert's conversion. He covered his head with ashes and put on sackcloth, hurrying from church to church, preaching and praying. In 983 he was consecrated bishop of Prague. The newly made prelate was a trial to himself and to his flock. He went about barefoot in a threadbare monk's habit, astonishing the people of Prague with his rigorous fasting, sleepless vigils, and self-mortification. He expected everybody to follow his example, but the flesh of his lambs was too weak.

From his pulpit he thundered against polygamy, refused to allow priests to wed or to keep mistresses, suppressed the heathen rites so dear to his people, and forbade the selling of Christian slaves to pagans. Things came to a head when a woman, accused of having committed adultery with a priest, fled to him for protection. Adalbert offered her sanctuary in a nearby convent. Stirred up by her husband, an angry crowd of armed men demanded her surrender, threatening to kill Adalbert if he would not deliver up the "whore." Adalbert refused, but his sacristan, frightened to death, let them have the keys, and they went into the convent and killed her. Soon afterward his enemies drove Adalbert from Prague.

Adalbert went to Rome where he met St. Nilus, another friend, but also taskmaster, of both Gerbert and Otto III. The future saint advised Adalbert "to dwell with the good bishop Leo who will help you in the daily battles every poor sinner has to fight on his way to the heavenly kingdom; and who will fan the flames of divine love within you into a white-hot fire, so that your heart will be a burnt offering upon the Lord's altar." Leo did just that, convincing Adalbert to become a monk. As a monk he insisted upon doing the meanest kind of work, such as emptying latrines, and he made himself the servant of the lowliest and poorest people so that the "holy spark was lit in the hearts of the brothers who said that with Adalbert God had entered among them."

Adalbert had a vision in which he saw himself walking between rows of martyred saints and holy people and hearing a voice from on high: "Between them shalt you take your meals and receive your food and honor."

Pope Gregory advised him, "Return to your sheep in Prague, and if they will not suffer you, go and preach the word of God to the heathen!" Adalbert chose the latter and joined Otto III on a crusade against the Wends. He became the young emperor's close friend, "filling his heart with the love of God and deep humility." In order not to become too proud as a result of Otto's favor, he secretly washed and cleaned the clothes and shoes of the lowliest servants. He experienced a second vision. In it he saw a chamber with two beds. Stretched out upon one was a beautiful woman with an inscription over her head, reading "Joys of the World." The other bed was shrouded in purple silk hangings with gold-embroidered letters bearing the message "this reward is offered to thee by the king's daughter." Adalbert perceived at once that *this reward* signified a martyr's crown. He threw himself upon his knees and prayed, "Hail to thee, Holy Virgin, that you are granting me what I wish for most of all."

In 997 Adalbert set out on his mission, taking leave of Otto with tears and kisses. He traveled first to Pomerania where people worshiped the images of horses and bears. He preached to great crowds, and converted many. Accompanied by two brothers he reached a sea port in the Land of Amber, probably Pillau in East Prussia. The people there spoke a Slav language that he could understand. The brothers were asked what they wanted. Adalbert answered that they had come to convert the people to the Christian faith. At once a terrific tumult broke out. A friendly merchant whispered into Adalbert's ear to leave quickly if he and his friends valued their lives.

For five days Adalbert and his companions, Gaudentius and Benedict, took shelter in a peasant's hut. The night before leaving, Gaudentius had a dream, which he related to Adalbert. "I saw upon an altar a golden cup filled with wine. When I tried to empty it, the altar's servant forbade it, saying, 'this cup is put here for Adalbert to drink tomorrow.'"

"May God bless us," answered Adalbert, "one should not believe in such kinds of dreams."

They wandered on in the morning, singing psalms, and were secretly followed by a Polish shaman with eight armed companions. Walking through a thick forest, the three brothers came to a clearing where Gaudentius read mass and Adalbert received communion. Then they ate a last small loaf of bread and lay down to sleep in the grass, only to be wakened by the clanking of their pursuers' arms. Adalbert and his companions were bound and dragged away. As Gaudentius reported later, "He was pale and uttered not a word." On a hilltop, possibly a heathen shrine, a man named Sicco berated Adalbert for being a spy and ran a spear through his body. The other men also pierced Adalbert with their weapons, cut off his head, and threw the body into the sea. They let Gaudentius and Benedict go. This happened on April 23, 997. The head was retrieved by his friends, and his body washed up on the Baltic shore. Both head and body were then buried at Gnesen (Gniezno).

According to one legend, St. Nilus saw all this the moment it happened, telling those who were near, "Dear sons, rejoice, our friend Adalbert has just been granted a most blessed death." When Otto heard the sad news in Magdeburg, he broke down weeping, at the same time praising God for setting Christendom such a glorious example. Otto later made a pilgrimage to Gnesen, a long and arduous journey, to pray at his friend's grave. He is also said to have paid Adalbert's weight in gold to his murderers for a decent reburial.

Adalbert was not the only saint, martyred by the Slavs, whom Gerbert had known personally. Bruno of Querfurt learned Slavic languages, traveled to King Stephen of Hungary and to Vladimir in Kiev, preached the word of God to savage Pechenegs, then fell a martyr beneath the axes of Poles.

Gerbert's concerns were different from those of his martyred friends, and he never involved himself with matters in the distant Slavic East. He was fully occupied with affairs in France, Italy, and Germany—matters that at times nearly overwhelmed him.

CHAPTER NINETEEN

From Pagan Chieftain to Royal Saint

BEFORE AND AFTER HE BECAME POPE, Gerbert played a conspic-
uous part in the conversion of Hungary, the country of the Magyars.
The Magyars were nomads who appeared out of the steppes of Central Asia. According to their own legends they came to Europe with
the Huns, a chieftain named Hunyor being their tribal ancestor. Their
name, *Magyars*, supposedly is derived from *mag*, meaning core or center
of the host and, possibly, from *magas*, meaning high, because they called
themselves a tall people. The late eighth century found them divided
into seven tribes, vassals of the Khazars, ranging along the edges of the
Caucasus. After freeing themselves from Khazar rule, they crossed the
Don on skin boats and roamed for a while between the Don and Ku-
ban rivers. They were described as bow-wielding horse riders who lived
from hunting, fishing, and raiding, and they were admired for their
extraordinary mobility. The Arab Al-Bekri called them a people living
in leather tents, forever in search of new pasture land. The Byzantine
emperor Leo the Wise described them as a proud, brave, hot-tempered,
and honor-loving people, inured to every kind of hardship, scornful
of luxury and comfort. The Magyars, for their part, called themselves
"rich in blue squirrel, white silver, yellow gold, golden millet, black
sable, and brown horses."

Chroniclers noted with some surprise that though, on a raid, Magyar men killed women, especially nuns, they refrained from raping them. Cursed as the Scourge of God, they were nevertheless chaste. They concluded no formal marriages yet were monogamous. Their old word for marriage was *nöszés*, meaning cohabiting. Originally brides were bought, and, upon reaching maturity, a maiden was called Eladó Léany—that is, "salable girl."

The Arab traveler Gardézi described the Magyars' marriage customs. The bride's father invited the parent of his prospective son-in-law to his tent. After the price for the girl had been paid in horses, the father gathered whatever he had in the way of sable, ermine, gray squirrel, and foxbelly furs, rolled them up in a carpet, and gave them to his guest to take home. Then the girl's family brought her to the suitor's tent, and that made the marriage, or, rather, honorable cohabiting, official.

Before settling down in the plain between the Danube and the Theiss rivers, the Magyars had no written language. After the introduction of Christianity, monks and priests, with the help of Gerbert, brought them the Latin alphabet, and a few nobles began sending their sons to learn reading and writing in the newly established churches and monasteries. The little ones did not like that at all, preferring to race their shaggy ponies or practice archery, and therefore the Magyar word *könyu* means tears as well as book.

Parents, grandparents, and old folks in general were venerated for their wisdom. Possibly they were admired also for merely having survived the brutal raiding, wandering years. Although plundering Pechenegs or European Christians was fine and praiseworthy, stealing within the tribe was taboo: "What is gotten after a dog's way will also be lost in the manner of dogs." Life was looked upon as a wandering that never reached a particular goal. For a man, to lead a good life meant to stop eating before being full; to abstain from taking advantage of a trusting young woman; to hear and see much, but to talk little; and not to burst out into nickering laughter, the mark of a fool. Bad men came to bad ends. Men looked upon bossy, domineering women with suspicion. "Beware of the bearded woman" was an old Magyar proverb. Death was simply a transfer to new pastures. After death the soul flew away in the shape of a bird. The dead were buried and a mound raised over their graves.

The Arab chronicler Al-Bekri wrote, "The Muhaffiyya [Magyars] are idolators and the name of their Malik [king] is kanda." Gardézi added that the Magyars were a race of Turks, that their leaders rode out at the head of twenty thousand horsemen, that their great chief was called *kanda*, that the chief who actually managed affairs was called *jula*, and that the people did what the *jula* commanded. The medieval Arab historians were astute observers, Magyars did indeed have a dual leadership. The nominal head of the combined tribes was the *kende*, while the chief administrator had the title of *gyula*. The *kende* might have been the ceremonial chief standing in relation to the *gyula* like the English monarch to the prime minister or the Japanese *tenno* to the *shogun* in feudal times. The Magyar ruler was also referred to by the Turko-Mongolian title of *kakhan*, meaning chief of chiefs.

The turul bird was the totem animal of the ruling family, and its image, carried on a pole, served as the nation's standard. It was said that "the sun walked before the *khan*," meaning that at the head of the *ordu* (army) rode a man with a huge kettledrum. In the earliest days, men and women were sacrificed at a *khan*'s death. While tenth-century Christian nobles continuously rebelled against their rulers, there are no reports of uprisings or assassinations of Magyar *kakhans*. Possibly their persons were looked upon as sacred. This changed as soon as they became Christians.

Ibn Rusta wrote that the Magyars worshiped the sun and the moon, while Gardézi reported that they were fire worshipers. Their chief deity was Ïsten, who might have been a fire god of Persian origin. Below Ïsten, were ranged a number of lesser gods—of winter, summer, rain, wind, forests, people, horses, water, day, night, sky, and earth. The evil principle was represented by Ördög, the bad god.

Magyars prayed to the images of their deities. Thietmar of Merseburg mentions that the late tenth-century *kende*, Géza, sacrificed to idols while at the same time praying to the true God of the Christians. Offerings, mostly in the shape of cattle, were made in sacred groves, on mountains, and near certain springs. During the most solemn ritual a white horse, noble and immaculate, was given to Ísten. Parts of it were probably ritually eaten at the sacrificial meal, *adlomás*, which was a part of the ceremony. Priests, called *táltos*, played an important role and often interfered in tribal politics. Seers, carrying bird-headed staffs, cast the shoulder blades of horses into the fire, predicting the future from cracks in the bones.

The swirling masses of Magyar light cavalry usually did not attempt to besiege or storm heavily defended walled towns, and thus, in a roundabout way, they contributed to the founding of cities throughout the first half of the tenth century. Their mode of fighting was the despair of the heavily armored Western knights on their heavy, slow horses. The Magyars preferred to advance in loose, mutually supportive bands, coalescing and splitting up with bewildering speed as the need arose. They fought from a distance with their short, powerful bows and light javelins, avoiding hand-to-hand battles, and they wheeled their horses in a way that confused their foes, now advancing, now retreating, outflanking their opponents, ambushing them, pretending to flee in order to entice an enemy from a strong position only to turn suddenly upon him when least expected. They practiced ever new stratagems against which their opponents were helpless. One despairing monk wrote that these Hungarian enemies of God and humans alike could so well hide a whole army that, at one moment, a wide plain could seem to be absolutely empty, only to be covered with Magyar horsemen in the next. A Christian army might be on the march, thinking them far away, only to see them rise suddenly, as out of nowhere, in its rear and on its flanks. The Magyars were like swarming hornets surrounding and stinging a poor lumbering cow. One could neither escape nor catch them. They were truly the whip with which God flayed Christendom for its many sins, and in countless churches trembling people prayed, "De sagittis Hungarorum libera nos, Domine!" (From Hungarian arrows free us, O Lord!)

In 895 the Magyars settled down in present-day Hungary under the leadership of a chieftain called Árpád, who became the founder of a dynasty. Árpád's throne had been the saddle, but after settling down the Magyars adopted the farming ways of their Western counterparts. At Árpád's death the Magyars, known henceforth as Hungarians, were no longer homeless tribespeople, but settled folk with their own country, and Árpád was able to hand on his chieftainship to his son Zoltan. All this did not mean that the Hungarians gave up their plundering raids. They continued to penetrate into every corner of Europe, but they now had a permanent base to which they could always return.

Until the reign of Zoltan (906–947), the Magyars were a loose confederation of semi-independent tribes with their own customs and peculiarities. Under Zoltan, tribal differences quickly disappeared, particularly after he married his son, Taksony, to the daughter of a chief commanding the powerful Kuman tribe.

Taksony reigned from 947 to 972. During his rule an incident occurred that could have changed European history as well as Gerbert's papacy. In 948, one of Taksony's chief *khans*, the *horka* Bulcsu, nicknamed the Man with the Bloody Hand, went to Constantinople to arrange an extension of the armistice between his people and Byzantium in exchange for tribute. On this occasion he let himself be baptized, receiving the title of Roman Patrician. Bulcsu would probably have brought Hungary within the orbit of the Byzantine church had he not, in 955, been taken prisoner during the great Battle of the Lechfeld. Otto I had him hanged and thereby changed the destiny of Europe. Hungary became part of the West, not of the East, and Gerbert, not the patriarch of Constantinople, finished the work of Christianizing the Magyars.

Géza ruled after Taksony with an iron hand. He was called a ruler pitiless toward his own people. With brute force he forged his Asian tribespeople into feudal Europeans. He broke the power of the tribal chieftains, since he believed that it was better to hang or blind a few scores of them now than be forced to execute thousands of rebels later.

After the Magyars' crushing defeat of the Lechfeld, Géza realized the primitive raiding days were over. The nomads had to become farmers, the *khans* feudal barons. Géza established a strong central government with the help of an army no longer tribal but loyal to him alone, consisting mainly of Rus Varangians and Slav mercenaries. To these he later added numbers of Germans and Italian knights. The tribal chieftains were replaced by *ispáns*, provincial governors responsible only to him. He exchanged embassies and concluded peace treaties with German emperors and Byzantine *basileii*.

To help make Hungary a part of the Christian West, he married one of his daughters to the doge of Venice, another to a Polish prince. For his son Vajk he obtained the hand of Gisela, a Bavarian princess. He encouraged Western builders and artisans to come to Hungary and invited monks and prelates to instruct his people in the Christian faith, more for political than religious reasons. In 974, Piligrin, bishop of Passau, is said to have baptized five thousand noble Hungarians during one single ceremony. As often happened, it was the ruler's wife who was most eager to spread the gospel. Géza had married Sarolta, daughter of the *gyula* of Transylvania, a most pious Christian woman. She managed to have herself and her husband baptized by German prelates.

Géza's conversion was hardly conventional. He continued to sacrifice to his ancient idols while, at the same time, praying to Christ and taking the sacraments, saying that he was rich enough to serve two different gods. Christian chroniclers were happy to record that the heathen Hungarians were tolerant. They forbade no one baptism, and those who had remained pagans lived in harmony with their Christian neighbors. It reminded one observer of the biblical passage: "The wolf and the lamb shall feed together, and the lion eat straw like the ox." During Géza's lifetime Christianity was strictly limited to the court and nobility, as the people at large so strongly resisted the Christian gospel that even Géza could not cram it down their unwilling throats.

According to legend, a lovely youth appeared to Géza in a dream, telling him that he was not destined to convert the Magyars because his hands were steeped in blood, but that his son was fated to complete the good work. But Géza was hardly the man to dream of lovely youths. A pious tale also has it that St. Stephen the Martyr appeared to Sarolta, foretelling that she would give birth to a saint, recognized as such by the Lord God even before being formed and quickened in her womb, and that his name would be Stephen. The son born to her, however, was called Vajk, or Bajnok, that is, "fighter."

Vajk was taught Western knightly ways by the Italian count Theodato de San Severino, while the saintly Bruno of Querfurt instructed him in matters of religion. Gerbert's friend and future saint, Adalbert, also preached the word to the Hungarians but, according to Bruno of Querfurt, turned them only a little from their heathen ways, casting over them but the shadow of Christianity. In 995 Vajk was solemnly baptized, it is said by Adalbert, and he was given the fitting name of Stephen. Thus the prophecy received by Sarolta was fulfilled. In the following year Stephen married Gisela of Bavaria, who had intended to become a nun but after some reflection decided that she could serve God better as a queen helping her husband to bring heathen Magyars to God. In 997 Géza died and was succeeded by Stephen. Géza had been born and raised in a tent; Stephen ruled his country from a German-style castle at Gran.

Throughout most of his reign Stephen had to fight many rebels resisting both Christianization and Westernization. His main opposition came from a powerful chieftain named Koppány who raised a rebellion in the name of Magyar freedom and the old gods. To differentiate between "good" and "bad" Magyars the Christians were called White Hungarians and the pagans Black Hungarians. In 998 Stephen defeated the Blacks during a great battle near Lake Balaton in which Koppány was killed. Stephen had Koppány's body chopped into four parts, which were nailed to the gates of four castles as a warning to other would-be rebels, but there were always more uprisings. In Thietmar's words, Stephen attacked the Black Hungarians "with force, intimidation, and love, bringing them to the true faith," but resistance continued for years, and many of Stephen's missionaries died a martyr's death. Stephen's own nephew, Prince Vazul, or Vászoly, planned to assassinate him. Betrayed, Vazul was sentenced to death but, being of blood of Árpád was allowed his life in exchange for "the sight of his eyes and the hearing of his ears."

In the year 1000, the Polish duke Boleslav sent envoys to Pope Sylvester II, that is to Gerbert, begging the pontiff to raise him to the dignity of a king and to bestow upon him a crown. Gerbert had a golden crown made and had already appointed a day when it should be delivered to the Polish ambassadors, but according to a legend the Lord's angel appeared to Gerbert in a dream, saying, "The Lord knoweth His own whom He hath chosen. Therefore He commands thee to deny the crown to a people still steeped in robbery and slaughter. Tomorrow will appear before thee the messengers of a new country, unknown to thee, to demand a crown hallowed by thine apostolic blessings, in the name of their lord whom God Almighty has chosen to be their anointed king. To them give the crown!"

Of course, neither Hungary nor its duke were "new and unknown" to Gerbert, who had been in close communication with Stephen for some time. A Hungarian embassy arrived a little later than the Poles and also demanded a kingship for their ruler. Gerbert received them with joy and, on the spur of the moment, gave the crown not to Boleslav but to Stephen. The pope surprised the Hungarian envoys by granting them more than they had asked for, going to extraordinary lengths to exalt the new son of the church. Not only a crown but also a precious cross would he send to his beloved Stephen, granting him and his successors the right to style themselves apostolic kings.

Together with the crown Gerbert sent Stephen a letter, reading in part, "My glorious son, all that which thou hath desired, we joyfully allow and grant thee by the authority derived from Almighty God and the Saints Peter and Paul, together with our own benediction. . . . And as thy Highness did undertake the apostolic office of proclaiming and spreading the faith of Christ, we feel moved to confer besides, upon thy Excellency and out of regard for thy merits that thou will be crowned with the crown we sent thee. We also beseech Almighty

God that He may abundantly water with the dew of His blessing the new plants of thy realm, that he may protect thee against thy open and secret foes, and adorn thee, after the vexations of thy earthly rule, with the eternal crown of His heavenly kingdom."

Still in existence, the famous crown consists of two parts. The upper part is Gerbert's original one. The lower, an open circlet, was a gift from the Byzantine emperor Michael Ducas, sent in 1073 to the then reigning Hungarian king as a token of friendship. The original consists of two hoops fastened together, surmounted by a globe, topped by a markedly bent cross—the result of having been dropped centuries ago. It is adorned by an image of Christ surrounded by the twelve apostles. The lower, newer crown is encrusted with pearls and a huge sapphire and representations of archangels, saints, and Greek emperors. Today, after many vicissitudes suffered during World War II Stephen's crown is back where it belongs, in Budapest. Its cross still leans to one side.

Having listened, amid shouts of approval, to the reading of Gerbert's letter bestowing apostolic blessings, the Hungarian lords and common people joyfully acclaimed Stephen their king. After being anointed with sacred oil, he was duly crowned on August 15, the day of the Virgin's ascension, in the year 1000, in the cathedral of Gran (Esztergom). Gerbert had made Hungary into a bulwark of Christian Europe and must have been well satisfied with what he had achieved. Stephen died in 1038 and was ultimately canonized as Hungary's patron saint. The twilight of the gods had given way to the eternal light. Ínten, the old fire god, had to lend his name to the God of the Christians, while Ördög, the god of evil, simply became the Christian's devil. Paganism had lost one of its last strongholds.

CHAPTER TWENTY

A World Astonished

WHEN, IN 997, HOUNDED from his see at Rheims, Gerbert arrived at Aix-la-Chapelle, Charlemagne's old *Kaiserpfalz*, he came as a refugee. Otto III received him joyfully with many marks of friendship and respect, putting his tutor's mind at ease. Aristotle had come back to Alexander, and all was well again.

Gerbert found things much changed. His old friend, the empress Theophano, was dead. For seven years she had administered the empire in her son's name with tact and firmness. She had, temporarily at least, overcome her feeling of ill will against her rival, the old empress Adelaide, and together they had safeguarded the child king's inheritance. The two empresses were jealous of each other, rivals not for the love of a man, but of a boy—their boy. In 991 Theophano had exclaimed with dark foreboding, "If I live another year, Adelaide shall not rule this world," but she did not live another year. After celebrating Easter with great pomp at Quedlinburg, she suddenly died on the 15th of June, at Nymwegen. She was in her early thirties and still beautiful as a Byzantine ivory carving. Her earthly remains were buried in the presence of her eleven-year-old son in the Benedictine abbey of St. Pantaleon at Cologne, which she herself had enlarged and endowed with many gifts.

Almost all the main figures in this narrative had their legends, and Theophano was no exception. She was hardly buried when she appeared to a German nun, begging her to say prayers for the soul of one who had been an empress but now suffered in purgatory for having worn so much silk, purple, and byzantine jewelry, seducing many good Saxon ladies to follow her pernicious example and to squander their wealth upon vain things.

Theophano's death prompted the swift return of her old rival, the temporarily retired Adelaide, who took the deceased's place as regent. Like a good Christian, the sixty-year-old Adelaide comforted young Otto for having lost such a wise and loving mother. She took up the regency with the help of the great nobles and prelates, particularly the all-powerful Archbishop Willigis of Mayence, but her stay at court did not last long. On his fourteenth birthday, Otto was declared to have come of age, and he made it known that he no longer wished to be ruled by women. As Thietmar wrote, "Led astray by bad advice by flippant young men, he told her to leave, and she did so with regrets." Bitten by remorse, Otto later wrote her a touching letter, thanking Adelaide for her motherly tenderness, expressing his gratitude for all she had done for him and beseeching her to further guide him. But he did not mean it.

The public life of the old empress, who had once turned men's heads and been the heroine of a romantic escapade, was not over. For the rest of her life she devoted herself to good and pious works, living among monks and nuns, assuming a new and last title: "Adelheida, by God's gift empress, by herself a poor sinner and God's maidservant." Nearing her end, she fell down upon the ground crying, "God, what shall I do? What shall become of my grandson? In my mind I see many dying with him in Italy and I, miserable woman, fear he too will die, my Otto, of royal blood. O, God of the Universe, save me from having to survive his death." God granted her wish. She did not have to witness the burial of still another Otto. She died in 999.

The young Otto much preferred Gerbert's company to that of his grandmother. He at once made him his *musicus*, not, as some thought, his musician, but his teacher of natural sciences. In Magdeburg both friends busied themselves with an astrolabe, read Boethius, and debated the finer points of philosophy. Gerbert even accompanied the young emperor on a campaign against the Slavic tribes. While Otto was still busy fighting Wends and Serbs, he made Gerbert a gift of the barony of Sassbac near Strassburg. Gerbert showed extravagant gratitude: "Magnificent thanks for the magnificent gift of the magnificent Sassbach." By letter he encouraged Otto, still on campaign: "what greater glory can there be for a prince, what more laudable in a leader, than to collect armies, plunging into the country of his foes, animating by his presence the defense against the enemies' onslaughts, exposing himself to the greatest danger for his country and faith, for his own and his country's salvation?"

Their mutual admiration was boundless. In the fall of 997, the young king penned a letter to his teacher: "To the most skilled of masters versed in all the branches of philosophy . . . We wish to have near our person your loving self. We would like to see you, O honored and excellent man, to better enjoy your wise guidance, the more so since your philosophical knowledge has always shown a great forbearance for our shortcomings. To put it simply, we are resolved to ask that you may instruct us, in word and letter, to tend us your priceless counsel in matters of state. With this request, which you may not deny us, we also express the desire that you strive without pity, against the rusticity of our Saxon nature and develop whatever of Greek elegance may dwell in our mind. Because you may yet discover a little spark of learning in us and are just the master to fan it into flame. Fan it, O Gerbert, with the mighty fire of your knowledge this tiny spark, waken within us, with the help of God, the Greek genius to shine forth." Otto added a little verse of his own to please Gerbert:

> Verses I have never penned
> Nor my mind to poetry bent.
> Should I bring this rhyme along
> So that I too can write a song,

So many songs to you I'll post
As are men in Gallia's host.

He concluded by "humbly asking His Paternity" for an answer, which was not long in forthcoming: "Your surpassing goodness, that you wish to have me in your service, I might possibly repay because of my vows, not due to any merit of mine. If a weak spark of knowledge burns within me, it is due to the favors your noble father has shown me, and which your revered grandfather first lit in my heart. We cannot bring you treasures of our own, but only give back to you what we merely held in trust. . . . Truly, it is a sign of God if a man, Greek by birth, Roman by his high office, claims as his own patrimony the treasures of Greek and Roman heritage. We obey your imperial command and shall never fail in serving you."

It was a strange relationship, that of the many-years-older scholar and the young visionary king, whom people had already begun to call Stupor Mundi (Wonder of the World) and A Prince to Astonish the Universe; an odd marriage of coolness with fire, age with youth, realism with unreality. Those who knew Otto well observed an inner strife raging in the mind of this gifted visionary—"strange in a common man, dangerous in a prince." Otto suffered from having a split personality, being at the same time humble and overproud, peaceful and warlike, deep and superficial, benign and terribly cruel, lusting for and shunning power. Angel or devil, he was one of the most fascinating of all medieval figures.

In war mighty,
in peace potent,
in either state
kindly was he;
amid victories
happy he was;
those whom his soldiers' arms
had not subdued,

renown of his name
conquered enough.

Though he was hardly mighty in war or potent in peace, no one
could deny that his brain produced high-flying ideas. Bernward, after
Gerbert his most respected and beloved teacher, wrote that "everything new and strange attracted the young king, so that he introduced
thoughts and arts never encountered in Saxony before. He penetrated
lightly, as if floating, into the most profound sciences, aspiring to
great deeds, he was high-strung like a bow about to break from too
much tension." Fluent in German, Latin, and Greek, he was described
as a graceful youth, the handsome son of a handsome father and
beautiful mother, and, with the first down of manhood on his cheek,
a young prince whom nobody could view without delight.

German historians judged him harshly for neglecting Saxony in
favor of Italy and for being more Roman and Greek than German.
Pflugck-Harttung wrote, "Otto grew up a stranger in the world he
was to rule, contemptuous of his people whom fate had entrusted to
his care, ignorant of the conditions within his empire which he was
supposed to master, a visionary youth living in a dream, who presumed
to heal a sick world which he haughtily contemplated from the dizzy-
ing heights of his unfulfilled ideals which were beyond his powers of
realization. He childishly destroyed the work of his ancestors which
his grandmother and mother had safeguarded so long with true states-
manship."

Actually, Otto spent more time in Germany than in Italy and
pursued his campaign against Wends and Obotrites as vigorously as
those against rebellious Roman nobles. But it was no wonder that a
dreamer like Otto should have bound himself from childhood on under the spell of the old *Romzauber*, the magic pull of Golden Rome—
his Rome and *his* Romans, as he was soon to call them. The idea of
becoming the new Caesar of a new-old universal empire fired his imagination and gave him an exaggerated view of his own power which,

so he said, could not be exercised in paltry campaigns in an empty country of miserable bogs against wretched Slavs. It was no wonder that the excitable teenager, burning with ambition and love of the spectacular, which Italy so well inspired, should in his mind already see himself as the favored successor of the great imperators of antiquity, an "aspiration which now had bound his heart in ever stronger bands."

In 996 the young King of Hosts (*Heerkönig*) set out on his first march to Rome, a triumphal procession over still snowbound mountain passes into sunny Italy. He was surrounded by a glittering retinue, the victory bringing Holy Lance carried solemnly before him. German historians saw it not as a triumphal march but as a saintly pilgrimage of penitents into a cloud-land of mirages. They characterized Otto as burning with a holy zeal to reform a corrupt church and to improve the morals of *his* Romans—not the proper task for a Saxon kaiser.

It was spring, and, for the moment, all was joy and optimism. Upon arrival Otto learned that Pope John XV had died of a "malefic fever" and that the Roman nobility and clergy waited humbly to receive from his hands a new Holy Father. What Otto was not aware of was that the great mass of *his* Romans had watched his grand entrance into their city with indifference or open hostility. He graciously consented to give Rome and the world a new pope, his very own cousin Bruno of Carinthia. Bruno, who was hardly older than the emperor, sat himself down upon the throne of St. Peter under the name of Gregory V. People uttered the obligatory hallelujas and hosannas, but the Romans whispered among themselves that a stranger had made a stranger pope and that from a stranger did a stranger receive the imperial diadem.

Otto, naturally, viewed things differently. He had come to take up the Teuton's burden, which the enfeebled Romans were no longer able to bear. He had come as their savior, and he expected their gratitude. He saw himself as a better custodian of the wondrous city with its monuments of ancient greatness than its fickle and enfeebled natives, "his children" no longer able to govern themselves. He was thrilled at the sights that greeted his eyes, thrilled at the thought that he possessed Rome, his rightful inheritance.

> O Rome, noble mistress and world ruler,
> All other cities in glory surpassing;
> Reddened with the roseate blood of martyrs,
> Aglow with the whiteness of virgin's lilies,
> Hail to thee we sing, now and forever,
> For all eternity be saluted and blessed.

On his coronation day, May 21, 996, Otto was, after the ancient custom, received in festive procession by the higher clergy and the representatives of the nobility and the people of Rome. Senators in splendid robes accompanied him, and the prefect of the city walked in measured steps before him, holding aloft the naked sword of justice. Almoners scattered coins among the mass of gaping, scrambling, exulting citizens. At the foot of the stairs of St. Peter's, he dismounted and ascended the steps to where the pontiff in the midst of his prelates awaited him. The emperor humbly kissed the Holy Father's foot and, in return, received the kiss of peace. Amidst prayers and hymns, enveloped in clouds of incense, he was dressed in shining garments and girt with the sword of temporal power until, at last, the pope fixed the heavy golden ring upon his finger and placed upon his brow the crown of Charlemagne. "Gloria" reverberated throughout the cathedral and praise songs intoned, "Life and victory to the emperor, to the German and Roman host!" The Saxon knights shouted aloud, "Heil Dir, Kaiser!" while the Romans burst out into such deafening cries that nobody could understand them.

Otto was crowned Emperor, Caesar, Augustus, and Roman patrician, the veritable Image of God (Imago Dei), or at least God's temporal lieutenant on earth: "The giant's greatest ascending in triumph to the stars." No wonder that it went to the head of the sixteen-year-old adolescent and that he indulged in a great deal of self-glorification.

All was smiles now and submissiveness on the part of the Romans. Otto even forgave the second Crescentius, the incorrigible intriguer against Saxon interests, his former misdeeds. Crescentius, for his part, swore henceforth to be faithful, laying his hands between those of the emperor as any good vassal was wont to do, and faithful he remained—just as long as Otto and his knights stayed in Rome. But the emperor and his army were needed back in Germany. Otto left reassured. Had he not made his cousin Bruno pope to look after things in his absence?

Back in Sassbach, Gerbert once again found out that playing the feudal lord did not suit his temperament. Taking advantage of Otto's occupation elsewhere, other claimants to the estate made life miserable for Gerbert and even drove him away. In despair he wrote to Otto, "I wish I had never owned it. To receive from your generous hands those splendid gifts and to lose them in so great a bewilderment! What am I to think?" He reminded the emperor of the services he had rendered his cause: "For three generations, to you, to your father and grandfather, amid battles and foes, have I always remained unwaveringly faithful. For your sake I have faced down raging kings and maddening crowds. Through wilderness and deserts, assailed by robbers, enduring hunger and thirst, plagued by cold and heat and all other trials have I stood firm, ready to die in order to see the son of Caesar, not captive, but on his throne, an emperor. I have seen him so, to my joy, hoping to rejoice to the end, finishing my days with you in peace!"

Soon the answer came, in the letter already quoted, in which Otto humbly asked Gerbert to come and stay with him. Though Gerbert never got Sassbach back, he would soon receive much larger and more splendid gifts in exchange.

In the meantime Gregory V, only twenty-three years old, held Rome for the emperor. The German pope, "a young man of letters, but somewhat fiery on account of his youth," had a formidable rival in Crescentius and soon was locked in a battle with the Roman over who should rule the city. Bruno was no match for such an experienced infighter as Crescentius, and he played into his opponent's hands by surrounding himself with his compatriots and raising them to the highest positions in the curia, a move that his Italian enemies considered an insult to Roman citizens. After the manner of Saxon barons, he was also hotheaded, impatient, and grimly determined on his goals, more like the warlike Nicholas I than the peaceful Gregory the Great whose name he had taken upon assuming the papacy. It was not difficult for Crescentius to stir up the nobles as well as the turbulent Roman mob, who forced the pope to flee for his life.

In the spring of 997, Crescentius was master of the city, having chased his third pope from the Lateran. Gregory V was riding posthaste to seek a shelter in Pavia with little more than his papal robes upon his back, leaving many of his German prelates behind in the hands of the enemy, who promptly cast them into the dungeons of the Castle of St. Angelo. Crescentius II now styled himself patricius, Dux, Senator, Comes, and Consul, Duke and Count of the Romans. The Saxons, not unnaturally, dubbed him Crescentius Tyrannus. Bold, unscrupulous, pertinacious, and keen, he now ruled as a despot, maker and unmaker of popes and terror of the church. He ensconced himself in the Castellum Sancti Angeli, the gloomy, massive, impregnable fortress that now became known as the Castellum Crescentii. The self-made consul and patrician now put a "hitherto respectable" person on the papal see under the name of John XVI, and thereby hangs a tale.

The new antipope was none other than John Philagathos of Calabria, bishop of Placentia, the empress Theophano's erstwhile favorite and Otto's godfather and instructor in Greek, who had even been given the task of procuring a Byzantine princess for the young emperor. Philagathos, "of Greek race, a man of pliant conscience, tortuous mind, and extraordinary astuteness," let himself be made pope to further an ambitious plan of his—no less than restoring Rome to the Byzantine Empire and placing the Catholic church under the supremacy of the patriarch in Constantinople. As a counter against the German emperor who was sure to come back at the head of his Saxon warriors, the new pope and the new duke needed the help of the ruler of the East, Basil II. Without it, they realized, they would be quickly overwhelmed by the army of German knights. And so they began negotiations with Basil which, they hoped, would lead to a formal alliance.

One should not judge Philagathos too severely. He was, after all, Greek in mind and heart. Having to choose between Otto and Basil, he would side with the latter. The plan came to nothing, since the hard-headed realist Crescentius was in this particular case even more naive than the romantic Otto. Basil was busy conquering Bulgaria and Armenia and was not about to launch another campaign in far-distant places. In the meantime, Gregory hurled the ban of excommunication at Crescentius and his antipope, but the matter was not be be decided by hurled paper scrolls but by hurled spears. Late in 997 Otto was again marching upon Rome, and this time he was not smiling. As the emperor's army approached, John Philagathos fled in terror to one of his hideouts in the Campagna. He was recognized, manacled, and dragged to Rome. The antipope's punishment was frightful. His eyes were gouged out, his nose, lips, and ears were sliced off, and his tongue was torn out by the root. He was then placed backward upon a miserable donkey, its tail was placed in his hand, and his head was crowned with a comical animal mask whose ears were sticking up. Thus he was paraded through the town to be pelted with ordure—a hideous example to other would-be traitors. He was then thrown into a dungeon in spite of his crippling wounds.

Some apologists have maintained that all this was done without Otto's knowledge; but this is hardly credible since Philagathos had called himself pope, was co-leader together with Crescentius of the anti-German rebellion, and had once been the emperor's tutor. One cannot imagine that the mutilators would have done their savage works without being sure of Otto's approval. Otto's later execution of Crescentius bears that out. Philagathos's punishment was so extreme probably because he had once been so close to Otto, and his actions were therefore looked upon by his former pupil as the worst kind of treachery and personal affront.

Rather than fleeing, Crescentius barricaded himself inside the Castle of St. Angelo, trusting in its gigantic walls, his men, and his stores of supplies. He hoped for help from the outside and was sure that he could hold out for a long time. But his men deserted one after another, his provisions dwindled, and the outside help never came. Secretly Crescentius stole away from his stronghold in disguise and sought out the emperor to reach a belated understanding. With a cold smile Otto told him to go back to his fortress and defend himself.

Some chroniclers say that Otto took the castle by treachery and that he had promised Crescentius life and limb if he surrendered. This might or might not be true. It is certain that Otto's commander, the margrave Eckhardt of Meissen, assaulted the castle day and night with catapults, battering rams, and siege engines of all kinds; and when these made no impression on the walls, he raised up storming ladders, taking the ramparts in grim, hand-to-hand fighting. On April 29, 998, retreating step by step to the roof of the castle, Crescentius finally gave himself up together with a few survivors. Twelve of them were hanged; he himself was beheaded on the highest point of the fortress. His head was impaled upon a spike and his body fastened to the crenelated ramparts for all to see. Oddly enough, his remains were buried on the Ianiculus, in the church of St. Pancratius, the guardian of vows and avenger of false oaths. He received a fitting epitaph:

Dust art thou, man, and ashes.
To mighty deeds you aspired.
Now a few feet of earth for you are enough.
Behold, he who ruled Rome,
Now a few feet of earth for you are enough.
When favored by fortune,
Now lies here, small and mean.
In splendor he sat,
Lord and duke of the Romans,
Of famed forefathers of the famous branch.
Whoever you art
Still today warmed by the sun,
Say: "Farewell" and know you will share his fate.

Gerbert had followed Otto to the gates of Rome but, wisely, no farther, so as to have no part in the cruelties perpetrated within the city. True to his nature, he always managed to be absent at the vengeance of the victorious. But the eighty-eight-year-old Nilus, hoary with age and already worshiped as a saint during his lifetime, came down from his hermitage in Gaeta to face the young victors, Otto and Gregory, sitting together in the Aventine Palace. They hastened to greet him, assisted him in climbing the marble stairs, kissed the hands of the holy hermit, and placed him on a chair higher than their own. A few months earlier, Nilus had warned Philagathos not to set himself up as antipope, advice that had fallen on deaf ears. Nilus now told pope and emperor that he had not come to ask favors for himself but for Philagathos, who had often distinguished himself in their service and had lovingly lifted them out of the baptismal font when they had been newborn infants, and whom they had repaid cruelly by robbing the poor man of his eyesight.

Humbly he begged them to put the pitiable, disfigured wretch in his care. Otto and Gregory instantly changed from a vengeful mood into maudlin repentance. They burst into tears and knelt before Nilus, saying "We will do all that your holiness demands of us." And so the saintly hermit took what was left of poor Philagathos out of prison and back with him to his cell, but not before telling Otto and Gregory, "As you had no pity on him, so the Lord will have no pity on you when you stand before His throne." Unlike Nilus, Gerbert had not lifted a finger on behalf of the Greek grammarian, but then he never claimed to be a saint.

Nilus had shaken Otto to his innermost core. From that time on the emperor showed a growing tendency to melancholy, self-mortification, fasting, punishing his flesh, retreating into dark caves, and praying for forgiveness. It was said that his asceticism was due to his remorse over the hideous treatment he had meted out to his Greek tutor. The whole sad business had a weird postscript. Otto, hitherto chaste and, for all that is known, still a virgin, became enamored and intimate with a woman—the widow of Crescentius.

He was young, so the legend went, and the wife of Crescentius was wonderfully fair. Her name was Stephania. She came weeping before him, mourning her lord, and she was beautiful in her grief. The young emperor saw her and pitied her and loved her, and he took her to his heart in sin. Though he repented daily, he daily fell again, while the woman offered up her body and her soul to be revenged for the fierce man she had loved. Eventually she found her opportunity against him and poured poison in his cup, kissed him, and gave it to him with a loving word. And he drank it and died, and thus the prophecy of the holy man Nilus, was fulfilled upon him.

In reality, Otto died in Patano of natural causes when the widow was nowhere near and their affair long forgotten, but about their relationship there can be no doubt. Bruno of Querfurt, Otto's friend and the last man to slander him, spoke darkly of an "adulterous beauty," of Otto's sins of "adolescent flesh," and of "the splendid youth, who never married, even though his flesh was weak, seducing him into a few trivialities."

Another chronicler, Petrus Damianus, put it more bluntly: *"Cuius [Crescentius's] uxorem imperator in concubinam accepit,"* which means that after executing him, the emperor made Crescentius's widow his concubine. It was a thing to be expected from a not quite twenty-year-old youth, particularly as, to quote Gibbon, men wearing the purple seldom sigh in vain. Still, it was a strange passion that drove Otto to take, of all the women in Rome, Crescentius's widow to his bed.

One day after Crescentius had been put to death, Otto named Gerbert archbishop of Ravenna to compensate him for the loss of Sassbach and his see at Rheims. Ravenna was, after Rome, the most important town and archbishopric in Italy, at one time the Eternal City's rival as the capital of late Roman emperors. Once it had even tried to replace Rome as the papal seat and endeavored to make its patron saint, San Apollinarius, into a thirteenth apostle, in spite of the fact that San Apollinarius had never existed; his name was originally that of a ditch in which those "slain by Apollo," that is, the plague, were buried. Be that as it may, Ravenna was a city of great magnificence, containing within its walls the famous round campanile, the mausoleum of the empress Galla Placida with its slightly transparent windows of alabaster, Theoderic's squat tomb, and, among several others, the three great churches of San Vitale, San Appolinare Nuovo, and San Apollinare in Classe. These were wonderful examples of Byzantine art and architecture, aglow with some of the world's finest mosaics.

Yet Gerbert was not happy in Ravenna. Though he held the highest ecclesiastic office, second only to the papacy, he was Ravenna's first non-Italian archbishop, and once again he was surrounded by enemies. He was in his midfifties, now, his health was deteriorating, and he was often in pain; but his discomfort was to last only a year.

In February 999, Pope Gregory, not yet thirty, died. It was rumored, with good reason, that he had been poisoned. In April, not losing any time, Otto raised his beloved teacher to the Holy See. Thus the humble monk of Aurillac became the Vicar of Christ, Pope Sylvester II. Gerbert chose the name of the pope who, according to tradition, had baptized the first Christian emperor, to symbolize that Otto was the new Constantine and he himself the new Sylvester, corulers of the new universal empire, two bodies with one single heart. Together they would rule the world in perfect harmony as God's viceregents, with the holy and imperial city as its center. Kings would bow before them in acknowledgment of their divine mission and authority. No more would the empire be a rugged bastion, held together by force, which his grandfather had created to dominate the West; no more even of Charlemagne's empire. This empire would live in the shadow of the cross, where pope and emperor would work, each in his own sphere, for the happiness and welfare of humankind. Forgetting his aches and pains, the new pope threw himself with youthful ardor into his task of reforming the church in head and body.

In a letter, Gerbert urged Otto on: "Things imagined by great minds . . . need great deeds to be realized. Italy should not deceive herself that civilization and wisdom of the ancients died in the emperor's castle, and Greece should cease to brag of the wisdom of her ruler. Greece is in error thinking that she inherited the power and greatness of Rome. Ours, ours is rich and fruitful Italy. We possess warlike Gaul and Germany and are served by stout Slavs. Above all we have you, emperor, you of Greek blood, towering above the Greeks, ruling Rome by rights of inheritance, superior both to the Romans and Greeks in mind and eloquence."

Gerbert addressed Otto as his "ever august Caesar my glorious Lord Otto," and "exalted Imperator of the Romans," trying to bolster the morale of Otto, who tended toward feelings of insecurity and inadequacy, scarcely hidden beneath a fragile but glittering surface. More and more the pope had to prop up the emperor with flattery to keep him going. But there is also a tone of exultation in Gerbert's letters, the exultation of a man who feels himself close to reaching his goal.

Otto was now ready to recreate in one body the senate of ancient Rome, the triumphs of Trajan, the glory of the Roman republic, and the pomp of Justinian's Byzantium. He built his palace on the Aventine, occupying the site of Nero's golden house. Spread out before him stretched the sprawling *civitas sacrosancte*, a world of churches, majestic ruins, and great palaces, a sea of broken marble and magnificent decay, but also unimaginable splendor, venerable structures hallowed by faith and history. Out of the rubble rose the mighty basilica called the Lateran, Santa Maria Maggiore, the Forum, the Colosseum, and the great *thermae*, empty shells now, but still impressive in their desolate grandeur. Below him he also recognized the towered lairs of Rome's nobles, cowed but always ready to leap again for his jugular; the house of the Crescentii; and, near his own palace, that of Marozia and Alberic, remade into a church. Humbly admiring, he stood before the giant sculptures of the horse tamers, depicted in heroic nudity, or the more than life-size statue of a goddess clasped in a tangle of snakes, who, it was piously explained, represented Mother Church. But most lovingly his eyes caressed the triumphal arches of Titus and Constantine and Trajan's column, feeling himself the heir of these great conquerors. He was becoming the victim of grandiose delusions, the counterpart of his inferiority complex, a megalomaniac insisting on being addressed as emperor of emperors, consul of the senate and people of Rome, renovator of the empire. The Saxon atheling made himself over into an oriental *basileus*; often he quoted Horace: "Greece, taken captive, captured her savage conqueror, carrying her arts into clownish Latium."

Otto was at heart an actor, and the Aventine became the grand theater in which he daily enacted the drama of the universal empire, casting himself as the star and his courtiers the supporting cast. He reinstituted the stiff Byzantine court ceremonial and ruled in Caesarian splendor, taking his meals in silent isolation at a semicircular table raised high above those of his followers.

He appeared clad in strange and outlandish garments—an over-large robe adorned with images from the apocalypse and a gold-embroidered dalmatic covered with the signs of the zodiac. He ordered everything in his wardrobe down to the minutest detail and demanded oriental devotions to his person. He was always surrounded by a large crowd of attendants who had to address him with such appelations as Saxonicus, Romanus, and Italicus. "The empty shades of consuls and senators were revived by him from their tombs." Shadowy offices were created—Magistri et Comites imperialis, Militiae et palatii imperialis, Protospatharii and praefectii navalis—imperial colonels and admirals.

He gave new names to old Saxon offices. Chamberlains and butlers became *Vestiarii* and *Protovestiarii*. Chief ministers were dubbed *Logothetes* and *Archilogothetes*. He forced his self-conscious, awkwardly grinning Saxons to wear flowing Byzantine costumes so that the court assembly became a masked ball. He recreated the rank of Roman patrician for imperial aides who wore golden headrings, but he also, more importantly, established trial by jury after the Saxon manner. Otherwise he made the law of Justinian paramount, proclaiming, "In accordance with this book will be judged Rome, Leo's city, and the whole universe." The seal on his imperial bulla read, "Roma, Mistress of the World, guides the reins of the terrestrial orb."

He was depicted in illuminated manuscripts as a blond, beardless, shining youth, eternally young, the new Apollo. His feet were shown resting on his universe. He held in his left hand the orb, the *sphaera mundi* surmounted by the cross of faith; in his right he wielded the Holy Lance of power, while the provinces of his realm, in the shape of beautiful women, bowed low before him. Thus he saw himself and thus he expected others to see him—destined, as he said, quoting St. Augustine, to prepare the end of all ends, the millennium of the apocalypse. The last trumpet might yet sound, so Otto to believed, and he felt himself responsible for the world's salvation, God's holy vessel chosen from on high.

CHAPTER TWENTY-ONE

A Pope Too Wise,
An Emperor Too Young

LESS THAN A MILE AWAY from the emperor's Aventine palace, at the Lateran and Basilica of St. Constantine, consecrated to Christ the Savior, Gerbert had created his own world. Some time before he became pope he had written down a little enigmatic hexameter, its meaning known only to himself: "Scandit ad R. Gerbertus ad R. post Papa vigens R." Some said the three Rs represented the three decisive stages in Gerbert's career—Rheims, Ravenna, and Rome—proving that he could foretell his own future and therefore was a practitioner of the occult arts.

In any event, his rule began well. "His ideal of papal power was no less splendid than Otto's dream of a world state," though considerably more rational. His papal reign began auspiciously with Otto's gift of eight counties to the See of St. Peter to set his friend up in style. Otto said of his gift, "Even as for love of Peter we have chosen our lord and teacher Sylvester, and by the will of God have appointed and created him our most serene pope, so for the love of the same Lord Pope Sylvester we now confer upon holy Peter from our own property these gifts, that our teacher may offer them to our Saint Peter, prince of the apostles."

Like Otto, Gerbert also lived in a world of mystery, a rational spirit in the midst of symbols. But what was for Otto a matter of choice was for Gerbert part of his job. He now was the keeper to the keys of the kingdom, the living link between humanity and God, successor of St. Peter, Romanus Pontifex, Sanctissimus Pater, Servus Servorum Dei, invested with the plenitude of power over the teachings, worship, and discipline of the church.

One imagines Gerbert celebrating mass in his papal vestments, performing the miracle of transubstantiation in which, so it was said, Christ set his own body as a mousetrap and his blood for a bait, and in which the flesh and blood of the Savior is transformed into bread and wine. He consecrated the holy wafer or host, containing, so the church taught, the body, blood, soul, and Godhead together with the hair, nails, beard, and all else pertaining to the comeliness of the glorious Body which Christ resumed at his wondrous Resurrection.

The church over which Gerbert ruled had many names steeped in symbolism. She was called the Body of Christ. She was hailed as a bride because Christ had betrothed her to himself. She was Mother Church, for daily in baptism she bore sons to God. Sometimes she was referred to as a widow, because "she sitteth solitary through her afflictions, and, like Rachel, will not be comforted." The church was even symbolized as a harlot, because "she is called out of many nations, and because she closeth not her bosom against any that return to her."

St. Peter's Basilica the site of so many mysteries and ceremonies, was itself a symbol, being the abode of God. The portal represented Christ who had said, "I am the door," while the pavement was an allegory for the foundation of the faith; the towers were the priests and prelates, bulwarks of the church; while the great golden cross in the center reminded the faithful to love the Redeemer from the bottom of their hearts.

Gerbert was also, at least theoretically, charged with guarding the church's relics, enough of them to fill a city, and of many kinds, both in Rome and throughout Christendom. Cities, the chapels of kings and dukes, and abbeys and convents were the repositories of vials of the Virgin's milk, of Christ's tears, of St. Joseph's breath and sweat, drops of wine left over from the wedding of Cana, hairs from Noah's and St. Peter's beards, nails from the true cross, manure from Job's pile, branches from the bush from which God spoke to Moses, hay from the manger, salt from the pillar into which Lot's wife had been changed when, incautiously, she looked over her shoulder,

The people of the Dark Ages fervently believed in relics. We do not know to what extent Gerbert did, as he never wrote about them; but Otto had absolute faith in their efficacy, swore solemn oaths upon them, and carried them into battle. The young emperor made a special pilgrimage to southern Italy in order to obtain the bones of St. Bartholomew from a monastery near Benevento. Unwilling to antagonize the emperor, the monks gave him the bones, and Otto returned in triumph to Rome; but the monks had tricked him by having substituted for the desired bones the much less valuable ones of St. Paulinus of Nola.

As pope, Gerbert wielded awesome powers. *Ecclesia*'s Zeus, he could at will hurl the thunderbolts of anathema and interdict at those disobedient to Mother Church. Anathema and interdict were punishments in the face of which even kings cringed and trembled. Serious offenders could be deprived of the Eucharist for one or ten years and until the hour of their deaths. During the period of penance the penitent was compelled to abstain from sex and to spend his life in religious exercises. He could be sent on a long and dangerous pilgrimage. Before readmittance to communion the sinner appeared before the assembled faithful in sackcloth with ashes strewn over his head, his hair shorn off; he confessed his sins on his knees, imploring the favor of absolution. The excommunicated man was cut off from all Christian ritual, ostracized by his neighbors, severed from relatives and friends. No Christian, on pain of being anathemized, might speak and eat with him or give him shelter. He was alone in this life and damned in the next. Gerbert himself had suffered cruelly under the weight of excommunication during his last year at Rheims.

In contrast to excommunication, which punished individuals, the interdict punished whole cities, provinces, and kingdoms for the fault of their princes. In a region under interdict, all churches were closed. Priests neither married their parishioners nor buried them. Public officials were forbidden to perform their office, judges to pass judgments, governors to govern, and everything came to a standstill. It was indeed a thunderbolt that brought mighty rulers to their knees.

Gerbert was not afraid to use such weapons against even the most powerful barons. The margrave Arduin, one of the greatest lords in Italy, had started a typical tenth-century war against his local rivals, temporal and spiritual, appropriating their land and laying waste to their estates. He stormed and set fire to the palace of the bishop of Vercelli, who died in the flames. He went on to attack the bishop of Ivrea, plundering his cathedral's treasury and ravaging church lands. Gerbert immediately pronounced a horrific sentence against him, putting Arduin under the ban: "You shall give up your sword, shall never eat meat, shall not kiss man nor woman, wear no linen, remain never longer than two nights in one place nor receive the body of Christ until the hour of your death." Arduin quickly came to heel. Gerbert was equally severe in the case of offending clerics, suspending one contumacious abbot from his office for two years, condemning him to fast for two days every week, not to take wine or any cooked food, and not to eat at all until he had recited the entire psalter.

Like others before him, the pope's attitude was changed by his high office. As Gerbert, archbishop of Rheims, he had resisted the pope's right to interfere in French church affairs. As Sylvester II he enforced that right. He restored his mortal enemy, Arnulf, to the See of Rheims, thereby admitting that his own tenure as archbishop there had been illegal and his excommunication just.

"We may assert with confidence that, while snatching a few happy moments for his books, Sylvester passed the too brief period of his pontificate in advancing the interests of the Church all over the world. Everywhere did he oppose the slightest tendency to heresy or schism. . . . He was prepared to resist schism with his very life if need should arise. Nor would he tolerate breaches of ecclesiastical discipline."

He maintained, even against Otto, that papal authority, derived from Christ, was higher than that of the crown, provided that the church was without stain. He condemned in the strongest words the selling of church benefices, bishoprics, and abbeys for money, the acquisition of church lands, and the holding of multiple clerical offices. In his epic battles against simony, he was likened to a Christian Hercules cleansing the Augean stables of the church.

Simony was the corrupt but almost universal practice under which a bishop paid the king or duke or archbishop who gave him his see. In their turn the priests paid the bishop who ordained them, and the parishioners paid the priests for marriages, weddings, and last rites. Bishops, often from noble houses, treated their parishioners like their feudal serfs, their parishes like family holdings they could dispose of as they pleased.

The term *simony* derived from the name of Simon the Magician in Acts: "And when Simon saw that through laying on of the apostles' hands the Holy Ghost was given, he offered them money, Saying, Give me also this power, that on whomsoever I lay hands, he may receive the Holy Ghost. But Peter said unto him, Thy money perish with thee, because thou hast thought that the gift of God may be purchased with money." The practice of simony plagued the church for centuries, as did the selling or bestowing of high church offices to minors and relatives, the evil of nepotism.

"How wretched and mad are those men who commit the cure of many thousand souls to their little nephews whom they would not trust with three pears lest they eat them! I have heard how one of these boys, after receiving an archdeaconry from his uncle, was set solemnly in his stall during the ceremony of installation, and was found not yet to have outgrown the needful ministrations of his nurse." Nepotism was rife in the tenth century. The horrid John XII was placed upon the papal see at the age of sixteen and, in turn, conferred an archdeaconship upon a child of ten.

It was natural that Gerbert, as pope, should despise and condemn these practices, since he himself had been driven from Bobbin, Rheims, and Ravenna for refusing to participate in them. His failure to succeed in these earlier appointments should not necessarily be interpreted as a sign of weakness or poor administration on his part; Bruno of Querfort, Adelbert of Prague, and even the mighty Willigis of Mayence all suffered the wrath of their subject nobles and priests at one time or another in their illustrious lives.

On the other hand, as Focillon wrote, "The error of hagiographers is to think that in a great life all things are great." Gerbert was not without blemish, though the fires of youth had now become the weak embers of advancing age. The conflict between the powers of good and evil also raged within his soul, and he knew well that Tyrannus, the representative of hell, can, given the chance, take up his abode in the body of a pope. Darkly Gerbert wrote that turning back from his earlier ways had liberated him from satanic powers. He could be scheming and avaricious. Sometimes the politician got the better of the pontiff. Focillon called him "old Gerbert, great in mind and great perhaps in intrigue, an honest man full of wise tricks, friend of the devil and prince in humanities." But, as the old saying went, "The light, even though it passes through pollution, is not polluted." For all his faults, Gerbert was still a great man and a very good pope.

Throughout his papacy, as throughout his whole life, Gerbert had to fight rumors that he was a sorcerer practicing the occult arts. Some detractors even went so far as to suggest that he was the Antichrist who was expected to make his appearance as the world neared its end. Gerbert had learned much in Spain that had not been known in the Christian West. Everything about him was suspect: the subjects he taught and wrote about; his many inventions, marvels to see and touch, made by his own hands—the spheres and astrolabes, the abacus, a

steam-powered organ, a new system of writing music, the Arabic numerals. In an age of superstition, his real achievements were soon over-
shadowed by the legends ascribed to him. He was said to have squared
the circle and to have constructed an artificial man as well as a monstrous, oversized human head that could speak and answer questions.
Such things could not be made by mortals without the aid of supernatural powers. As Gerbert grew old and famous, he also grew infa-
mous. He had gained his wisdom by means of detestable arts learned
from heathen Saracens, it was whispered, or by having sold his soul to
the devil.

It was even asserted that there existed a regular brotherhood of
evil magicians, churchmen among them, who brought up generation
after generation of sorcerers. Of them all, Gerbert was the most prominent; otherwise, it could not be explained how such a man of low, even
suspect, birth, whose wisdom derived from accursed Islam, could ever
have become God's Vicar on Earth.

It was written that Gerbert was the son of a Burgundian nobleman, wiser and more learned than all other men. Studying at Rheims,
the story went, he fell in love with the beautiful daughter of his teacher,
Praeposius, but the maiden rejected his impure advances. He then
tried to seduce her with the help of love potions designed to make
him irresistible, but, being a beginner at the practice of the occult, his
magic backfired and rendered him impotent. Distraught, Gerbert took
to drink and gambling, losing all his money.

One day, wandering in the forest, he stumbled upon an alluring
maiden dressed in diaphanous veils "which hide nothing," sitting amid
heaps of gold coins. She spoke to him: "I am Meridiana, of noble
birth, and desire thee for my lover. I shall take thee to my bed and
make thee rich beyond all imagination, because I am madly inflamed
by fleshly passion for thee."

The damsel made Gerbert "as rich as Solomon," and he established himself in a palace. His knowledge of the occult now improved,
he also succeeded in making Praeposius's daughter his mistress. Meridiana found this out and forced Gerbert to sign, with his own blood,

a paper promising to be hers forever. Poor Gerbert did not know that the ravishing creature was, in reality, Diabolus Meridianus, the devil's tool, and that by signing the document he had sold his soul to the fiend. "Thus the wisest of men are brought low by lustful concupiscence and the wiles of the female sex being forever at Satan's service."

With her infernal arts, Meridiana taught Gerbert more than mortal Christians should know and helped him to become abbot, bishop, and pope. Too late he recognized her true nature. By having had carnal knowledge of the devil's wood sprite, he had himself been turned into a demon.

In a German version of this legend, the Devil Abacus was said to have helped Gerbert win all scholarly disputations with the most learned men of his age, so that his fame spread throughout the world and the emperor could not help but make him pope. In return, he had sold his soul to the devil. A French tale accused Gerbert of being an adept in Muhammadan necromancy, which he had studied at Hispalis (Seville). It described him as a limb of the fiend (*suppot du diable*), who could understand the language of birds and many unclean beasts.

The most famous of Gerbert's detractors was William of Malmesbury, who wrote, "To the papacy succeeded Sylvester, also called Gerbert, about whom it will not be absurd to write these facts which are generally related about him. Born in Gaul, from a lad he grew up a monk at Flory; afterwards, either disgusted at a monastic life or seized by lust of glory, he fled by night into Spain, chiefly designing to learn astrology, and other sciences of that description from the Saracens. Gerbert then, coming among these people, satisfied his desires. There he learned what the singing and flight of birds portended; there he acquired the art of calling up spirits from hell. There is no necessity to speak of his progress in the lawful sciences of arithmetic and astronomy, music and geometry, which he imbibed so thoroughly as to show they were beneath his talents, and which he revived in Gaul, where they had for a long time been wholly obsolete.

"Being the first to acquire the abacus from the Saracens he gave it rules which are scarcely understood by the most learned mathematicians. He stayed with an infidel philosopher whose good will he obtained by paying him money. The Saracen had no scruples selling his knowledge; he would talk to him of matters deep or trivial, and lend him books. There was however one volume, containing the knowledge of his whole art, which he could never be enticed to lend. Gerbert was consumed by desire to possess this book by any means, 'for we ever press more eagerly towards what is forbidden.' He implored the Saracen for the love of God, and by his friendship and offered many things in exchange for the book, but all in vain. He plied him with wine and, with the help of the Saracen's daughter through carnal intimacy, stole the book from under the infidel's pillow and fled.

"Waking up, the Saracen pursued the fugitive by his arcane knowledge of the stars and heathen magic. Gerbert, discovering his danger by the very same arts, hid himself under a wooden bridge, neither touching earth nor water, Thus he reached the sea coast. There, with incantations, he called up the devil, and made a pact with him to be under his power forever, if he would save him from the Saracen, who was gaining on him, and whisk him away to another, far coast. This the devil did."

As the feared day of the presumed end of the world approached, many Romans were afraid that it would reveal Gerbert in his true shape of the devil's familiar. Trembling, they watched as this Pope Sylvester II stood motionless, arms upraised, at the conclusion of the Mass on New Year's Eve in the year 999. The great bell struck twelve "and still nobody stirred. But after a while all came to life, as after a long dream. The choir intoned the 'Te Deum Laudamus,' and then all broke into one great shout of exultation, praising God and the holy father, singing, crying, laughing, tears of joy streaming from their faces." Outside the basilica the multitude stood for a moment transfixed but, in the twinkling of an eye, was swept away in a frenzy of universal joy amid the ringing of innumerable bells, great and small. Humanity had been given a new lease on life upon an earth reborn. The year of fear and trembling had passed. A new day had dawned.

CHAPTER TWENTY-TWO

And Behold,
All Was Vanity

THE LAST DAY OF THE YEAR 999 and the first day of the year 1000 had come and gone. Yet still the earth stood and people still lived. On the night of awe and mystery, singing and praying crowds, waving torches and palm branches, had filled the Forum and the Capitol, their flickering brands performing a ghostly dance like eerie swamp lights scurrying to and fro, the incantations of numberless men and women sounding like a swarm of giant bees. The bell had tolled in the new year: "I praise the true God, I call the people, I assemble the priests, I mourn the dead, I put Satan to fight and I ring in the Last Judgment." Then many imagined that they saw the face of the Lord in the nocturnal sky, but it was only a cloud, and no trumpet had sounded. And when the sun at last rose upon a new century, somebody quoted a poet, whose name has been forgotten:

> Why do you weep,
> Birth-giving Roma?
> Come, dry your tears,
> Behold, you are saved.

Skeptics, though, had their misgivings. The secular-ecclesiastic rule of Otto and Gerbert did not work well because the emperor, weak, eccentric, and vascillating, could not hold up his part. "The sin of this king," wrote Bruno of Querfurt after it was all over, "was that he would not look upon his native land, delectable Germany, for the love of Italy, where savage destruction runs armed with a thousand deaths. The land of Romulus, feeding on its children, still lured him on with adulterous beauty."

Otto did return briefly to Germany, having fallen into one of his mystical moods. In the year 1000, on the Sunday of Pentecost, he was in Aix-la-Chapelle, standing in Charlemagne's fabled dome, "like a relic from the sea encrusted with shells and parasites, by additions in various styles, over which a thousand years roll in vain." The young emperor was resolved to look upon the face of the long-dead emperor, the great Karl himself. He ordered the sealed crypt in which the illustrious Frankish ruler lay buried to be opened and the marble slabs covering its entrance removed. Those charged with this task did so with awe and trepidation. As soon as Otto with a few chosen companions entered the crypt, they were enveloped by a strange musty odor, and they fell on their knees, praying to the dead emperor. When they dared to lift up their eyes they beheld Charlemagne sitting upright on his throne, as he had in life, a golden crown upon his bony brow, his right hand resting on his fabled sword, the irresistible *Joyeuse*, his left hand holding scepter and orb, the emblem of a dominion which was coextensive with the globe itself. A pilgrim's pouch, symbol of humility, still dangled from his belt, while on his knees had been placed the Gospels, with a gem-encrusted cover and pages illuminated in leaf gold and glowing colors. The royal roseate dalmatic covered his flesh-less shoulders, while the hands were covered with white gloves through which the nails had grown. None of the body had decomposed except the tip of the nose, which Otto was to replace by another made of gold. He also had the nails cut and the moldering body dressed in new white linen. He pulled a tooth from the skull to keep for himself as a relic and also took from Charlemagne's neck a golden cross. When all this had been done and everything put in order, the young emperor and his retinue tiptoed wordlessly out of the dark burial chamber into the somber light of the church, after which the crypt was once more closed and sealed. Among Otto's attendants were many who thought it was a sacrilege to disturb the dead emperor's eternal sleep, spreading the tale that the crowned skull had spoken to Otto, warning the young prince of his imminent death and prophesying that Otto would die without heirs to his body.

Later in the year 1000, Otto set up his permanent court in Rome. Gerbert was glad to have him and his knights back, as without them he had hardly been able to maintain himself against the once-again plotting Italian nobles. On the Aventine, however, things were not right with Otto, who sat darkly brooding at his raised marble table. Under his gold-embroidered dalmatic, he now wore a hairshirt and a belt of thorns. Instead of Caesar and Augustus, he insisted on being called The Peaceable, God's Slave, and Iesu Christi Servus Servorum— Christ's servant of servants. More and more he exhibited a contempt for the things of this world, the *contemptus saeculi*, passing back and forth from pride to humility. Rising from the depths of self-deification, lust, vengeance, and killing, the reaction had set in. Otto felt himself abandoned by heaven, no longer in a state of grace, a miserable sinner against God and humanity. Remorse over the hard fate he had dealt out to his enemies gnawed at his vitals. The headless Crescentius and the mutilated Philogathos haunted his dreams. More and more often he crept away from the splendors of his palace to the Cave of San Clemente, scourging his body until the blood flowed, and, exhausted, he rested upon its cold, dank stone floor.

Extreme in all things and unable to compromise, his self-mortifications and self-imposed penances were as extravagant as his Byzantine self-glorifications had been. He fasted until he looked like a living corpse, spent sleepless nights on bleeding knees, and tried to fall asleep on beds of thorns, enduring these self-tortures until he fell down in a faint. Lightheaded from these rigors, he endured visitations from hideous monsters and visions of the Babylonian whore. He began to hallucinate. For a while only his trusted companion, Bruno of Querfurt, future martyr and saint, knew to what lengths Otto had gone in his quest for forgiveness. Finally, it could no longer be hidden. Gerbert was at a loss to understand it. Self-flagellation and fasting in caves were not his idea of healthy penance. Sternly he admonished Otto, the old teacher asking the young pupil, "What shall become of you, of me, of our empire, of your Saxons surrounded by enemies in a strange and hostile land?" His chiding was in vain. Gerbert's power to soothe, to persuade, to rule Otto's mind was gone. The emperor was no longer listening to human voices but to the spirits of his dreams.

Otto had ready answers for those who pled for his return to reality. Did not many rich nobles, atoning for their sins, give all they possessed to the church or to the poor? Had not the doge Orseolo of Venice left the splendor of his exalted office to become a hermit? Did not holy anchorites find shelter from an evil world in dark and hidden grottoes? Could an emperor, weighed down by enormous misdeeds, do less?

Rather than heeding Gerbert or his Saxon commanders, Otto made pilgrimages to living saints, above all to St. Nilus of Gaeta or St. Romuald of Ravenna. Nilus, the Calabrian Greek and John Philagathos's rescuer, had once been of the world, "stricken by lust like a wounded deer." Married and the father of two children, he had been seized by the holy fire of renunciation, deserting wife and family to live in a cave. He preached against carnal human nature, saying that couples should not participate in any church festival if they had bedded together the night before, warning that hell had a special lake of molten lead awaiting those who had done so. Better not to marry, better not to bed together at all. Nilus had first gone to Monte Cassino, asking the abbot to find him a rough and wild place where he could live the exemplary life of Christian devotion in a tiny cell or cleft in a rock wall. He fasted often and never ate meat. He wore only a goat skin, which teemed with vermin because he changed it only once a year, but he allowed himself the luxury of taking walks, reading, singing hymns, and practicing calligraphy. People said that Nilus was endowed with supernatural gifts that gave him spiritual power over rich and poor, high and low.

Otto made a pilgrimage to Nilus, hoping that the hermit might be able to put his mind at rest. Saint and sinner, the almost ninety-year-old recluse and the not quite twenty-year-old emperor had a long talk. Nilus spoke of bad deeds, of blinding, of killing, of the sin of pride. Otto burst into tears, calling himself Nilus's unworthy son. He offered the old man veneration, riches, abbacies, his own monastery in Rome. He placed his own golden circlet, which he always wore as a symbol of his royalty, into the hermit's trembling hands as a sign of abject submission. Nilus wanted none of these things. He spoke to Otto of death, of the Last Judgment, of the need for salvation, of truly repenting before it was too late. He said that the only things he wished for were Otto's prayers and that he should prepare himself for a worthy death and the day when even emperors had to account to God for their deeds. Strange things to say to one as young as the adolescent Saxon.

On his knees, the emperor begged Nilus to come with him to Rome, where the light of his holiness would act like a spreading balm, turning many hearts from the world to heaven. Nilus would not hear of it. He consented only to go with Otto as far as the nearby abbey of Monte Cassino. When they approached it, Nilus heard the sounds of a lute coming from the refectory and learned that the monks had taken a bath. He turned back in horror. Before parting, he forgave and blessed Otto, who went away barefoot, weeping and lamenting.

During his mental crises of the year 1000, Otto turned in despair to Romuald, another stern, uncompromising hermit and future saint. Romuald had fled the world to atone for a life of luxury, pleasure, and perversion. He found a refuge in Ravenna's monastery of San Apollinare in Classe, but his never-ending exhortations to the brothers to repent, to do penance, to stay awake longer and eat less, to spend more and more time on their knees, and to make things ever harder for themselves got on their nerves so much that they threatened to kill him if he did not leave. Romuald then formed a small hermit colony in swamps and salt marshes near Ravenna. For him there were no short-cuts to salvation, no easy ways to attain the kingdom. He had once flogged his own father to force him to return to a monastery the old man had deserted. Romuald was a man after Otto's heart.

Easter Sunday of the *annus mirabilis*, the miracle year, found Otto cowering at Romuald's feet, beating his breast, confessing, praying, staying with the hermits in a separate cell. It became Romuald's great-est ambition to have among his recluses not only a doge of Venice but also a Saxon emperor. If Romuald was hard on Otto, Otto was even harder on Romuald. At all hours, night and day, tortured by evil dreams and memories, the emperor interrupted the hermit's devotions or dis-turbed his sleep. Hour after hour he haunted Romuald, begging him to show him a way out of guilt and despair. Terrible like a sword, irres-istible like a raging flood was Romuald's eloquence: "Renounce the world for your soul's sake!" he exhorted Otto again and again, and the emperor responded, "Verily, God's spirit talks to me through your mouth." He addressed Romuald's band of ascetics: "From this hour I promise God and His Saints that within a certain span of time, dur-ing which I shall try to undo the errors of my reign, I shall hand over the government to one better and worthier than myself. I shall renounce the world, become a monk and make a pilgrimage to the Holy Sepul-cher in Jerusalem." But for the present, he told Romuald, he had to leave. Victory and revenge over the unfaithful Romans, who had once again risen against the holy empire, had to come first. "Victory and revenge!" Romuald was outraged. Otto tried to appease him by fol-lowing Christ's example of fasting and mortifying his flesh for forty long days in the Abbey of San Apollinare. Romuald was not in the least mollified. "If you go back to Rome," he thundered, "you shall never see me or Ravenna again!"

Otto never fulfilled the vow made to Romuald. Bruno of Quer-furt, Otto's alter ego in otherworldliness, urged him from time to time to keep his promise, but Otto was in no hurry. He just smiled and said, "I have not forgotten." For a short time it pleased him to be emperor again, and it was at this time that, persuaded by the bishops Peter and

Leo of Vercelli, he issued his terrible decree that no serf of the church should ever be free to aspire to liberty. Also, he had a problem. A Byzantine princess, Stephania—not to be confused with Crescentius's widow—had been promised him as a bride and was expected to arrive in Italy any day. If he married her, as he now intended, he could not very well become a monk. Otto hoped that time and fate would resolve the matter; so he let things drift.

In January 1001 the town of Tivoli revolted. Otto besieged it and the rebels surrendered. The emperor forgave them upon their promise to henceforth be loyal to him, but Tivoli sparked a much larger uprising in Rome. For three days the Roman mob, stirred up by the nobles, invested Otto in his palace on the Aventine and finally stormed it. Aided by a few men, Otto fought his way through to his soldiers in the Castle of St. Angelo. From its walls he addressed a raging, frenzied crowd: "Are you not my Romans, for whose sake I left my fatherland and friends? Whose fame I would have carried to the ends of the earth? You were my favorite children. See how you have rewarded me, your father, by slaughtering my companions. And yet I cannot banish you from my heart, you whom I have cherished with a parent's love."

His must have been a charismatic speech; the unpredictable Romans suddenly burst into cheers and, on the spur of the moment, killed two of their ringleaders and swore, as so often before, eternal fidelity. But a few days later, they had changed their minds again. Filling the streets and screaming curses, they killed every German they could lay their hands on. The Roman nobles ordered all the gates of the city closed and barricaded to prevent Otto from being reinforced and laid siege to the Castle of St. Angelo. At a council of war, Otto was persuaded by his handful of vassals to try to cut his way through and out of the city. After having received the sacraments from the hand of his friend, Bishop Bernward, Otto seized the Holy Lance. He was about to lead the sally out of the fortress when word was received that his companions outside the city had made an arrangement with the rebels. The emperor and pope were guaranteed unopposed departure, providing that every German left inside Rome would leave with them.

Silently, Otto mounted his horse and, together with Gerbert and Bernward, rode off through the Porta Flaminia which, not so long before, had seen his triumphal entry into the city. Many Romans, even rebels, wept when they saw him leave. Always there had been a curious love-hate relationship between them. This happened on February 16, 1001. Otto was never to enter his *urbs regia* again.

He made Ravenna his new headquarters, as the rest of Italy remained loyal. Thietmar wrote with great bitterness, "The emperor held all the country, all of Lombardy in faithfulness; except only Rome, which he loved and treasured above all." In June, Otto was once more before the city, but confidence in himself and his destiny had been shattered. He soon gave up the siege, saying that Rome was too strong, his forces too small. He was unlike the shining, eager Caesar to whom his men had become accustomed, and his dejection undermined their morale. Nobody believed in his dreams anymore. Otto turned his back on Rome, which no longer cast its siren spell over the spurned lover.

After that, nothing mattered any more. He had simply given up. He was losing his will to live because there was no longer anything to live for. In vain Gerbert tried to cheer him up, offering him the consolation of philosophy: "You are young, all this will pass." But the days when a chapter from Boethius could set things right had passed.

Otto now tired easily, ate little, and withered before Gerbert's eyes. He no longer had the power to decide whether to go back to Germany, where he was needed, or to stay in Italy, where he was not wanted. He did not know what to do but would no longer listen to advice. He told Gerbert that the air of Italy did not agree with him, that its nature was in enmity with the nature of his body. In January 1002 he rode restlessly back and forth through the hill country north of Rome, a shivering ghost oppressed by dark thoughts beneath dark winter clouds. He complained of the cold, asking for one more fur coat to cover his shoulders. He could hardly keep his saddle. Ashen-faced, he sought shelter in the castle of Paterno, a massive chunk of stone rising from the flank of Mount Soracte. Painfully stiff, he dismounted in the courtyard but managed to smile and jest with Paterno's lord, the ever faithful Count Tammo. The following morning he could hardly get up. His friends watched him as he staggered, holding on to walls for support. He received bad news from Germany, where, due to his long absence, everything seemed to be falling apart. He was "shaken by a light fever," nothing serious, it was said, just a case of swamp fever.

Soon it became clear that the sickness was overwhelming him. He was consumed by the Roman fire brought on by "harmful effluvia." Thietmar wrote of ulcers or abcesses breaking open, but he was not personally present. Some thought it was smallpox or a single case of the plague. Otto himself believed it was poison. To make matters worse, his enemies laid siege to the castle, so that the defenders faced starvation. His body was covered by a rash. He told Thankmar that he was burning up. Propped up in a chair and wrapped in blankets a message reached the stricken emperor that his long-awaited Greek bride had finally landed at Bari. Her arrival no longer mattered. Otto took to his bed, never to rise again. He asked for and received the last rites, handing over the empire's insignia to Bishop Heribert of Cologne, awaiting the end calmly and with dignity, "cheerful and strong in the faith, departed the empire's crown from this world." So departed Romanorum Ultimus, the Last of the Romans. Otto's last words were, "The rope is broken and I am free." He passed away, it was said, in the arms of Gerbert, who gently closed his eyes.

The emperor died only a short day's ride from his beloved Rome, which had rejected him: "Homeless expires the king born in purple before the gates of the city." He was twenty-two years old at the time of his death. Otto left no heirs. With him died the house of Otto and the dream of his universal empire of all Christians. In obedience to his last wish, he was to be buried in Aix-la-Chapelle, next to the great Charlemagne. The cortege carrying his remains northward fought its way for seven days through swarms of enemies until it reached Verona and safety. Although he was buried according to his instructions, no one has been able to pinpoint the exact site of Otto's grave.

His Greek bride loitered for a while at Bari, shrugged her shoulders, and sailed back to Constantinople. Gerbert returned to Rome, occupying once more the Chair of St. Peter; but his life, too, had lost its purpose, since with Otto the church had lost its right arm to carry the sword of temporal power. To be born was misery, to live was anguish, and to die was trouble, but at the end of the road the gate of light stood open. Not disease but the death of his dream had killed Otto, and it was Otto's death that killed Gerbert. Pope Sylvester II passed away due to unknown causes on May 12, 1003, barely one year after his pupil. Some say that "Pope Sylvester lingered another year at Rome and then was swept away by a violent and mysterious death."

Virulent mythmakers wrote endings to their dark legends about his life and death. He was pronounced to have been the antichrist, whose satanic powers had postponed the Second Coming of the Savior. It was written that before his death he no longer dared to partake of the Savior's flesh and blood when celebrating mass. Preaching inside Rome's Jerusalem chapel he perceived Meridiana—the devil's wood sprite—clapping her hands for joy; by this he knew that his end was near. Repenting, Gerbert called his prelates and bishops together, confessed his sins before all the people, and ordered that from that hour on all popes must receive the body of Christ publicly. He also ordained that, after his death, his body should be cut to pieces and thrown into the streets for the devil to pick up as his due, so that his soul could be saved.

William of Malmesbury wrote, "Some may regard this as a fanciful tale, but the horrific choice of his death confirms me in the belief that he was indeed allied with the devil; else, when dying, why should Gerbert, like a pagan gladiator, mutilate his own person, unless weighed down by an enormous crime? Accordingly, in an ancient volume which came into my hands, I found written: 'Sylvester, who also called Gerbert, came to a shameful end.'"

The huge human head that Gerbert had magically constructed was said to remain mute unless spoken to by him, but then it only spoke the truth, answering yes or no. When Gerbert inquired, "Shall

I be pope?" the head answered yes. He also asked, "Shall I die before I read mass in Jerusalem?" The head answered no. By this, Gerbert was deceived into thinking that, as long as he did not go to the Holy Land to celebrate a mass, he would be immortal. For this reason, he would not renounce the devil or do penance for his sins. Gerbert did not know that at Rome there was a church called "Jerusalem," "because whoever flies thither finds safety, whatsoever crime he may be guilty of." Gerbert happened one day to celebrate the church's most sacred rite in this place and, recognizing his mistake too late, fell sick and died.

In some legends, Meridiana promises Gerbert that he will not die before he has said mass in Jerusalem:

> I shall be by thee both early and late,
> So that sicknesses shall not thee take.
> From death you shall right escape
> More or lesse
> Until in Jerusalem have sungen messe.
> He said: "That shall never betide,
> Into that land shall I never ride,"
> If that I may.
> "Then shall you live," she said, "until doomsday."

Most tales point out that Gerbert failed to recognize that by *Jerusalem* the demon meant the church of Santa Croce in Gerusalemme, only a short walk from the Lateran, one of seven churches visited, one after another, by pilgrims, because they contain pieces of the true cross. When Gerbert discovered the trick Meridiana had played upon him, after mass in "Gerusalemme," then:

> So thick the devils came from hell.
> That no tongue of them might tell.
> Fire and brimstone from them fell
> With stink of might;
> The bright sun withdrew and gave no light.

"Not, O Gerbert, will Abacus and pagan ciphers help thee now!" and: "Then the Pope Gerbert wept full sore." According to one legend the stricken pope fought with seven devils, to each of whom he gave a piece of his flesh; this satisfied them, so that they left him his soul. Holy Mary then descended from heaven, telling Gerbert that he had been forgiven and after a period in purgatory would attain paradise.

In 1240, the Cistercian monk Alberic wrote that Gerbert was buried under a slab of marble that sheds tears whenever a pope was about to die, and that those who kneeled at his graveside, "for every Lord's Prayer they say for him, a year in purgatory is forgiven them."

The most persistent legend was a distillation of all the others. It told of how the devil appeared at Pope Sylvester's side one day as he was celebrating a mass in the church of Santa Croce de Gerusalemme. Sylvester broke out into a cold sweat and died the same day, ordering that his body be cut up into small pieces so that the Evil One should not carry it off. Afterward, the legend stated, a cold sweat spread over his tomb and his bones rattled every time a pope entered the agony of death. Perhaps as a result of this persistent legend, Sylvester's tomb was opened in 1648, revealing Sylvester intact, hands crossed on his breast, and miter on his head.

It is refreshing that not all medieval chroniclers repeated these absurd tales. Some followed the lead of Dietrich of Reims who in 1390 simply commented, "The Romans hated this excellent pope for his great knowledge and wisdom and for this reason slandered him as having practiced the devilish arts." In truth, rather than practice "devilish arts," Gerbert and the Ottonians presided over the twilight of the old pagan gods. The years around Anno Domini 1000 saw the kings of Denmark, Norway, Sweden, Poland, and Hungary accept the Christian faith.

The German historian Gregovorius summed it up best: "A German and a Frenchman swept away the barbarism which so long prevailed at the Lateran. Gerbert in Rome is like a solitary torch in the darkness of the night. The century of grossest ignorance closed strangely enough with the appearance of a renowned genius. . . . But Rome can merely claim the honor of having served as the scene of his studies which have met with no response. If the Romans noticed their aged pope watching the stars from his observatory in a tower of the Lateran, or surrounded in his study by parchments and drawing geometrical figures, designing a sundial with his own hand or studying astronomy on a globe covered with a horse's skin, they probably believed him in league with the devil."

Today, the little town of Aurillac stands in the shadow of an old castle, one of the few remaining relics of Gerbert's days. His bronze statue, erected in 1851, still stands. It depicts on its socle a scene showing little Gerbert with a rudimentary telescope that he has fashioned out of a hollow tree branch in order to study the stars.

The little monk from Aurillac, born of "humble and obscure" parents, had done much to lead the West out of the darkness of the Century of Lead and Iron into a new age, the age of Lanfranc, Anselm, and Abelard. The scholars, humanists, chroniclers, and philosophers who came after him called Gerbert the light of Christendom. Some of his light still shines.

Bibliography

GENERAL

Artz, Frederic B., *The Mind of the Middle Ages A.D. 200-1500*. New York: Alfred A. Knopf, 1958.

Barraclough, Geoffrey. *The Crucible of Europe*. Berkeley and Los Angeles: University of California Press, 1976.

Boissonnade, P. *Life and Work in Medieval Europe*. New York: Harper & Row, 1964.

Brooke, Christopher. *Europe in the Central Middle Ages*, 1964.

Buckley, Theodore [Sir Emerson Tennent]. *Great Cities of the Middle Ages*. London, 1862.

Cambridge Medieval History. Vol. 3. 1922 and 1966.

Coulton, G. G. *Life in the Middle Ages*. 4 vols. in one. Cambridge University Press; New York: MacMillan, 1930.

Daniel-Rops, Henri. *The Church in the Dark Ages*. Translated by Audrey Butler. London: J. M. Dent & Sons; New York: Dutton, 1959.

De Ferdinandi. *Der Heilige Kaiser: Otto III und seine Aluum*. Tübingen: Rainer Wunderlich Verlag, 1969.

Duckett, Eleanor. *Death and Life in the Tenth Century*. Ann Arbor: University of Michigan Press, 1962.

Durant, Will. *The Age of Faith*. New York: Simon & Schuster, 1950.

Fliche, A. *L'Europe Occidentale de 888 a 1125*. Paris: 1940.

Focillon, Henri. *The Year 1000.* New York: Ungar, 1969.

Funck-Brentano, François. *The Middle Ages.* New York: Putnam, 1923.

Genicot, Leopold. *Das Mittelalter, Geschichte und Vermächtnis.* Graz, Austria: Verlag Styria, 1956.

Gibbon, Edward. *Decline and Fall of the Roman Empire.* 1892.

Hall and Foster. *Stories and Studies from Chronicle and History.* New York: John C. Ricker, 1852.

Heer, Frederic. *The Fires of Faith.* Milestones in History, vol. 2. New York: Newsweek Books, 1970.

Herlihy, David. *The History of Feudalism.* New York: Walker & Co., 1970.

Lacroix, Paul. *Military and Religious Life in the Middle Ages.* London, 1872.

Lecky, W. E. *History of European Morals.* New York: George Braziller, 1925.

Lopez, Robert S. *Byzantium.* London, Variorum Press, 1978.

———— *Some Tenth Century Towns.* 1959.

———— *The Birth of Europe.* London: Phoenix House, 1962; Boston: Lippincott, 1967.

———— *The Tenth Century.* 1959.

MacKinney, Loren Carey. *The Medieval World.* New York: Farrar & Rinehart, 1938.

McCall, Andrew. *The Medieval Underworld.* London: Hamish Hamilton, 1979.

Munro, Dana Carlton. *The Middle Ages.* New York: Century, 1923.

Osborn, E. B. *The Middle Ages.* New York: Doubleday, Doran & Co., 1928.

O'Sullivan, Jeremiah, and John F. Burns. *Medieval Europe.* New York: F. S. Crofts & Co., 1943.

Painter, Sidney. *A History of the Middle Ages.* New York: Knopf, 1964.

Pfister, Kurt. *Die Welt des Mittelalters.* Vienna: Bergland Verlag, 1952.

Pflugk-Harttung, Dr. Julius von. *Geschichte des Mittelalters.* Historischer Verlag Baumgartel, vol. 2. Berlin, 1891.

Pirenne, Henri. *Economic and Social History of Medieval Europe.* London: Kegan Paul, Treanch, Trubner & Co., 1936.

———— *Les Villes du Moyen Age.* Bruxelles: Maruice Lamertin, 1927.

Power, Eileen. *Medieval Women.* Cambridge, Postan, 1975.

Rowling, Marjorie. *Everyday Life in Medieval Times.* London: B. T. Botsford; New York: Putnam.

Roy, Jules. *L'an Mil.* Paris: Hachette, 1946.

Taylor, H. O. *The Medieval Mind.* 2 vols. London, 1927.

Thompson, James Westfall. *Economic and Social History of the Middle Ages.* New York: Unger, 1952.

Thorndike, Lynn. *The History of Medieval Europe.* Boston, 1949.

———— *A History of Magic and Experimental Science,* 2 vols. New York: MacMillan, 1923.

APOCALYPSE

Berlitz, Charles. *Doomsday 1999 A.D.* Garden City, N.Y.: Doubleday, 1981.

Cohn, Norman. *The Pursuit of the Millenium.* London: Paladin, 1970. Also published in French as *Les Fanatiques.*

Fülöo-Miller, René. *Leaders, Dreamers and Rebels.* New York: Viking, 1935.

Glaber, Raoul. *Les cinq Livres de ses histoires* ed. M. Prou: Paris, 1866.

Harnak, Adolf. "Millenium," *Encyclopaedia Britannica,* 1936.

Mcginn, Bernard. *Visions of the End.* New York: University of Columbia Press, 1979.

MacKay, Charles. *Extraordinary Popular Delusions.* London, 1841; Boston: L. C. Page & Co., 1932.

Plaine, Dom Francois. "Les Pretendue Terreurs de L'An Mil." *Revue des Questions Politiques* (1873).

E. Pognon. *L'An Mil.* Paris, 1947.

Roy, Jules. "L'An Mil: Formation de la Legende de L'An Mil." État de la France de L'An 950 a 1050. Paris, 1881.

Sendy, Jean. *Les Temps Messianiques.* Paris, 1979.

von Eiken, H. *Die Legende von der Erwartung des Weltuntergangs.* Forchungen zur Deutschen Geschichte, vol. 23. Munich, 1883.

GERBERT DE AURILLAC, POPE SYLVESTER II

Adalbero. *Adalbero, Remenssis Archiepiscopus: Epistulac.* Patologia Latina 137.

Allen, R. S. "Gerbert, Pope Sylvester II." *English Historical Revue* 7 (1892): 625-68.

Bastid, Paul. "Le Millénaire de Gerbert." *Revue Politique et Parlementaire* 176 (July-August-September 1938): 230-46.

Bayle, Montaigu Pierre. "Le Millenaire de Gerbert." *Revue Universelle* 74 (1938): 493-503.

Darlington, Oscar G. "Gerbert the Teacher." *American Historical Review* 52, no. 3 (April 1947) 456-76.

Döllinger, J. I. *Die Papst-Fabeln des Mittelalters.* Munich, 1863.

Eichengruen, Fritz. *Gerbert als Persönlichkeit.* Leipzig: B. G. Teubner, 1928.

Havet, Julian, ed. *Lettres de Gerbert.* Paris: 1889.

Lattin, Harriet Pratt. "The Policy of Gerbert in the Election of Hugh Capet." Thesis, Ohio State University, 1926.

————— ed. *The Letters of Gerbert.* Columbus, Ohio: O. H. L. Hedrick, 1932.

Leflon, le chanoine Jean. "Gerbert: Humanisme et Chrétienté au Xe Siècle." *Editions Fontenelle* (1945).

Mann, Horace K. *Lives of the Popes.* London: Kegan, Paul, Trench Trul ier & Co., 1925.

Nagl, Alfred. "Gerbert." *Kaiserliche Akademie* 116 (Vienna 1888): 861ff.

Olleris, A., ed. *Oeuvres de Gerbert.* Paris: Paris & Clermont, 1867.

Picavet, F. *Gerbert, Un Pape Philosophe.* Paris: Ernest Leroux, Editeur, 1897 and 1917.

Pivec, K. "Briefsammlung Gerberts." *Mittelungen des Instituts für Österreichische Geschichstforschung MIOG XLIX* (1935).

Schultes, K. *Papst Sylvester als Lehrer und Staatsmann.* Hamburg, 1891.

Schultess, Dr. Karl. *Die Sagen über Sylvester II.* Hamburg: Sammlung Wissenschaftlicher Vortrage, 1893.

Tannery, P., ed. *Memoires Scientifiques* 5, Toulouse-Paris, 1922. Articles 5 and 10.

Thorndyke, Lynn. "Gerbert and the Introduction of Arabic Astrology." *A History of Magic and Experimental Science.* New York: Columbia University Press, 1923-1956.

Thurston, Herbert. "The Magical Arts of Pope Sylvester II." *The Month* 118 (July-September 1911): 177-91.

Tout, T. F. *The Empire and the Papacy: Period 11.* London: Rivingtons, 1914.

Weigle. *Die Briefsammlung von Rheims.* Berlin: Weidmannische Verlagsbuchhandlung, 1966.

William of Malmesbury. *Historia Novella.* Translated by K. R. Potter. London, 1955.

————— *The Chronicle of the Kings of England.* London: Henry bohn, 1897.

————— *De Rebus Gestis Regum Anglorum.*

GERMANY, DITTONIANS

Barraclough, Geoffrey. *The Origins of Modern Germany.* Oxford: Oxford University Press, 1957.

Bauer, Albert and Reinhold Rau. *Quellen zur Geschichte der Sächsischen Kaiserzeit* (Widukind, Adalbero, and Luitprand). Darmstadt; Wissenschaftliche Buchgesellschaft, 1971.

Becker, J. "Luitprand of Cremona." Translated into English by F. A. Wright. *Scriptores rerum Germanarum; Patrologia Latina CXXXVI,* 1915. From Monumenta Germaniae Historica.

Bergman, Sister Mary Bernardine. *Hrosvithae Liber Tertius,* St. Louis: St. Louis University, 1942.

De Ferdinandi, Michael. *Der Heilige Kaiser.* Tübingen: Rainer Wunderlich Verlag, 1969.

Dupre-Theseider, E. "Otto I und Italien," *Institute für Osterreichische Geschichts Forschung* 20. Vienna, 1962.

Fife, Robert Herndon. *Hroswitha of Gandersheim.* New York: Columbia University Press, 1947.

Giesebrecht, Wilhelm von. *Die Deutschen Kaiser.* Velhagen & Klasing, Leipzig: 1881.

Gmelin, Otto. *Der Ruf zum Reich.* Munich: F. Bruckmann, 1956.

Grundmann, Herbert. *Betrachtungen zur Kaiserkrönung Ottos I.* Munich: Bayerische Akademie der Wissenschaften, 1962.

Haight, Anne Lyon. *Hroswitha of Gandersheim.* New York: Hroswitha Club, 1965.

Halphen, Louis. *La Cour d'Otton III, Mélange d'archeologie et d'histoire de l'école Français a Rome.* Paris, 1905.

———— *La Cour d'Otton a Rome (998-1001): A travers d'histoire du moyen age.* Paris: 1950.

Hirsch, P. "Widukind, monachus Corbeiensis: Res gestae Saxonicae." *Scriptores rerum Germanarum; Patologia Latina CXXXVII,* 1935.

Holtzmann. "Thietmar von Merseburg." "chronicon." *Monumenta Germaniae Historica,* 1955; *Scriptores rerum Germanarum; Patrologia Latina CXXXIX.*

Holtzmann, Robert. *Geschichte der Sächsischen Kaiserzeit.* 4 vols., 1961.

Holtzmann, Walther. *König Heinrich I under die Heilige Lanze.* 1947.

Hroswita of Gandersheim, *Carmen de gestis Oddonis.* Hanover & Berlin: Monumenta Germaniae, 1826, vol iii & iv.

Koepke, R., and F. Duemmler, *Kaiser Otto der Grosse*. Leipzig, 1876.

Labande, E. "Mirabilia Mundi: Essai sur la personalité d'Otton III. *Cahiers de Civilisation Médiévale* 6 (1963).

Pflugk-Harttung, Dr. Julius von. *Nord und Süd* 20 (1882).

Ruotger. "Vita Brunonis Archiepiscopi Coloniensis." Edited by Irene Otto. *Scriptores rerum Germanarum*, n.s. 20 (1951).

Schramm, E. P. *Die Deutschen Kaiser und Koenige in den Bildern ihrer Zeit*. Leipzig.

————— *Kaiser, Rom und Renavatio*. 2 vols. Berlin: Sturdlien der bibliothek Wartburg 17, 1929.

Ter Braak, M. *Kaiser Otto III; Ideal und Praxis im Fruehen Mittelalter*. Amsterdam, 1928.

Tout, T. F. *The Empire and the Papacy*. London: Rivingtons, 1914.

Uhlirz, Mathilde. "die Italienische Kirchenpolitik der Ottonen." *Mitteilungen des Instituts Österreichische Geschichtsforschung*. 48 (1934).

Wilmans, R. Otto III. *Jahrbücher des Deutschen Reiches*, 1954.

Wright, F. A. *The Works of Liutprand of Cremona*. London & New York, 1930.

ROME, PAPACY, CHURCH, MONASTICISM

Amann, Émile and Auguste Dumas. *Histoire de L'Église* Vol. 7. Paris, 1948.

Benedict of Nursia, Saint. *The Rule*. Translated by Abbot J. McCann. London: Burns, Oates, 1952.

Bland, David. *A History of Book Illustration*. New York: World Publishing, 1958.

Crawford, Francis Marion. *Ave Roma Immortalis*. New York: Macmillan, 1898.

Daly, Lowrie J., S. J. *Benedictine Monasticism*. New York: Sheed and Ward, 1965.

Delatte, Paul. *A Commentary on the Rule of St. Benedict*. Archabbey Press, 1950.

Diringer, David. *The Illuminated Book*. New York: Philosophical Library, 1958.

Doyle, L. J. *St. Benedict's Rule for Monasteries*. Collegeville, Minn.: St. John's Abbey, 1948.

Funk, F. X. *Lehrbuch der Kirchengeschichte*. Paderborn, 1907.

Gebhart, E. "L'Etat d'âme d'un Moine de l'An Mille." *Revue des deux Mondes* (September 1891): 600ff.

Gilson, Étienne. *The Spirit of Medieval Philosophy*. New York: Scribners, 1940.

Gontard, Friedrich. *The Chair of St. Peter: A History of the Papacy*. New York: Holt, Rinehart & Winston, 1964.

Gregorovius, F. *Geschichte der Stadt Rom*. Stuttgart 1903.

Jackson M., and E. Hodder. *The Seven Sovereign Hills of Rome.* London: Longmans, Green & Col, 1936.

Lanciani, Rodolfo. *Pagan and Christian Rome.* Boston: Houghton Mifflin. 1896.

Papencordt, F. *Geschichte der Stadt Rom.* Berlin, 1867-68.

Reumont, A. von. *Geschichte der Stadt Rom* I. Berlin, 1867.

Smith, Lacy M. *Early History of the Monastery of Cluny.* London: Oxford, 1920.

Thompson, James W. *The Medieval Library.* New York: Hafner, 1957.

Van Zeller, Dom Hubert. *The Holy Rule.* New York: Sheed and Ward, 1958.

Voigt, H. G. *Adalbert van Prag.* Leipzig, 1898.

Watts, Alan W. *Myth and Ritual in Christianity.* New York; Scribners, 1940.

SCIENCE, SCHOLARSHIP, ART

Boeckler, A. *Kölner Ottonische Buchmalerei: Beitälge zur Kunst des Mittlealters.* Berlin, 1950.

Boeckler, Albert. *Deutsche Buchmalerei Vorgotischer Zeit.* Die blauen Bucher, konigstein a /Taunus, 1952.

Focillon, Henri. *The Art of the West in the Middle Ages.* Vol. I Romanesque Art, New York: Cornell University Press, 1963.

Frazer, James George. *The Golden Bough.* New York: Macmillan, 1949.

Gilson, Etienne. *The Spirit of Medieval Philosophy.* New York: Scribners, 1940.

Gimpel, Jean. *The Medieval Machine.* New York: Holt, Rinehart & Winston, 1976.

Grabar, Andre, and Carl Nordenfalk. *Early Medieval Painting.* New York: Editions Albert skira, 1957.

Hyman, A., and J. Walsh. *Philosophy in the Middle Ages.* New York: Harper & Row, 1967.

Knowles, Davis. *The Evolution of Medieval Thought.* New York: Random House, Vintage Books, 1962.

Lacroix, Paul. *Science and Literature in the Middle Ages.* New York: Frederic Unger Publishing, 1964.

Schramm, Percy Ernst. "Zur Geschichte der Buchmalerei in der Zeit der Sächsischen Kaiser." *Jahrbuch für Kunstwissenschaft* I (1923).

Thorndike, Lynn. A History of Magic and Experimental Science. 2 vols. New York: Macmillan, 1923.

SPAIN

Altamira, Rafael. *A History of Spanish Civilization*. London: Constable & Co., 1930.

Aschbach. *Geschichte der Omaijaden in Spanien*. Frankfurt am Main, 1860.

Bonassie, Pierre. *La Catalogne* (du milieu du Xe a la fin du XI e siécle, Tome I). Universite de Toulouse, 1957.

Brockelmann, Carl. *Der Islam: Ullsteins Weitgeschichte Geschichte des Orients*. Berlin: Ullstein, 1910,130-208.

——— *History of the Islamic Peoples*. Toms River, N.J.: Capricorn books, 1960.

Browne, E. G. *Arabian Medicine*. Cambridge University Press, 1962.

Castro, Americo. *The Structure of Spanish History*. Princeton, N.J.: Princeton University Press, 1954.

Coppée, Henry. *History of the Conquest of Spain*. 2 vols. Boston: Little Brown & Co., 1881.

D'Olwer, Nicolau. *La Catalogne a L'Epoque Romane*. Paris, 1932.

Dozy, Reinhart. *Spanish Islam*. Totowa, N.J.: Biblio Dist., 1972. Reprint of 1913 edition.

Hitti, Philip K. *History of the Arabs*. New York: MacMillan, 1964.

Lane, Edward W. *Arabian Society in the Middle Ages*. London: Chatto, 1883.

Lane-Poole, Stanley, *The Moors in Spain*. London: T. Gisher Unwin, 1887.

Makkari. *History of the Mohammedan Dynasties in Spain*. Translated by De Gayangos. London, 1840.

Millas Vallicrosa, J. M. *Neuve Estudios Sobre Historia de to Ciencia Española*. Barcelona, 1960.

Scott, S. P. *History of the Moorish Empire in Europe*. Philadelphia and London, 1904.

BYZANTIUM

Baynes, Norman H. *The Byzantine Empire*. Oxford: Oxford University Press, 1958.

Byron, Robert. *The Achievements of the Byzantine Empire*. Russel & Russel, 1964.

Diehl, Charles. *Manual d'Art Byzantin*. 2 vols. Paris: 1957.

——— *Byzantium: Greatness and Decline*. New Brunswick, N.J.: Rutgers University Press, 1957.

——— *Byzantine Portraits*. New York: Knopf, 1957.

Gibbon, Edward. *The Decline and Fall of the Roman Empire*. Vol. 2. London: J. B. Bury, 1896; New York: Modern Library, 1936.

Kiefer, Otto. *Kaiser und Kaiserinnen von Byzanz*. Berlin: Reimar Hobbing, 1937.

Lopez, Robert S. *Byzantium and the World Around it: Economic and Institutional Relations*. London: Variorum Press, 1978.

Ohnsorge, W. "Byzanz und das Abendland im 9 und 10 Jahrhundert." *Saeculum* 5 (1954).

Oman, Charles. *The Byzantine Empire*. London, 1892.

Ostrogorsky, George. *Geschichte des byzantinischen Staates*. Berlin: 1940; Munich: 1952.

———— *History of the Byzantine State*. Oxford: Blackwell, 1956.

Psellus, Michael. *Fourteen Byzantine Rulers*. London: Penguin Classics, 1979.

Rice, D. Talbot. *Byzantine Art*. Oxford, 1935; Pelican Books, 1954.

Schlumberger, G. *Nicephore Phocas: Un Empereur, Byzantin au Xe siécle Nicephore*. Paris, 1890 and 1923.

Schneider. A. M. *Die Hagia Sophia zu Konstantinopel*. Berlin, 1939.

Vasiliev, N. *A History of the Byzantine Empire*. 2 vols. Madison, Wis.: University of Wisconsin Press, 1929.

Vryonis, Speros, Jr. *Byzantium and Europe*. New York: Harcourt Brace & World, 1976.

ENGLAND

Churchill, Winston. *The Birth of Britain*. New York: Dodd, Mead & Co.; Bantam Books, 1956.

Davis, ed. *Medieval England*. Darby, PA: Arden Library, 1984.

Duckett, Eleanor. *Saint Dunstan of Canterbury*. New York: W.W. Norton, 1955.

Page, R. I. *Life in Anglo-Saxon England*. New York: Putnam's Sons.

William of Malmesbury. *Chronicle of the Kings of England*. London: Mead & Co., 1897.

FRANCE

Glaber, Raoul. *Les Cinq Livres de ses Essaies Histoires*. Edited by M. Prou. Paris, A. Picard, 1866.

Guizot, Francois. *History of France*, Vol. I. New York: Peter Fenelon, Collier & Son, 1890.

Lavisse, E. *Histoire de France*. Paris, 1900.

Michelet, Jules. *Histoire de France*. 17 vols. Paris, 1833-1856.

Petit, E. "Raoul Glaber." *Revue Historique* (Paris, 1892).

Prou, M. Raoul Glaber: *Les Cinq Livres de ses Histoires* (900-1044). Vol. 3. Paris, A. Picard, 1866.

Richer. *Histoire de France*. Vol. 2. Paris: Editions Champion, 1930.

Richer, Monk of Rheims. *Histoire de France*. Edited and translated by Robert Latouche. Paris: Societe D'Edition "Les Belles Lettres," 1937.

VIKINGS, SCANDINAVIA

Bronsted, Johann. "The Norsemen in North America Before Columbus." *Smithsonian Institution* (1953), 367 ff.

————— *The Vikings*. London: Pelican Book; Penguin Books, 1960.

Du Chaillu, Paul. *The Viking Age*. 2 vols. New York: Scribner's sons, 1889.

Haskins, Charles Homer. *The Normans in European History*. Boston: Houghton Mifflin, 1915.

Hermann, Paul. *Conquest by Man*. New York: Harper & Row, 1954.

Jewett, Sarah. *The Story of the Normans*. New York: Putnam's Sons, 1886.

Jines, G. *The North Atlantic Saga*. London: Oxford University Press, 1964.

La Fay, Howard. *The Vikings*. Washington D.C.: The National Geographic Society, 1972.

Laing, Samuel. *Heimskringla: The Olaf-Sagas by Snorre Sturlason*. New York: Dutton, 1898.

Mowat, Farley. *West Viking*. Boston: Little, Brown & Co., 1965.

Oxenstierna, Count Eric. *The Norsemen*. Greenwich, Conn.: New York Graphic Society Publishers, 1965.

Sawyer, P.H. *The Age of the Vikings*. New York: St. Martin's Press, 1962.

Trykare, Tre. *The Viking*. New York: Time-Life Books, 1966.

von Wolzogen. *Die Edda*. Leipzig: Philipp Reklam, 1900.

SLAVS, RUSSIA

Cross, Samuel H. *Slavic Civilization Through the Ages*. London: Russel & Russel, 1948. Also Cambridge 1948.

————— *The Russian Primary Chronicle (Chronicle of Nestor)*. Cambridge: Cambridge University Press, 1953.

Die Reyse des A'med ben Foszlan, ben Abbas, ben Raschhid, ben 'Hammad, Gesandten des Chalifen Muktadir's an den König der Slaven. Leipzig: Arabische Studien, 1837.

Dvornik, F. *The Slavs: Their Early History and Civilization.* New Brunswick, N.J.: Rutger's University Press, 1962.

———— *The Slavs in European History and Civilization.* New Brunswick, N.J.: Rutgers University Press, 1961.

Grekow, B. *Kiev Rus.* Moscow: Foreign Language Publishing House, 1959.

Jacob, G. "Arabische Berichte von Gesandten an Germanischen Fürstenhöfen aus dem 9. und 10. Jahrhundert." *Quellen zur Deutschen Volkskunde* I (1927).

Kluchevsky, V. *History of Russia.* London: Russel & Russel, 1912

Laehr, G. "die Angänge des Russischen Reiches." *Historische Studien* Vol. (1930): 122-23.

Leger, L. Translation of the *Chronicle of Nestor* into French. Paris, 1884.

Paszkiewicz, Henryk. *The Making of the Russian Nation.* London: Darton, Longman & Todd, 1963.

Pokrovsky, M. *History of Russia.* New York: 1931.

Spector, Ivar. *An Introduction to Russian History and Culture.* New York: 1961.

Stählin, Karl. *Geschichte Russlands von den Anfangen bis zur Gegenwart.* Vols. I & II. Graz, Austria: 1961.

Vernadsky, G. *Kievan Russia.* New Haven, Conn.: Yale University Press, 1948.

Zeki Validi Togan, A. "Ibn Fadlans Reisebericht." Leipzig: *Abhandlungen für die Kunde des Morgenlandes.* Vol. 24:3 (1939).

HUNGARY

Fessler, J. *Geschichte der Ungarn.* Vienna, 1842.

Jekelfalussy, Josef. *The Millennium of Hungary.* Budapest, 1897.

Kosary, Dominic G. *A History of Hungary.* Cleveland: Benjamin Franklin Bibliophile Society, 1941.

Luttich, Rudolf. "Ungarnzüge in Europa im 10. Jahrhundert." *Historische Studien* 84 (1910).

Majlath, Janos. *Geschichte der Magyaren.* Regensburg, 1852.

Marczali, Hendrik. *Ungarns Geschichtsquellen.* Vienna, 1894-1902.

Szilagyi, Sandor. *Hungarian Historical Biographies.* Budapest, 1884.

———— *History of the Hungarian Nation.* Vols. I and 2. Budapest, 1898.

Teleki, Pal Grof. *The Evolution of Hungary.* New York: MacMillan, 1923.

Vambery, Arminium de. *The Story of Hungary.* London: T. Fisher Unwin, 1883.

Index

Other Seastone Titles

AMERICAN INDIAN GENESIS: THE STORY OF CREATION
Percy Bullchild
Introduction by Mary Crow Dog
Written as it has been spoken for generations in the Blackfeet style, this provocative work provides a Plains Indian history of the world's creation. *Hardcover. $16.00*

APOCALYPSE 2000: THE BOOK OF REVELATION
John Miller, Editor
Introduction by Andrei Codrescu
Brings the fascinating Book of Revelation to life with rich illustrations and modern reflections about the apocalypse by notable contemporaries. *Hardcover. $17.95*

BEFORE HE WAS BUDDHA: THE LIFE OF SIDDHARTHA
Hammalawa Saddhatissa
Introduction by Jack Kornfield
Written in a lucid, flowing style, this biographical profile reveals the strength and gentleness of Buddha's character and brings to life the compassion that gave his teachings universal appeal. *Hardcover. $16.00*

DAVID: POWER, LUST AND BETRAYAL IN BIBLICAL TIMES
Jerry M. Landay
The personal story of a man of ambition, complexity, talent and human frailty, one of the most popular heroes of the ancient world is portrayed here with the care of a historian and the color of a novelist. *Hardcover. $18.00*

DEAD SEA SCROLLS: THE COMPLETE STORY
Dr. Jonathan Campbell
Dispels rumors surrounding the Scrolls and recounts the actual events of their unearthing, laying the groundwork for a vivid investigation of the relevance of the Scrolls to our times. *Trade paper. $12.95*

JESUS THE MAGICIAN: CHARLATAN OR SON OF GOD?
Morton Smith
Introduction by Russell Shorto
Challenging the accepted Christian image, *Jesus the Magician* introduces us to a complex and enigmatic man whose contemporaries perceived him as a magician, even a trickster. Smith relies both on the Gospels and on what was said of Jesus by those who did not believe in him. *Trade paper. $13.95*

JESUS AND BUDDHA: THE PARALLEL SAYINGS
Marcus Borg, Editor
Introduction by Jack Kornfield
Traces the life stories and beliefs of Jesus and Buddha, then presents a comprehensive collection of their remarkably similar teachings on facing pages. *Hardcover. $19.95*

MUSIC OF SILENCE
David Steindl-Rast with Sharon Lebell
Introduction by Kathleen Norris
A noted Benedictine monk shows us how to incorporate the sacred meaning of monastic life into our everyday world by paying attention to the "seasons of the day" and the enlivening messages to be found in each moment. *Trade paper. $12.00*

ZOO OF THE GODS:
THE WORLD OF ANIMALS IN MYTH AND LEGEND
Anthony S. Mercatante
This fabulous bestiary reveals a wealth of tales from every culture, time and place. Underlying scores of animal stories are the relationships the author draws between beastkind and humankind. *Trade paper. $14.95*

To order these or other Seastone books call 800-377-2542 or 510-601-8301, e-mail ulysses@ulyssespress.com or write to Ulysses Press, P.O. Box 3440, Berkeley, CA 94703-3440. There is no charge for shipping on retail orders. California residents must include sales tax. Allow two to three weeks for delivery.

About the Authors

RICHARD ERDOES was born in Frankfurt and educated in Vienna, Berlin, and Paris. He is co-author of *Lakota Woman*, author of *The Sundance People*, and co-editor of *American Indian Myths and Legends*. He lives in Santa Fe, New Mexico.

KAREN ARMSTRONG, author of the introduction, has written several books on religion including the *New York Times* bestseller, *A History of God*.